MULTINATIONALS IN A CHANGING ENVIRONMENT

MULTINATIONALS IN A CHANGING ENVIRONMENT

A Study of Business-Government
Relations in the Third World

by
Adeoye A. Akinsanya

PRAEGER

PRAEGER SPECIAL STUDIES • PRAEGER SCIENTIFIC

New York • Philadelphia • Eastbourne, UK
Toronto • Hong Kong • Tokyo • Sydney

Library of Congress Cataloging in Publication Data

Akinsanya, Adeoye A.
    Multinationals in a changing environment.

    Bibliography: p.
    Includes index.
    1. International business enterprises—Developing
countries. 2. Industry and state—Developing countries.
I. Title.
HD2932.A34 1984   338.8′881724   83-24592
ISBN 0-03-059866-4 (alk. paper)

Published in 1984 by Praeger Publishers
CBS Educational and Professional Publishing,
a Division of CBS Inc.
521 Fifth Avenue, New York, NY 10175 USA

456789 052 9876545321

Printed in the United States of America
on acid-free paper

To Okuadebo, my Mother.

She made me what 'am today.

Preface

This book was written under strains and stresses. Several people, by words or through letters, have encouraged me to plod on. Of particular mention are my mother (to whom I have dedicated the entire book) and Betsy Brown, my former editor. My appreciation goes to Betsy for her patience, particularly as the publication of this book is more than a year behind schedule. In the process of writing this book, I have, albeit unwittingly, neglected Olubukunola and Oluwatobi, my daughters. I wish they could know how much I cared and still care for them.

Some of my colleagues and friends have helped in one way or another to sharpen my thoughts on this book. They include Professor Timothy Shaw (Dalhousie University, Halifax, Canada), Professor M. A. Ajomo, Dr. Adesina Sambo, Dr. Adele Jinadu, and Dr. 'Remi Anifowose, all of the University of Lagos. I am grateful to them all. I take this opportunity to express my deepest appreciation to Professor I. W. ("Bill") Zartman of the School of Advanced International Studies, The Johns Hopkins University, Washington, D.C., for making my stay at SAIS as a Fulbright Scholar interesting and rewarding; to Dr. Edward Cox and his family for extending warm courtesies to my family and me when I was a Visiting Professor of International Studies at the University of South Carolina, Columbia, South Carolina, during the 1980-1981 academic session.

The research on which this book is based is partly financed from a grant provided by the Ford Foundation. My appreciation goes to Dr. E. O. Akinluyi (Director of Planning, University of Lagos); Dr. Robert Drysdale (Ford Foundation Representative in West Africa); and Dr. A. C. A. Ogunsanwo (University of Lagos): Dr. Akinluyi for being instrumental in securing the Ford Foundation grant; Dr. Drysdale for showing interest in my work; and Dr. Ogunsanwo for drawing my attention to the possibilities of a Ford Foundation research grant and a one-year teaching position at the University of South Carolina. I shall be eternally grateful.

As usual, Pamela Hodges (London School of Economics) shouldered the onerous responsibility of typing and retyping the manuscript. She not only did an excellent job, in spite of all odds, but also cheerfully and competently rendered other services related to the book. She is, indeed, a friend. Finally, my gratitude goes to friends, too numerous to mention, for many invaluable services, inspiration, support, and encouragement in the course of preparing the manuscript. Special mention must be made of 'Bimpe Adeniji, 'Kunle Okunuga, Dr. Arthur Davies, Sam Ijalana, and Bob Hage (ex-First Secretary of the Canadian High Commission in Lagos). Needless to say, none of them is responsible for any shortcomings of this book.

Acknowledgments

The author gratefully acknowledges kind permission extended by the following to reprint from the books, periodicals, and journals indicated in parentheses: American Political Science Association (excerpts from the American Political Science Review); Basic Books (excerpts from Raymond Vernon, Sovereignty at Bay); Cambridge University Press (excerpts from Gerald Helleiner, A World Divided); George Allen and Unwin (excerpts from John Dunning, Studies in International Investment); The Johns Hopkins University Press (excerpts and tables from Isaiah Frank, Foreign Enterprise in Developing Countries); Macmillan Press (excerpts from Harry Johnson, Technology and Economic Interdependence; and Alasdair MacBean and V. N. Balasubramanyam, Meeting the Third World Challenge); Macmillan Publishing Company (excerpts from Jagdish Bhagwati, Economics and World Order); Massachusetts Institute of Technology Press (tables from Thomas J. Biersteker, Distortion or Development? Contending Perspectives on the Multinational Corporation); Nigerian Economic Society (tables from Oil and the New International Economic Order); Board of Editors of the Nigerian Journal of International Studies); Oxford University Press (tables from Grant L. Reuber, et al., Private Foreign Investment in Development, and African Affairs); Philip Allan Publishers (excerpts from David Colman and Frederick Nixson, Economics of Change in Less Developed Countries); Prentice-Hall (excerpts from Abdul Said and Luiz Simmons, New Sovereigns); Princeton University Press (excerpts from World Politics); Praeger Publishers (excerpts from Adalberto Pinelo, The Multinational Corporation as a Force in Latin American Politics); Royal Institute of International Affairs (excerpts from International Affairs); St. Martin's Press (excerpts from Charles Kegley, Jr., and Eugene Wittkopf, World Politics); Time Incorporated (excerpts from Fortune); and Westview Press (excerpts from Karl Sauvant and Farid Lavipour, Controlling Multinational Enterprises).

Contents

List of Tables

1.

Introduction

The multinational corporation is one of the most controversial, most visible, and most frequently studied actors in the contemporary world economic system. In general, this business enterprise is regarded not only as the vehicle through which capital and technology are transferred from the major economic powers to the developing countries but also the vehicle through which the natural resources, particularly petroleum, bauxite, iron ore, copper, and uranium, of the developing countries are developed. Thus, bauxite in Guyana and Jamaica has been identified with the Aluminum Company of Canada (Alcan), the Reynolds Aluminum Company of the United States, and Revere; petroleum in Peru has meant the International Petroleum Company, and in Bolivia it has meant the Standard Oil Company of New Jersey and the Gulf Oil Corporation; copper in Chile has been synonymous with Kennecott and Anaconda, while Iran since 1954 has been wedded to the Seven Sisters.[1] However, things are changing. By the late 1960s serious misgivings and concerns had been expressed about the economic, social, and political consequences of the operations of multinational corporations (MNCs). These concerns have engaged the attention of scholars, public functionaries, and international bodies all over the world; they have inspired not only a vast literature but also a host of initiatives designed to curb the activities of MNCs at the national and international levels.[2]

1

MULTINATIONALS: BLESSING OR CURSE?

In assessing the impact of multinationals on
Third World development, many scholars have focused,
almost exclusively, on the impact of multinationals
on Latin American social, economic, and political
life. But this is very much expected. In general,
Latin Americans, Africans, and Asians have been very
critical about the activities of MNCs; to them,
multinationals have made a negative rather than a
positive impact on their national development. On
the impact of United States-based MNCs on the ownership patterns in Latin America, it has been said
that as local subsidiaries of these multinationals
become established and dominant, they

> co-opt whatever local entrepreneurial
> talent is available, thus, transforming
> the national bourgeoisie into a "trans-
> national technocracy." . . . The middle
> class is also affected; part is incorpo-
> rated into the new economic structure
> and part is left out--effectively barred
> from upward mobility and terrified by
> the prospect of proletarianization. The
> working class is simply divided--those
> few who find employment with the Ameri-
> can subsidiary companies become a privi-
> leged elite within the working class.
> The balance of the labour force is left
> to endure the problems of unemployment
> and marginal economic existence.[3]

The point to be emphasized here is that while the
polarization of the working class makes it difficult to organize labor, the co-optation of the
"available" local talent inhibits the development
of an indigenous bourgeois class.
     The view that multinationals are the vehicles
through which scarce capital is transferred from
"capital rich to capital poor regions" has been
challenged not only by some Western scholars but
also by many Third World scholars and public functionaries.[4] Commenting on the contention that the

Eco-
perspective

ent Salvador Allende Gossens was
vate foreign capital, presumably
opriatory" measures,[5] the Chilean
iited States, Orlando Letelier,
:

rms, we have been <u>exporting</u>
mporting it. . . . Between
. . . $450 million flowed
direct investments. Now de-
tion for such investments
eriod, which the companies
of the country, and the net
figure would be only $257 million. In
the same period, the outflow of profits
and dividends just on investments was
$1.056 billion, about four times the net
investment.[6]

In essence, contrary to widely held views, the developing countries are capital exporters rather than
capital importers. For example, while the flow of
United States direct foreign investments to the developing countries between 1960 and 1968 stood at $1
billion, the outflow of capital from the developing
countries to the United States in the form of profits
and dividends amounted to $2.5 billion during the
same period.[7] According to Raymond Vernon, the latter figure, that is, the outflow of capital, could
be greater if we include royalty payments and fees.
To be sure, the Secretariat of the United Nations
Conference on Trade and Development (UNCTAD) estimated that the developing countries were paying about
$1.4 billion at the end of the 1960s for the use of
patents, licenses, know-how, and trademarks, and
that these costs could grow six-fold to $9 billion
during the 1970s.[8]
    Table 1.1 shows that the average rate of re-
turns on United States direct foreign investments in
the developing countries was 17.5 percent while that
for developed market economies stood at 7.9 percent.
More significant is Africa, where the rate of return
was higher than the 7.9 percent recorded for developed market economies and 10.7 percent for the whole
world. It was small wonder, therefore, that the

late 1960s and early 1970s in several African countries were characterized by politics of economic
nationalism. In fact, one of the reasons frequently
advanced by African leaders for indigenizing private
foreign investments, particularly through host government's acquisition of majority equity interests
in local subsidiaries of MNCs, is to maximize local
retention of profits.[9] Table 1.2 indicates royalty
payments and fees by six developing countries and
their relationship to gross domestic product and export earnings, while Table 1.3 shows the inflow of
direct foreign investments to Africa and the outflow
of income on these investments between 1965 and 1970.
For each of the years considered in Table 1.3, Africa
as a whole recorded a negative balance. But positive
balances were recorded for the non-oil-producing
African countries between 1965 and 1967 while negative balances were recorded for the years 1968-70.
For the oil-producing African countries, substantial
negative balances were recorded for the entire period.
The point emphasized here is that MNCs have been able
to minimize the overall amount of taxes paid to the
host government and, by extension, maximize returns
on their investments through a variety of means (dividends; interest and royalty payments; capital transfers; transfer-pricing; "triangular trade"; payments
for goods, services, and knowledge; etc.). While
these issues will be fully examined in Chapter 3,
there is no doubt that capital outflows have far-
reaching implications for the balance of payments of
the countries concerned.

    There are some arguments advanced in defense
of MNCs. For example, it has been argued that a
process known as "import substitution" takes place
when a local subsidiary of an MNC establishes producing facilities in a developing country. This
means that products that were previously imported
into that country are henceforth produced locally.
In essence, the advantage that the home country of
the multinational has in net capital flow "is minimized if not reversed."[10] This argument assumes,
albeit wrongly, that "import-substitution" would not
and could not have taken place without direct foreign investments. In any event, there is only minimal import-substitution in the case of extractive industries geared for exports. For example,

TABLE 1.1

Average Rate of Returns on United States and United Kingdom Direct Foreign Investments 1965-68

Area	All Sectors	United States (%)*	United Kingdom (%)*
Africa	22.3	7.7	--
African/Asian/European Developing Countries	--	--	10.4
Developing Countries	17.5	11.0	9.8
Developed Market Economies	7.9	9.6	9.3
Total	10.7	10.0	9.5

*Excluding petroleum.

Source: Akin. Ogunpola and Oladeji Ojo, "The Role of Multinational Corporations in the Economic Development of African Countries," Nigerian Journal of International Studies 1 (1975): 78.

TABLE 1.2

Payments of Royalties and Fees by Selected Less-Developed Countries and Their Relationship to Gross Domestic Product and Export Earnings

Country	Year	Royalties and Fees Paid ($ million)	Share of GDP (%)	Payments Exports (%)
Argentina	1969	127.7	0.72	7.9
Brazil	1966-68	59.6	0.26	3.4
Colombia	1966	26.7	0.50	5.3
Mexico	1968	200.0	0.76	15.9
Nigeria	1967	33.8	0.78	4.2
Sri Lanka	1970	9.3	0.51	2.9
Total (above and nonweighted average)		457.1	0.68	7.3

Source: Ogunpola and Ojo, p. 79.

TABLE 1.3

Africa: Inflow of Direct Foreign Investments and Outflow of Income
on Cumulative Direct Foreign Investments 1965-70
($ million)

	Year					
	1965	1966	1967	1968	1969	1970
Oil- and non-oil-producing countries						
Inflow	182.2	163.7	241.5	201.6	235.5	270.7
Outflow	380.8	718.8	7.8.8	936.7	024.3	006.2
Balance	-198.6	-55.1	-467.1	-762.1	-688.8	-725.5
Non-oil-producing countries						
Inflow	133.5	74.7	61.5	53.6	46.5	42.7
Outflow	49.3	53.8	56.6	57.7	56.3	60.2
Balance	84.2	20.9	4.9	-4.1	-9.8	-17.5
Oil-producing countries						
Inflow	48.7	89.0	180.0	148.0	189.0	228.0
Outflow	331.5	665.0	652.0	906.0	868.0	036.0
Balance	-282.8	-576.0	-472.0	-758.0	-679.0	-708.0

Source: Akin. Ogunpola and Oladeji Ojo, "The Role of Multinational Corporations in the Economic Development of African Countries," Nigerian Journal of International Studies 1 (1975): 79.

> A . . . factor severely limiting the con-
> tribution of the aluminum industry to host
> economies is that mining operations, as a
> rule, are not integrated into the national
> economy and instead exhibit the typical
> characteristics of an enclave. Hardly any
> forward or backward linkages to the rest
> of the economy exist because, on the one
> hand, production is, as a rule, exported,
> while, on the other hand, the equipment
> required for mining is technologically too
> sophisticated to be manufactured locally.[11]

More important,

> Investment in infrastructure usually is
> limited and specific to the needs of the
> mining operations; and upgrading of
> skills remains company-specific and
> tends not to be disseminated throughout
> the economy. Thus, despite some positive
> inputs into the host economy . . . in the
> form of employment, government revenue,
> and foreign exchange, mining operations
> are more integrated into the world-wide
> operations of the parent company than
> into the economic system of the host coun-
> try. The implications of such a situation
> are that the enclave country not only
> foregoes substantial income but also the
> beneficial spin-off effects associated
> with advanced production.[12]

Consequently, leaders of many developing countries
not only believe that the economic gains from the
continued operations of MNCs are questionable but
also have become increasingly circumspect about the
contributions of multinationals to economic development.

MULTINATIONALS AND RELATIONS
WITH HOST STATES

Leaders of many developing countries are not
just concerned about the economic power that multi-

nationals seem to exercise over the lives of peoples and governments. They are much more concerned about the political consequences of the operations of these business entities. This concern is expressed not only by the developing countries that emerged from colonial bondage in the 1960s but also by countries, such as those in Latin America, which achieved political independence more than a century ago. Generally, these countries perceive themselves to have remained in a dependent economic relation to developed market economies. Regardless of when political independence was attained, this concern has focused increasingly and almost exclusively around the role of MNCs in the economies of these countries. Therefore, not only do developing countries see multinational corporations as a threat to their national sovereignties; MNCs also are often seen as instruments of foreign power.

In effect, do multinationals distort the precarious balance of power within the host country? Do MNCs intervene in the politics of their host countries? Are multinationals instruments of the foreign policies of their home countries, and if not, do multinationals have their own foreign policies that may be at variance with the "national interests" of their home countries? Do MNCs lobby their home governments for policies (such as the Hickenlooper Amendment) that support them in their disputes with host governments? Do they influence their home governments to embark on a policy of intervention in their disputes with host governments? On these and many other related questions, opinions are sharply divided, and often they appear irreconcilable.

On the one hand are those who not only deny that MNCs intervene in the politics of the host states but also consider it improper and inappropriate for MNCs to influence the politics of the host states. Contributing to the debate, Geoffrey Chandler has noted:

> If an affiliate of an international
> group were to meddle in internal poli-
> tics in order to serve its own ends,
> this would amount at least to folly and
> at the most to suicide which would pro-
> voke no sympathy.[13]

He asserted, and quite rightly, that a company "is a part of the society in which it operates, and it will expect to remain in business for the long term; it cannot do this if it essays to interfere with political processes."[14] Nevertheless,

> This is not to say that the management
> of a company will not argue its case to
> the full. . . . But the strength of
> its argument will rest on the economic
> factors it can adduce to encourage or
> discourage measures affecting itself.[15]

Finally, Chandler dismissed the widely held view that MNCs offer bribes to influence local officials in order to circumvent host laws and regulations. He maintained that "bribery, even if arguments of morality are rejected, is inexpedient: lasting marriages are not based on venal affection."[16]

In his testimony before the United States Senate Foreign Relations Subcommittee on Multinational Corporations and United States Foreign Policy, George Clark, Senior Vice-President of the First National City Bank, New York, outlined four principles governing Citibank's operations in the Third World:

1. We must never lose sight of the fact
   that we are guests in foreign countries. We must conduct ourselves accordingly. We recognize the right
   of governments to pass local legislation, and our obligation to conform.
2. Under these circumstances, we also
   recognize that we can survive only
   if we are successful in demonstrat-
   ing to the local authorities that
   our presence is beneficial.
3. We believe that every country must
   find its own way, politically and
   economically. Sometimes, we feel that
   local policies are wise; sometimes,
   we do not. However, irrespective of
   our own views, we try to function as
   best we can under prevailing circumstances.

4. We have always felt free to discuss
   with local governments matters directly affecting our interests, but we
   recognize that they have final regulatory authority.[17]

This view tallies with the position taken by Chandler,
who, until his appointment as the Trade Relations Co-
ordinator for Shell International Petroleum Company,
was the Chairman and Managing Director of Shell
Trinidad Limited. A similar view has been expressed
by William Ogden, Executive Vice-President, Chase
Manhattan Bank. Asked by Senator Charles Percy (then
a member of the Church Committee on Multinational
Corporations) whether it is a typical pattern for
United States-based MNCs to participate actively in
the politics of the host states, the Chase Manhattan
executive replied in these words:

I certainly do not feel this is a pattern for the multinational corporation
or bank. To the best of my knowledge,
not only is it not a pattern but it is
just not done. For no other reason . . .
it is not only bad in a general sense
but it does not work. We tend to think
of ourselves as guests in the country.
They are sovereign, we are there, and
we have to be particularly careful about
it. In our bank we sometimes think that
we bend over too far. We don't do things
that we think maybe we should be doing.
We strive to avoid even the slightest
hint of getting involved in a country's
domestic politics.[18]

Other company representatives testifying before the
Church Committee felt that it was improper for a
foreign-owned company to interfere in the politics
of the host state. According to Miles Cortez of the
International Business Machines World Trade Corporation, a policy of intervention in the affairs of a
host state is "totally abhorrent" to the policy of
IBM,[19] while William Bolin, Senior Vice-President of
the Bank of America, disclosed that a policy of

political involvement "would have been directly contrary to our own interests."[20] He declared:

> Dependence upon our host makes it unthink-
> able to run the risk of political involve-
> ment. It is the global policy of the
> Bank of America to avoid completely any
> type of political position in the coun-
> tries where it operates. In all of the
> countries where we operate abroad, we
> carefully refrain from partisan politi-
> cal announcements, campaign contribu-
> tions, loans to political groups, and
> all other political activities.[21]

In essence, spokesmen of the banking and oil
industries are of the view that their employers do
not meddle in the politics of the host state. More
significant, they contend that it was unwise and improper to do so. However, this "utilitarian morality," if it ever exists, must be a "relatively recent development." According to Adalberto Pinelo,
it was Royal Dutch/Shell, incidentally Chandler's
employer, that financed the coup d'état that brought
Augusto Leguia and the Civilistas to power in Peru
at the turn of the century. Royal Dutch/Shell financed the coup in the hope of receiving favorable
concessions from Leguia, the Civilistas President of
Peru from 1908 to 1912.[22] Subsequent events demonstrated that Shell's move was crass "folly" (apologies to Chandler); and this is because Leguia made a
better deal with Shell's major rival, namely, the
Standard Oil Company of New Jersey (Exxon), which
holds 99.5 percent of the stock of the International
Petroleum Company. This incident, if anything,
proved that Shell was outmaneuvered in Peru. In any
case, to argue, as some corporation executives have
argued, that "political meddling and bribery is unwise does not prove that it does not take place."[23]

Consequently, there are those who contend that
MNCs have intervened in many important ways in the
politics of the host states. Multinationals, it has
been alleged, have taken several measures within
host states to favor friendly governments and oppose
unfriendly governments, to obtain concessions that

are favorable to their continued operations, and to
block host governments' efforts at restricting or
regulating corporate activity) For example, in 1962
when Honduras passed an important agrarian reform
measure providing for the redistribution of large
tracts of uncultivated United Fruit property,

> The company . . . responded vigorously,
> moving unilaterally to curtail Honduras'
> major export by ceasing to plant a
> disease-resistant banana strain. At the
> same time, it activated local organiza-
> tions that were apprehensive about eco-
> nomic reforms. . . . Still, the company
> wanted diplomatic assistance, including
> the threat to stop foreign aid if the
> Hondurans proceeded. . . . Under these
> pressures, the Embassy informed Honduras
> of the [Hickenlooper] amendment and its
> serious implications.[24]

More important,

> Because these actions by United Fruit
> and the U.S. Government were simultaneous
> and mutually reinforcing . . . Honduran
> President Morales reversed his previous
> stand and agreed to substantially amend
> the agrarian reform law. Later, he
> wrote to United Fruit President Thomas
> Sunderland that the company could safely
> expand production and need not fear ex-
> propriation or confiscatory taxes--a
> promise kept by subsequent Honduran
> governments.[25]

Thus, the threat of foreign-aid sanctions (against a
country carrying out urgently needed social reforms)
could complement corporate efforts aimed at protecting private foreign investments.

The MNCs have also been accused of (1) making
illegal contributions to political parties; (2) offering bribes to local officials with a view to inducing them "to do or omit to do something in violation"[26] of their lawful duties; (3) refusing to

comply with host laws and regulations; (4) using such extra-legal methods as international boycott to blackmail unfriendly governments;[27] and (5) being used to promote the foreign policy interests of their home governments such as providing cover for intelligence operations and enforcing such laws as the United States' Trading with the Enemy Act and the Export Control Act.[28] On the issue of offering bribes to local officials, the United States Securities and Exchange Commission and a U.S. congressional investigation revealed improper payments of more than $100 million by 100 U.S. corporations.[29] As tools for promoting the foreign policy interests of their home states, U.S.-based MNCs have been used by the Executive Branch to apply the Trading with the Enemy Act against the People's Republic of China, Cuba, North Korea, then-North Vietnam, and Iran while the decision by the U.S. government in 1950 in allowing oil companies to exempt royalty payments from U.S. taxes was a device by the Executive Branch to provide bilateral assistance to Middle Eastern oil-producing countries at a time when such bilateral assistance would not have been approved by Congress.[30]

Finally, the corporate views recognizing "the right of governments to pass local legislation and our obligation to confirm" may not always and entirely be true, particularly in situations where host laws are inconsistent or incompatible with the interests of the multinational firm. Reference has been made to United Fruit Company's reaction to a Honduran agrarian reform measure. Again, at the peak of the La Brea y Parinas tax controversy in Peru,[31] the government of President Jose Pardo, through the Peruvian Ambassador in Washington, requested

> that the government of the United States
> kindly use its good offices to the effect
> that the British Government recommended
> the aforementioned oil companies to ob-
> serve the laws of Peru.[32]

In essence, the Pardo administration was brought to its knees; to be sure, Lima begged Washington to "use its good offices" with London so that Lobitos Oil-Fields Company would comply with its orders,

namely, "to transport 20 percent of the oil it usually exported to Canada to Callao."[33]
   More significant, it has been claimed that
MNCs not only have used their power in the politics
of the home state to obtain foreign policies that
are favorable to corporate interests but also at
times have sought governmental support for their opposition to unfavorable regimes in host states.
Those who make this claim have argued that

> U.S. investments in underdeveloped coun-
> tries are a primary determinant of U.S.
> foreign policies towards these countries.
> The results . . . are foreign policies
> that are protective both of these in-
> vestments and of opportunities for their
> future expansion, which therefore are
> profoundly counter-revolutionary in
> their intent, and which undertake for-
> eign interventions and military alliances
> in pursuit of these ends.[34]

Thus, the proxy intervention of Guatemala in 1954
has been explained by the interests of the United
Fruit Company, including the fact that several U.S.
policy makers had close connections with United
Fruit; the proxy interventions in Iran in 1954 have
been explained by U.K. and U.S. oil interests, including the fact that General Fazollah Zahedi who
led the coup that ousted Prime Minister Mohammed
Mossadegh received covert support from Western European intelligence agencies and the United States'
Central Intelligence Agency led by Kermit Roosevelt,
grandson of President Theodore Roosevelt, who later
became one of the vice-presidents of Gulf Oil Corporation.[35] Additionally, the proxy intervention in
Cuba in 1961 has been explained by the $1 billion in
U.S. investments there; the proxy intervention in
British Guiana (Guyana) in 1963 has also been explained by U.S. investments in bauxite, while the
military intervention in the Dominican Republic in
1965 has been explained by U.S. sugar interests, and
again, including the fact that several U.S. policy
makers or advisers had close connections with the
major sugar corporations such as the National Sugar

Refining Corporation and Sucrest Corporation.[36] The point we need to emphasize here is that proxy intervention in Iran, Guatemala, and Brazil (1964), to mention but a few instances, was followed by increased direct foreign investments. For example, the proxy intervention in Brazil was followed by a major mining concession to the Hanna Mining Company as well as major increases in the already large U.S. investments in Brazilian manufacturing: $700 million in 1964 and $1.4 billion in 1971.[37] Again, the proxy intervention in Iran was followed by a deal arranged with a consortium of oil companies including Anglo-Iranian Oil Company and Gulf Oil Corporation.

Perhaps one of the most notorious instances of intervention in the politics of the home state by an MNC, and certainly one that explicitly demonstrates the dangers and political threats posed by MNCs, was the role of the International Telephone and Telegraph Company in Chilean politics in the early 1970s. According to the ITT Papers and the Reports of the Church Committee on Multinational Corporations and United States Foreign Policy, ITT--ranked twenty-first on the Fortune List of the world's 50 largest industrial corporations in August 1981, with annual sales of $18.53 billion--actively sought to prevent the election of Unidad Popular (Popular Unity) Presidential candidate, Salvador Allende Gossens. And, at a meeting on July 16, 1970, arranged between Harold S. Geneen (Chairman and Chief Executive Officer of ITT) and William C. Broe (Director, CIA's Clandestine Services for the Western Hemisphere) by John A. McCone (a former CIA Director, Consultant to the CIA and a member of the ITT Board of Directors), the ITT Chief Executive proposed an "election fund" of $1 million "controlled and channeled through the CIA . . . to support Jorge Alessandri,"[38] the Conservative Presidential candidate since the incumbent, Eduardo Frei, cannot legally succeed himself. According to Broe's testimony, he (Broe) refused Geneen's offer; however, both the ITT and the CIA agreed to exchange information on the Chilean situation.[39]

In spite of ITT's support to the conservative newspapers opposed to the election of Allende,[40] ITT's efforts to swing the September 4 popular election of Alessandri failed: Allende received 36.3 percent of the votes while Alessandri and Radomiro Tomic, the Christian Democratic candidate, got 35.3 and 28.4 percent, respectively.[41] Thus, Allende had a plurality. Under the Chilean Constitution, "When nobody gets a majority, the two highest candidates go to the Congress. The Congress then votes in a secret ballot and elects the President."[42] Because it was almost certain that Allende's election as President would be confirmed by the Chilean Congress in a run-off election on October 24 since it has become a convention for the Congress to elect as the President the candidate with the largest number of votes,[43] ITT devised an astute plan that would block Allende's victory in the congressional run-off election. This plan was the so-called Alessandri Formula. But just what is the Alessandri Formula, and how ITT hoped to implement it are known only to ITT insiders and top officials of the Nixon Administration, particularly Dr. Henry Kissinger, President Richard Nixon's National Security Adviser, and the U.S. Ambassador to Chile, Edward M. Korry.[44] To be sure, some conservative members of the Chilean Congress were to be warned of the "disaster" that "could fall on Chile if Allende & Co."[45] were to take over the reins of government. With these grave warnings, they

> would be persuaded to vote for Alessandri.
> Once elected by Congress, Dr. Alessandri
> would go back to his old pledge and resign
> the presidency. This would result in
> new elections in which Frei would be
> eligible for another presidential term.
> Frei's stature is such, most Chileans
> believe, he would defeat any opposition
> candidate.[46]

To this end, the ITT Board of Directors voted $1 million in support of any plan that was adopted by the government for the purpose of bringing about a coalition for the opposition to Allende so that when confirmation was up . . . this coalition would be united and deprive Allende of this position."[47] McCone offered Kissinger and Richard Helms, CIA Director,

$1 million to block Allende's election while Jack
Neal, ITT International Relations Director, made
similar offers on behalf of Geneen to Peter Vaky,
the State Department's Latin American Adviser to
Kissinger.[48] Both offers, all evidence shows, were
turned down.

Undaunted, ITT, in cooperation with some members of the CIA, tried to organize U.S. corporations
operating in Chile to cooperate in creating "economic
chaos," which in turn could be used by "select members of the Chilean Armed Forces" (who had been ap-
proached) to justify a coup against Allende. But in
a memorandum dated October 7, 1970, from William
Merriam (ITT Executive Representative for International Trade) to Edward Gerrity (ITT Senior Vice-
President for Corporate Relations and Advertising),
Merriam lamented that "repeated calls to firms such
as GM, Ford, and banks in California and New York
have drawn no offers of help."[49] Two days later,
Merriam informed McCone that

> Practically no progress has been made in
> trying to get American business to co-
> operate in some way so as to bring eco-
> nomic chaos. . . . According to my
> source, we must continue to keep the
> pressure on business.[50]

The "source" to which Merriam referred in his memorandum of October 9, 1970, was "our contact at the
McLean Agency," namely, the CIA.

At this stage, ITT received an unexpected
boost from the CIA. Put simply, the CIA, in the
person of Broe, wanted ITT's assistance for a plan
to stop Allende from becoming President by causing
economic disruption in Chile. Explaining the raison
d'être for the move, Broe noted:

> Members of the Congress were showing in-
> dications of swinging their full support
> to Allende. . . . It was felt that if
> a large number of Congressmen, Christian
> Democratic Congressmen, swung their
> support for him, he would take office
> with a mandate from the majority and he

would be in a very strong position. At
the same time, the economic situation
had worsened . . . and there were indi-
cations that this was worrying the Christian Democratic Congressmen. There was
a thesis that additional deterioration
in the economic situation could influence a number of Christian Democratic
Congressmen who were planning to vote
for Allende.[51]

Based on the "recommendations" of ITT men "on the
spot," namely, Robert Berrelez (ITT Director, Inter-
American Relations) and Hal Hendrix (ITT Public Relations Director, Latin America), Broe advised:

1. That foreign banks should not renew
   credits or should delay in doing so;
2. That companies operating in Chile
   should delay shipments of spare parts,
   and withdraw all technical assistance; and
3. That there should be a "run" on Savings and Loan Associations, thus,
   forcing them to close their doors to
   customers.[52]

Such measures, Broe hoped, would cause internal un-
rest, and therefore, would swing the congressional
votes to Alessandri or lead to military intervention.
However, Gerrity regarded the "Broe Plan" as "unwork-
able" and rejected it ab initio. In spite of this
position, ITT solicited the views of other U.S. corporations operating in Chile about the "Broe Plan."
    On October 24, 1970, the Chilean Congress con-
firmed Allende's election as President in spite of
ITT's and U.S. government's efforts to stop him.[53]
This issue is discussed in detail in Chapter 4. Meanwhile, ITT moved to the third stage of intervention,
namely, the overthrow of Allende, presumably by a
coup d'état. For a start, it organized an Ad Hoc
Committee on Chile consisting of representatives of
Anaconda, Kennecott, Grace, Pfizer Chemical, Ralston
Purina, Bank of America, and ITT, namely, those companies that "were very concerned about the possibil-

ity of nationalization of their Chilean investments in the very near future."[54] At its first meeting on February 9, 1971, in Merriam's Washington office, it was decided, among other things:

1. That pressure should be applied on the United States' Government through Kissinger's office rather than the State Department "to make it clear that a Chilean takeover would not be tolerated without serious consequences following";[55] and,

2. That pressure should be applied in international lending institutions such as the World Bank and the Inter-American Development Bank "to cease activities in countries that threaten or actually expropriate private investments whether it is done overtly or by 'creeping expropriation.'"[56]

That ITT hoped to accomplish its "mission" by imposing an "invisible economic blockade" on Chile or by making the "economy scream" (apologies to former President Nixon) was clear from a memorandum Merriam sent to Peter Peterson, Executive Director of the Council on International Economic Policy. Dated October 21, 1971, the memo proposed the establishment of a Special National Security Council Task Force on Chile containing an 18-point program, which was not only outrageous but also specifically designed to foment an internal uprising against Allende. The program included restrictions on public and private credits; delaying the purchase of Chilean copper for six months as well as delaying the delivery of fuel, arms, and ammunition to the Chilean Armed Forces; suspension of U.S. bilateral and multilateral assistance; instituting press propaganda against Allende directly or indirectly through support for Chilean conservative newspapers; making contacts with other investor states, particularly Chile's creditors, with a view to taking a concerted action against Chile; and above all making approaches to "reliance sources" in the Chilean Armed Forces as well as discussing with the CIA "how it can assist the 6-month

squeeze."[57] An attachment to the memo advises that
"everything should be done quietly but effectively
to see that Allende does not get through the crucial
next 6 months."[58]

At this stage we do not know the role of ITT
in shaping U.S. policy toward Allende's Chile. What
is clear, however, is that one major reason for
ITT's involvement in Chilean politics can be explained by its $153 million investment in Compania
de telefons de Chile (Chilteco), and the fact that
Allende had campaigned on a platform of the nationalization (or socialization) of the means of production, particularly the copper mines, banks, and public utilities including Chilteco, and these without
compensation or "adequate" compensation. In March
1972, syndicated Washington Post columnist Jack
Anderson published documents revealing attempts and
efforts by ITT to prevent the election of Allende
and, subsequently, to overthrow his government. Two
months later, the United States Senate Foreign Relations Committee voted to investigate Anderson's as-
sertions. As a result, Allende broke off negotiations with ITT regarding compensation for Chilteco.
Inquiries by the Church Committee revealed the extent of ITT's involvement in Chilean politics.[59] On
September 11, 1973, Allende was overthrown in a
bloody military coup.

Undoubtedly, while many or most multinationals
do not pursue such ruthless and persistent politics
of intervention as did ITT in Chile, there are enough
examples of such interventions to suggest that multinationals are in a position to exercise significant
political influence in their home states and often
use that position to favor whatever the corporation
perceives its corporate interests to be. In essence,
therefore, multinationals have posed serious threats
to the national sovereignties of many developing
countries and compounded North-South relations. To
be sure, revelations of political intervention by
multinationals in the politics of the host states
have not only unified Southern outcry against MNCs
and led to a United Nations investigation of these
business enterprises[60] but also have led to a new
spurt of public opinion against MNCs in the host
countries, particularly among government bureaucrats,

radical intellectuals and student bodies, national bourgeoisie, and organized labor.[61]

MULTINATIONALS IN A CHANGING ENVIRONMENT

⟨ Economic nationalism in developing countries is often characterized by the desire to increase control over their economies; it is also often characterized by the desire to secure greater control over alien-owned enterprises that play a very key role in the economy and the development of these countries. The position of many governments in less-developed countries is that the political gains from regulating or controlling the activities of alien-owned enterprises, particularly local subsidiaries of MNCs, will outweigh any economic costs in terms of creating new employment opportunities; local expenditure on goods and services; contribution to government revenues, gross domestic product, and foreign exchange reserves; and transfer of technology. Many of these countries emerged from colonial domination in the 1960s only to discover, to their chagrin, that political independence was not synonymous with economic independence. Put differently, many of these countries emerged from colonial domination in the 1960s only to discover, most painfully, that political independence was often accompanied by a more subtle form of economic dependence that could be as binding as more formal political links. However, concern about economic dependence is not limited to the emergent states of Africa, Asia, and the Caribbean. There is an increasing concern as well in countries such as those in Latin America, which achieved political independence more than a century ago but see themselves as having remained in a dependent economic relation to developed market economies, particularly the United States. In any event, regardless of when political independence was gained, this concern has focused increasingly around the role of MNCs in the economies of these countries. ⟩

In the main, these business entities have been the vehicles through which the natural resources of developing countries have been developed: bauxite

in Guyana and Jamaica, as noted earlier, has been
identified with Alcan, Reynolds, and Revere, while
copper in Chile has meant Anaconda and Kennecott.
More significant, the majority of the imports of developing countries, particularly intermediate and
capital goods, originate with MNCs while a large
proportion of their exports, directly or indirectly,
pass through them (i.e., MNCs). To be sure, "intrafirm" or "related-party trade forms an important
proportion of the total trade undertaken by MNCs.
In 1970 alone, half of the manufactured goods exported by U.S.-based MNCs seemed to have been traded
on an intrafirm basis between parents and majority-
owned subsidiaries while 32 percent of U.S. imports
from developing countries in 1973 were intrafirm deliveries from majority-owned subsidiaries. Additionally, 32 percent of U.S. imports in 1975 were
intrafirm deliveries from majority-owned subsidiaries
while 13 percent were related-party deliveries from
minority-owned affiliates, namely, companies in
which U.S.-based MNCs own between 5 and 49 percent
of the voting stock. In fact, no less than 88 percent of U.S. bauxite imports, 80 percent of rubber
imports, 68 percent of cotton imports, and 67 percent of banana imports are related-party deliveries.[62]
 The MNCs control many of the most important
export commodities of developing countries, and a
high proportion is exported on an intrafirm basis.
Thus, the mining affiliates of U.S. MNCs in Latin
America and the Caribbean export up to 80 percent of
their total sales to their parent companies. More
important, available data suggest that the bulk of
world production and processing of a number of export commodities is controlled by very few MNCs:
while three multinationals share 70 percent of the
world's production, marketing, and distribution of
bananas, six multinationals control 60 percent of
bauxite production capacity as well as 70 percent of
aluminum production capacity; additionally, fewer
than ten MNCs share the world's production and processing of copper, iron ore, lead, nickel, tea, tin,
tobacco, and zinc. In some cases, such as the Dominican Republic and Haiti, the whole of a country's
output (i.e., bauxite) is exported on an intrafirm
basis.[63]

The role of MNCs in the manufacturing sector
has been more important in relation to the imports
of developing countries than their exports. For example, imports by subsidiaries of MNCs into the six
newly industrialized countries in Latin America exceed that of exports by a ratio of 3 to 1; in Mexico
alone, the imports of MNCs are more than double
those of nationalized (state-owned) enterprises.
However, as far as manufactured goods are concerned,
the bulk of the exports of developing countries consist of labor-intensive products, although a rapidly
increasing proportion consists of machinery, transport equipment, and miscellaneous light manufactured
goods. Indeed, a significant proportion of these
exports is manufactured by subsidiaries of foreign-
based MNCs, and in 1976 a large proportion of these
products in Brazil, Argentina, Mexico, and India
were intrafirm deliveries from majority-owned subsidiaries of German-based MNCs.[64]
        Critics of the role of multinationals in devel-
oping countries have commented on the effect of
direct foreign investment on local competition and
entrepreneurship. In the introduction to his classic
study on the role of the International Petroleum Company in Peruvian development, Adalberto Pinelo lamented on the impact of U.S.-based MNCs on the ownership patterns in Latin America.[65] Specifically,
there are two aspects to this issue. The first is
the effect of the entry of foreign-owned enterprises
on existing or potential local enterprises in the
same business, while the second concerns the effect
of the marketing practices of foreign enterprises in
shaping or "distorting" local tastes and creating a
form of cultural dependency. For example, Isaiah
Frank comments on "how local entrepreneurs are
smothered when multinationals, with their tremendous
technological and financial resources, establish
subsidiaries in developing countries."[66] He adds:

> Existing firms may be forced out of
> business or may decide to sell out to
> the multinationals. Moreover, barri-
> ers are created to the entry of new,
> indigenous entrepreneurs as a conse-
> quence of the advertising, promotion,

and product-differentiation practices
of multinationals.[67]

According to Garret Fitzgerald, "a survey of 396
transnationals operating in developing countries
showed that close to 60 percent of 2,904 subsidiaries existing in the late 1960s had been set up
by acquisition rather than by new investment."[68]
While the marketing practices of multinationals
place barriers on the entry of new, local business-
men, such practices often lead to another "dimension
of the Third World's concern: the stimulation by
multinationals of a demand for types of products too
sophisticated for, or otherwise inappropriate to, a
poor country's stage of development."[69] Thus, the
marketing practices of the multinationals are therefore "seen as suppressing local entrepreneurs not
only by direct competition but also by capitalizing
on and reinforcing a strong prejudice in favor of
foreign products. . . . This is regarded as objec-
tionable not only in economic terms but also because
it perpetuates a form of sociocultural dependence
rooted in the colonial experience from which the developing countries seek emancipation."[70]

Multinationals control many of the most important export commodities of developing countries, and
a large proportion of these exports are intrafirm
deliveries from majority-owned subsidiaries. However, the market power of MNCs is reinforced by col-
lective or cartel agreements with other firms, particularly with other multinationals operating in
similar markets. According to Fitzgerald, studies
in the United Kingdom and the Federal Republic of
Germany indicate that MNCs "participated in approximately 70 percent of all export cartels" in both
countries. These cartel agreements, declared Fitzgerald, "include provisions for the allocation of
export and import markets as well as quotas for production, frequently including price-fixing, collec-
tive actions such as boycotts to deter new entrants,
and notification clauses to enable members of the
cartel to engage in collusive tenderings in regard
to imports."[71]

Finally, "spheres of influence" are not only
evident in the exports of MNCs in small developing

countries, meaning that these countries must pay more for imports of manufactured goods (such as machinery, chemicals, and steel) than are paid for comparable imports by larger developing countries; "spheres of influence" are also evident in the location of manufacturing subsidiaries as well as the percentage of direct foreign investments in the Third World. Data show that in 12 former British colonies in Africa, five in Asia, one in the Middle East (South Yemen and Aden), and one in the Western Hemisphere (British Honduras), over half (in a majority of cases, well over three-quarters) of direct foreign investment at the end of 1967 was British;[72] at the same time, over two-thirds of direct foreign investments in 14 former French colonies in Africa, one in Asia (French Polynesia), and two in the Western Hemisphere (French Antilles and French Guyana) represented French investments[73] while between 85 and 88 percent of direct foreign investments in Burundi, Ruanda, and Zaire was Belgian.[74] A similar degree of dominance by the United States was evident in a large number of Latin American countries as well as certain countries in the Middle East, Asia, and Africa although the distribution of direct foreign investments in some of these countries is changing.[75] For example, at the end of 1967, the percentage of the United States share of direct foreign investments in Argentina, Brazil, Colombia, Mexico, South Korea, Thailand, and the Philippines stood at 55.8, 35.6, 86.2, 76.4, 92.3, 20.1, and 92.3, respectively; however, the percentage of the United States share of direct foreign investments in the years indicated stood at 39.5 (1971), 32.2 (1976), 48.1 (1975), 68.7 (1975), 14.0 (1975), and 47.9 (1976), respectively.[76] Finally, in South Korea and Thailand, the percentage of the Japanese share of direct foreign investments in 1975 stood at 66.5 and 41.0, respectively, while the percentage of Japanese share of direct foreign investments in Indonesia in 1976 stood at 36.9.[77] To be sure, 70 percent of Japanese subsidiaries in the late 1960s and early 1970s were to be found in Asia and Oceania. Undoubtedly, the concentration of British investments in the former British colonies or the concentration of U.S. investments in Latin America and

Asia or the dominance of Japanese investments in
Asia reflects past colonial or semicolonial relationships.

Certainly, these are some of the features of
the activities of MNCs that have given rise to a
number of proposals that their activities be regulated, controlled, or monitored to ensure that their
operations are not at variance with the interests
and goals of developing countries. Consequently, we
have witnessed in the past two decades or so a rash
of "creeping expropriations," expropriations of the
assets of MNCs without "prompt, adequate, and effective" compensation, or unilateral termination of
concession agreements or state's contracts (with
aliens). These measures are symptomatic of a changing balance of power between MNCs and host countries.
The home countries of these business entities which
are subject to "expropriatory" measures increasingly
find themselves inhibited from the kind of interven-
tionism which they have resorted to in the 1950s.
But they have devised elegant measures aimed at protecting and defending their nationals' investments
abroad.

As a consequence, then, of the new economic
nationalism that has characterized the politics of
developing countries since the late 1960s as well as
the changing circumstances governing the relationship between MNCs and host countries on the one hand
and between developing countries and developed market economies on the other, we can expect a continua-
tion, indeed an intensification, of the conflicts between the North and South, and above all between the
nation-state and the MNC. Yet, an effective col-
laboration between governments and business is a sine
qua non for dealing with most of the major problems
facing the international community today. For many,
it appears self-evident that MNCs jeopardize the
sovereignty and independence of nation-states. Thus,
the publication of the ITT Papers on the purported
subversive activities of the International Telephone
and Telegraph Company in Chile created much sensation
not only in Chile but elsewhere in the world. There
are several instances when assets of alien-owned enterprises whose annual revenues sometimes exceed the
total outputs of the host countries have been nation-

alized by the host governments without a moment's hesitation. More significant, while the AFL-CIO and the sponsors of the Burke-Hartke Bill claim that U.S-based MNCs export jobs and capital from the United States,[78] leaders and radical intellectuals of developing countries maintain that MNCs exploit their irreplaceable natural resources for the benefit of their home countries. Certainly, all these propositions cannot be simultaneously true, if only because MNCs cannot at the same time be exporting benefits from the home countries and from host countries. Thus, "the benefits in question have to end in one geographical area or the other."[79] But this is not the place to join in the debate on the effects of direct foreign investments on the home and host countries. Nowhere is the study and understanding of the business-government relationship more important than in relation to MNCs. There lies the significance of this study.

NOTES

1. Adeoye A. Akinsanya, The Expropriation of Multinational Property in the Third World (New York: Praeger, 1980), pp. 115-86; Anthony Sampson, The Seven Sisters: The Great Oil Companies and the World They Made (London: Hodder and Stoughton, 1975), pp. 70-75, 128-54.
2. Raymond Vernon, Story Over the Multinationals: The Real Issues (Cambridge, Mass.: Harvard University Press, 1977); Isaiah Frank, Foreign Enterprise in Developing Countries (Baltimore, Md.: Johns Hopkins University Press, 1980); Sanjaya Lall and Paul Streeten, Foreign Investment, Transnationals, and Developing Countries (London: Macmillan Press, 1977); United Nations, Multinational Corporations in World Development, Publication no. E.73.II, A.11, 1973; Akinsanya, pp. 333-42; Patrick M. Boarman and Hans Schollhammer, Multinational Corporations and Governments: Business-Government Relations in an International Context (New York: Praeger, 1975).
3. Adalberto J. Pinelo, The Multinational Corporation as a Force in Latin American Politics: A Case Study of the International Petroleum Company in Peru (New York: Praeger, 1973), p. x.

4. See Dale F. Johnson, John Pollock, and Jane Sweeney, "ITT and the CIA: The Making of a Foreign Policy," The Progressive (May 1972): 16. The authors noted that U.S.-owned mining corporations "took out billions of dollars in profits over the years with minimal reinvestment of earnings for the benefit of the Chilean economy. U.S. Department of Commerce figures for 1953-1968, for example, indicate that mining and smelting operations in Chile (about ninety percent copper) earned $1.036 billion while new investments and reinvestment of profits together totaled only $71 million." Also, Akin Ogunpola and Oladeji Ojo, "The Role of Multinational Corporations in the Economic Development of African Countries," Nigerian Journal of International Studies 1 (1975): 67-88; Akinsanya, The Expropriation of Multinational Property in the Third World, p. 97.

5. An "expropriatory" measure refers to any measure taken or authorized by legislation or a ministerial order that has the effect of (1) unilaterally terminating, repudiating, or modifying a state's contracts or concession agreements (with aliens); (2) effectively taking control or management of private alien-owned enterprises or effectively impairing operations of such enterprises; and (3) establishing a state monopoly in certain sectors of the economy.

6. Pinelo, The Multinational Corporation, p. x (emphasis in original).

7. Ibid.

8. Vernon, Sovereignty at Bay--The Multinational Spread of U.S. Enterprises (New York: Basic Books, 1971), p. 172; Garret Fitzgerald, Unequal Partners (New York: United Nations, 1979), Publication no. TAD/INF/PUB/78.6, p. 18.

9. Akinsanya, "Host-Government's Responses to Foreign Economic Control: The Experiences of Selected African Countries," International and Comparative Law Quarterly 30 (1981): 769-90; Id., Economic Independence and Indigenization of Private Foreign Investments: The Experiences of Nigeria and Ghana (Columbia: Institute of International Studies, University of South Carolina, 1982).

10. Pinelo, The Multinational Corporation, p. xi.

11. Michael Morris, Farid G. Lavipour, and Karl P. Sauvant, "The Politics of Nationalization: Guyana vs Alcan," in Controlling Multinational Enterprises, ed. Karl P. Sauvant and Farid G. Lavipour (Boulder, Colo.: Westview Press, 1976), p. 119.

12. Ibid., pp. 119-20.

13. Geoffrey Chandler, "The Myth of Oil Power: International Groups and National Sovereignty," International Affairs 46 (1970): 717.

14. Ibid.

15. Ibid.

16. Ibid., p. 718.

17. U.S. Congress, Senate, Multinational Corporations and United States Foreign Policy. Hearings Before the Subcommittee on Multinational Corporations of the Committee on Foreign Relations on the International Telephone and Telegraph Company and Chile 1970-71, 93d. Cong., 1973, Part 1 (Washington, D.C.: Government Printing Office, 1973), pp. 342-43.

18. Ibid., p. 371.

19. Ibid., p. 379.

20. Ibid., p. 388.

21. Ibid., p. 385.

22. Pinelo, The Multinational Corporation, p. xii.

23. Ibid.

24. Charles H. Lipson, "Corporate Preferences and Public Policies. Foreign Aid Sanctions and Investment Protection," World Politics 28 (1976): 405-6. Under the Hickenlooper Amendment, the United States President is required, by law, to suspend U.S. bilateral assistance to any country that expropriates U.S. investments and does not provide "prompt, adequate and effective" compensation within six months. Under this amendment, foreign aid sanctions are automatic, and under it, the U.S. government formally suspended U.S. bilateral assistance to Sri Lanka, following Sri Lanka's oil expropriations affecting U.S. oil interests. U.S. bilateral assistance to Peru was quietly suspended without a formal application of the Hickenlooper Amendment. See Akinsanya, The Expropriation of Multinational Property in the Third World, pp. 170-73, 275-300.

25. Lipson, p. 406.

26. Theodore C. Sorensen, "Improper Payments Abroad: Perspectives and Proposals," Foreign Affairs 54 (1976): 722.

27. Because the major oil companies control the market, it was possible to enforce a boycott of Iranian oil following the expropriation of the Anglo-Iranian Oil Company in May 1951. This boycott and other measures contributed to the coup d'état organized by General Fazollah Zahedi with the covert support of the U.S. Central Intelligence Agency and other Western European intelligence agencies. See Richard M. Nixon, The Real War (New York: Warner Books, 1980), p. 83.

28. The Trading with the Enemy Act of 1917 empowers the President to regulate all commercial and financial transactions by U.S. nationals with foreign countries or nationals in time of war or national emergency while the Export Control Act of 1949 and its successor, the Export Administration Act of 1969, vest the Executive Branch with the authority to "prohibit or curtail" all commercial exports including technical know-how to communist countries from U.S. companies or their foreign affiliates. However, the U.S. government seems to have restricted the application of the Trading with the Enemy Act to "non-strategic trade," as permission has been granted to U.S. companies to trade with Cuba and other communist states. The attempt by the U.S. government to prevent Fruehauf, a U.S. company manufacturing trucks in France, from selling trailer trucks to a French company which had planned to sell them to the People's Republic of China, was resisted by the French government while the French courts considered the application of the Trading with the Enemy Act in France as abus de droit (abuse of a legal right). See Joan E. Spero, The Politics of International Economic Relations (New York: St. Martin's Press, 1977), pp. 101-2; William L. Craig, "The Application of the Trading with the Enemy Act to Foreign Corporations Owned by Americans: Reflections on Fruehauf v Massardy," Harvard Law Review 83 (1970): 579-601.

29. Lloyd N. Cutler, Global Interdependence and the Multinational Firm (New York: Foreign Policy Association, 1978), p. 18.

30. Spero, Politics, p. 200.

31. Pinelo, The Multinational Corporation, pp. 3-30.

32. Ibid., p. 19.

33. Ibid.

34. James R. Kurth, "The Multinational Corporation, U.S. Foreign Policy, and the Less Developed Countries," in The New Sovereigns: Multinational Corporations as World Powers, ed. Abdul A. Said and Luiz R. Simmons (Englewood Cliffs, N.J.: Prentice-Hall, 1975), pp. 143-44.

35. Sampson, pp. 113-39; Robert Scheer, "Eisenhower's Role Recounted. How CIA Orchestrated '53 Coup in Iran," Los Angeles Times, March 29, 1979, Part I, pp. 5-8. The author is grateful to Harold S. Kerbo (California Polytechnic State University, San Luis Obispo) for bringing his attention to this publication.

36. Kurth, "The Multinational Corporation," pp. 149-50.

37. Ibid., p. 150.

38. U.S. Congress, Senate, Multinational Corporations and United States Foreign Policy, p. 246.

39. Ibid., p. 247.

40. These included El Mercurio, Diaria Illustrado, and La Segunda, which, according to Hal Hendrix (ITT Public Relations Director for Latin America), "were getting thinner and thinner for lack of advertising." See U.S. Congress, Senate, Multinational Corporations and United States Foreign Policy, p. 127.

41. The results of the election are as follows: Allende 1,075,616 votes; Alessandri 1,036,278 votes; and Tomic 524,849 votes. See U.S. Congress, Senate, Multinational Corporations and United States Foreign Policy, p. 10.

42. Akinsanya, The Expropriation of Multinational Property in the Third World, p. 303.

43. The congressional election of Allende as the Chilean President was almost certain after the Christian Democrats led by Tomic decided on October 5, 1970, to support his candidacy in the run-off election. See Bertrand Russell Peace Foundation, Subversion in Chile: A Case Study in U.S. Corporate Intrigue in the Third World (Nottingham, England:

Bertrand Russell Peace Foundation, 1972), pp. 14, 16, 21.

44. See U.S. Congress, Senate, Multinational Corporations and United States Foreign Policy, pp. 11, 154-55, 160, 282-83.

45. Ibid., pp. 13, 250-51.

46. Ibid., p. 11.

47. Ibid., p. 102.

48. At the June 1970 meeting of the "Forty Committee" chaired by Kissinger, the committee, which had responsibility for approving CIA covert global operations, authorized a CIA fund of $400,000 to support anti-Allende media campaigns. See James F. Petras and Morris M. Morley, How Allende Fell (Nottingham, England: Bertrand Russell Peace Foundation, 1974), p. 29.

49. Bertrand Russell Peace Foundation, p. 51.

50. Ibid., p. 52.

51. U.S. Congress, Senate, Multinational Corporations and United States Foreign Policy, pp. 250-51 (emphasis added).

52. Ibid., p. 172.

53. Initial efforts by the U.S. government to stop Allende from becoming the President through a military coup d'état cost the life of General Rene Schneider, Commander-in-Chief of the Army. See Clark R. Mollenhoff, Alleged Assassination Reports Involving Foreign Leaders: An Interim Report of the Select Committee to Study Governmental Operations with Respect to Intelligence Activities (New York: Norton, 1976), pp. 225-54; see also Abraham F. Lowenthal, "The United States and Latin America: Ending the Hegemonic Presumption," Foreign Affairs 55 (October 1976): 199-213.

54. U.S. Congress, Senate, Multinational Corporations and United States Foreign Policy, p. 44.

55. Ibid.

56. Ibid.

57. Ibid., pp. 41-42; also U.S. Congress, Senate, Multinational Corporations and United States Foreign Policy, Part 2, pp. 940-42.

58. U.S. Congress, Senate, Multinational Corporations and United States Foreign Policy, Part 1, p. 40 (emphasis added).

59. See U.S. Congress, Senate, Multinational Corporations and United States Foreign Policy, Part 1; U.S. Congress, Senate, Multinational Corporations and United States Foreign Policy, Part 2.
60. United Nations, Multinational Corporations in World Development, Publication no. E.73.II, A.11, 1973; Id., The Impact of Multinational Corporations on Development and International Relations, Publication no. E.74.II, A.5, 1974.
61. See Akinsanya, "Host-Governments' Responses to Foreign Economic Control," pp. 769-90; Id., Economic Independence and Indigenization of Private Foreign Investments.
62. Fitzgerald, Unequal Partners, p. 11.
63. Ibid., pp. 11-12.
64. Ibid.
65. Pinelo, The Multinational Corporation, p. x. The International Petroleum Company, until its expropriation by the Velasco regime in October 1968, is a wholly owned subsidiary (99.5 percent) of Standard Oil Company (New Jersey), the world's largest industrial corporation, with annual sales of $103.1 billion according to the August 1981 Fortune List of the world's 50 largest industrial corporations.
66. Frank, Foreign Enterprise, p. 43.
67. Ibid.
68. Fitzgerald, Unequal Partners, p. 12.
69. Frank, Foreign Enterprise, p. 43.
70. Ibid., p. 44.
71. Fitzgerald, Unequal Partners, p. 13.
72. United Nations, Multinational Corporations in World Development, pp. 182-85.
73. Ibid.
74. Ibid., pp. 182-83.
75. Ibid., pp. 182-85.
76. Frank, Foreign Enterprise, pp. 14-15.
77. Ibid., p. 15.
78. See Dana T. Ackerly, "The Multinational Corporation and World Economic Development," American Journal of International Law 66 (1972): 14-22.
79. Boarman and Schollhammer, "Preface," in Multinational Corporations and Governments, p. vi.

Multinationals in a Changing Environment: The Nature of the Problem

Studies of economic nationalism in developing countries suggest that, aside from fundamental changes in form of governments,[1] its causes are to be found in such factors as:

1. Changes in the bargaining power between MNCs and host states in cases of investment in natural resources. Put differently, as developing countries experience rapid economic growth, they gradually become aware of their increased bargaining power with MNCs. More important, as local firms acquire the much-needed skills and technology-- indeed, as the host states acquire the much-needed capital and technology through a variety of sources-- the basis for the incentives initially given to foreign firms is severely undermined, thus, neces- sitating the need for regulation and control.
2. Increasing support for the widely held view that developing countries are too dependent on alien enterprises which export vital and irreplace- able natural resources; that alien enterprises, particularly local subsidiaries of MNCs, through various devices take a disproportionate share of their profits out of the host state; and that alien enterprises generally exercise undue influence and power over host governments and lives of people.
3. Increasing political sensitiveness of the leaders of developing countries to the demands by

various interest groups that the activities of foreign enterprises be regulated, controlled, and monitored.[2]

In Africa, Asia, Latin America, and the Caribbean as well as the Middle East, the resentment of alien control of the economy and the fear of exploitation of vital natural resources by local subsidiaries of MNCs are very deep. In many developing countries, the economic benefits of direct foreign investment are not particularly visible to the masses, perhaps only to a few members of the local elite. Many people in developing countries believe that their valuable, vital, and irreplaceable natural resources have been exploited and are being exploited for the benefit of alien enterprises and their stockholders, as well as their home states rather than for the host states. More significant, although local subsidiaries of MNCs provide jobs and capital, they do not provide the technology that can be readily used in the host economies; additionally, they force small local firms out of business and distort local tastes through massive expenditures on advertising. Finally, domestic and financial policies of many developing countries can easily be subverted by international capital flows controlled by multinational corporations.

Therefore, the drive to regulate the activities of local subsidiaries of MNCs and, by extension, increase national control over the economy, is manifested in a rash of creeping expropriations (near-confiscatory or prohibitive taxes); expropriation of assets of alien firms; renegotiation or revocation of concession agreements/state contracts (with aliens); or intervention of alien firms (i.e., taking over the management of such firms without an ultimate determination of legal ownership).

THE SOVEREIGN RIGHT TO EXPROPRIATE PRIVATE FOREIGN INVESTMENTS AND THE OBLIGATION TO PAY COMPENSATION

When a sovereign state, in the exercise of the power of <u>dominium eminens</u> (eminent domain), takes

over or expropriates the assets of local subsidiaries of MNCs, it is expected that the taking
state will discharge its obligations under customary
rules of international law, namely, by making repa-
rations to the deprived alien investors. The rule,
which has developed over the years, albeit largely
by the major investor states, is that a state's
sovereign right to expropriate alien-owned enterprises is qualified by four conditions. The first
is that the state can only expropriate assets located within its territorial jurisdiction. Second,
the taking must be in the public interest, that is,
the state must not act in an arbitrary or retaliatory manner in exercising its power to expropriate
alien investments. Third, the taking must not be
directed against particular racial or national
groups. And, fourth, the taking state must pay compensation, which, according to the U.S. Secretary of
State Cordell Hull, must be "prompt, adequate and
effective."3

Generally, there seems to be no disagreement
among scholars and states (socialist or free enterprise) on the first two conditions. However, some
controversies have centered on the latter two conditions. Thus, while some (Western) scholars and
investor states have interpreted the rule on nondiscrimination to mean that the taking state must
not discriminate between nationals and aliens,
other scholars and taking states have interpreted
the rule on nondiscrimination to mean that the taking state must neither discriminate between aliens
nor direct its expropriatory measures against particular national or racial groups.4 Interestingly
enough, it is the latter view that seems to have
been accepted by most states and scholars.

Therefore, the point of disagreement is on the
requirement and measure of compensation. To be
sure, conflicting public policies on the requirement
and measure of compensation can be discerned in the
practices of states. While the major investor
states still hold the view that the legality of an
expropriatory measure is contingent on the payment
of "prompt, adequate and effective" compensation
(see, for example, Nixon Doctrine of Economic
Assistance and Investment Security in Developing

Nations, January 19, 1972),[5] the Soviet-bloc nations
generally reject the view that the taking state has
any obligations to pay compensation although it may,
for reasons of political expedience, pay some compensation that is far from being "prompt, adequate
and effective." The problem is compounded because
developing countries, that more often than not expropriate alien assets, do not have any uniform
public policies on the payment of compensation.
While some developing countries make provisions for
the payment of "just," "equitable," or "prompt"
compensation in their constitutions, investment
laws, or bilateral treaties (i.e., the so-called
Treaties of Friendship, Commerce, and Navigation),
other developing countries hold the view that compensation could be paid by the taking state subject
to deduction of "excess profits" or "back taxes."
But other developing countries reject any obligations on the part of the taking state to pay compensation for general and impersonal expropriations,
pleading the principle of national treatment or
equality of treatment. Yet other developing countries, while recognizing an obligation on the part
of the taking state to pay compensation in accordance with municipal law rather than international
law, contend that the payment of compensation must
reflect the circumstances of the taking or the economic conditions and the realities of the taking
state, meaning that compensation need not be
"prompt, adequate and effective."[6]

   In any event, when a state expropriates alien
assets and pays compensation to the deprived alien
investor or reaches a compensation settlement, a
potential investment dispute is resolved to the
satisfaction of both parties. It is when a taking
state, such as Mexico in the 1920s,[7] maintains that
international law does not require the payment of
compensation for expropriations of a general and
impersonal character or contends that aliens cannot
demand and receive compensation when this right
(i.e., to compensation) is denied to its own na-
tionals--pleading the principle of equality of
treatment,[8] indeed, it is when a taking state re-
fuses to pay any compensation or when compensation
is illusory or when there is a manifest "denial of

justice"--that the investor state, as a matter of
right and duty notwithstanding "Calvo clauses" entrenched in state's contracts (with aliens), calls
on the taking state to discharge its obligations
under customary international law.

SOME HYPOTHESES

     Certain basic assumptions underlining this
study must be stated at this point. The first is
that most "expropriatory" measures taken by Third
World countries can be defended or justified on
grounds of "public interest," a wide term that is
likely to comprise "economic necessity." Expropriation of alien assets have generally not been
questioned by investors or investor states even if
the measures were retaliatory or arbitrary (or when
the expropriation proceedings involve a manifest
perversion or denial of procedural justice) provided
there is a bona fide offer to pay compensation.
Essentially, left-wing or right-wing regimes in the
Third World have expropriated alien assets, thus,
showing that expropriation, more often than not,
is a phenomenon of economic nationalism. This is
particularly significant because some capital-
exporting countries, while concerned about the
security of their nationals' investments abroad,
are equally concerned about extensive foreign control of their economies. For example, while the
Canadian government is worried about the country's
domination by United States-based MNCs, it is
equally concerned about the security and safety of
Canadian direct foreign investments, particularly
in the Caribbean.[9]
     Second, private investors engage in business
abroad not for humanitarian reasons but to make
profits. Therefore, if they make profits, they expect, not unnaturally, that they will be entitled
to keep them subject to the payment of taxation,
and that they will be allowed to carry on with their
own operations subject only to the "superior"
needs of the host state.[10]
     Third, when assets of local subsidiaries of
MNCs are expropriated on grounds of public interest,

we expect a "conflict of interests" between the
taking state and the deprived alien investor. In
the main, the conflict centers on the quantum of
compensation. Consequently, while the taking state
usually, and not unnaturally, favors the book value
because this guarantees less than adequate compensation (since the alien firm uses book value for
tax purposes), the alien investor usually, and not
unnaturally, favors going-concern values or market
value, since this guarantees adequate compensation.
This conflict is, by no means, irreconcilable;
sometimes the bargaining power of the deprived
alien investor is enhanced if there is a strong convergence of interests between the investor and a
major investor state which need not be its home
state. For example, when Guyana announced the nationalization of Demba (a subsidiary of Alcan) in
February 1971, Alcan put Demba's gross value at $114
million although its book value for Guyanese tax
purposes stood at $46 million. Because the
Guyanese compensation formula contains provisions
that the U.S. government felt would be tantamount
to expropriation without compensation, a view that
coincided with Alcan's, the U.S. Executive Director
of the World Bank in June 1971 abstained from voting on a Guyanese application for a $5.4 million
World Bank loan for sea defense dikes and ultimately
killed the application. Because of U.S. action,
the compensation settlement of July 14, 1971, fa-
vored Alcan: Alcan received $80 million ($53.5 million basic compensation and $26.5 million from
interest payments minus withholding tax).[11] Finally, not every taking of alien assets generates
diplomatic controversy between the taking state and
the investor state; thus, much depends on the volume
of investments expropriated, the influence and power
that can be wielded by the investors in the politics
of the home state, and the way the home state perceives the taking in terms of its overall foreign
policy interests.
     Having said that much, what then are the con-
sequences of expropriating the assets of local subsidiaries of MNCs? This question is very easy to

formulate but difficult to answer. But three hypotheses lend themselves to inquiry.

Hypothesis 1: Whereas expropriations of the
service sectors (banking, insurance, hotels, etc.)
do not generate much diplomatic controversies between the taking and investor states because the
assets involved are usually valued only in hundreds
of thousands of dollars, expropriations of the
mining (extractive), power, communications, and
agricultural sectors usually and generally generate
much-heated diplomatic controversies between the
taking and investor states and could lead to
government-to-government confrontation, particularly
if such investments carry government insurance
coverage.

Hypothesis 2: Whereas it is in the interest
of developed market economies (core societies) and
their MNCs (hereafter referred to as core actors)
not to support political violence in developing
countries (periphery societies) when the domestic
conditions in these countries continue to protect
and promote their (core societies') interests, when
developing countries (periphery societies) attempt
to "opt out of the world system" or attempt to restructure the economic relation favorable to the
core societies, then economic actors (MNCs) in core
societies work with their home governments to cause
economic and political disruptions in the periphery
societies (developing countries), disruptions that
could be used as a pretext for foreign military
intervention (ostensibly to protect political and
strategic interests) or used as an excuse by the
military establishment to stage a coup d'état and
restore the old political order. Put differently,
when assets of local subsidiaries of MNCs are expropriated, thus ending or eliminating the exploit-
ative or dependent relationship between the core and
the periphery, the independent power of economic
actors in the core societies can be combined with
their home governments' instruments of pressure
(some subtle, some blunt) to cause economic and
political disruptions in the periphery, disruptions

which can be used as a pretext for foreign military intervention (ostensibly to protect political and strategic interests) or used as an excuse by the military establishment to stage a coup d'état and restore the old political order.

Hypothesis 3: As a corollary to Hypothesis 2, foreign military intervention, whether overt or covert (proxy) or foreign-directed and foreign-influenced, a coup d'état following expropriations of assets or acquired rights of local subsidiaries of MNCs, more often than not, leads to increased foreign "business activity," in terms of increased private foreign investments and/or restitution of expropriated assets.

Should this study show,

1. That expropriations of assets in the mining, power, communications, and agricultural sectors rather than expropriations of the service industries generate much-heated diplomatic controversies and have led to government-to-government confrontation;
2. That economic actors in the core societies following the expropriations of their assets in the periphery societies often work in concert with their home governments to cause economic and political disruptions in the periphery, disruptions that can be used as a pretext for foreign military intervention (covert or overt) or used as an excuse by the military establishment to stage a coup d'état and restore the old political order; and
3. That foreign military intervention or foreign-directed and foreign-influenced coup d'état following expropriations of the assets of economic actors in the core societies

> have led to increased foreign busi-
> ness activity in terms of increased
> private foreign investments and/or
> restitution of expropriated assets,

then, we would have been in a position to determine
whether and under what circumstances business benefits from a government's foreign interventions,
whether covert or overt. Put differently, we would
have been able to determine the effects of inter-
ventionism on foreign business activity and the
interrelations of business and governmental
activity.[12]

SCOPE AND SIGNIFICANCE OF THE STUDY

As stated in Chapter 1, nowhere is the study
and understanding of the business-government relationships more important than in relation to MNCs.
Perhaps a prime issue in North-South relations for
the remainder of the century is the ongoing confrontation between two gigantic forces, namely,
"the political power of nation-states and the economic power of multinational corporations."[13]
Samuel Pisar has noted:

> Relations between national economic
> power and multinational economic power
> are profoundly ambiguous, rather like
> an erratic love and hate affair. The
> states need the multinational enter-
> prises because they stimulate the lo-
> cal business activity, create jobs and
> bring in tax revenues. At the same
> time, the states dislike this anonymous
> force which, true only to its own aspi-
> rations, remains outside their control.
> Governments want to protect their own
> national interests against decisions
> taken elsewhere that can affect the
> everyday life, the economic climate
> and even the social stability of their
> countries.[14]

Consequently, since the nation-states and the MNCs need each other, it seems clear that the basic problem is how to create a meaningful balance between economic and political power and between economic and political responsibility. That is why a number of specific proposals have been suggested to deal with some of the problems posed for developing countries by the activities of MNCs.

A subject of central importance and concern to governments and leaders of the Third World as well as some developed market economies (such as Canada and Organization for Economic Cooperation and Development/European Economic Community, OECD-EEC, member states)[15] that are concerned about the domination of their economies by U.S.-based MNCs, this study focuses on the problematical and sensitive issues of private foreign investments in the Third World and the policy implications for domestic political instability, economic independence, and modernization. Additionally, while this study will obviously and certainly throw more light on the relevance of the "dependency" theory to the political economy of Third World countries, a general explanation of expropriation patterns as well as the reactions of investor states can become a guide to action on the part of both the taking and investor states. To be sure, such an explanation can be used to evaluate, for policy purposes, the form and the scope that direct foreign investments should take; it can also be used to estimate the likely consequences of expropriation of assets of alien investors. Furthermore, while some studies have focused on the role of MNCs in international relations and development, and these invariably have been confined to Latin America,[16] this study takes a global view of MNCs as international political actors. Finally, although a growing number of studies on MNCs have been written by economists, business management scholars, and operational research specialists, until the early 1970s students of politics have ignored these business entities. This study, therefore, is another in the series carried out by students of politics on the role of MNCs in international politics.

However, there are two issues or aspects to which this study will not address itself. First, this study will not concern itself with the evolution of MNCs. The evolution of MNCs or the multinational spread of companies is too well-documented to merit any discussion in a study of this nature. Consequently, any discussion of the evolution of MNCs or the multinational spread of companies would be a mere academic exercise.[17] Second, we are equally not concerned about the legality or otherwise of expropriation of multinational assets or for that matter whether the law of state responsibility for injuries to aliens is or should be a universal principle of international law. This subject is best handled by international lawyers, although various studies do show that this is an aspect of international law on which opinions are sharply divergent. It is small wonder, therefore, that the debates continue.[18]

PROBLEMS OF DEFINITION AND DESCRIPTION

Now a word about the terms multinational corporation and Third World. Although the term multinational corporation is commonly used, sometimes references are also made to "international," "supranational," "global," or "transnational" corporations, and even "cosmocorps."[19] Various scholars have tried to make distinctions between these terms. But the state of the art is that one man's "multinational" enterprise is another's "transnational" one, and his "supranational" enterprise is the second's "international" enterprise or the third's "multinational" business enterprise. According to Vernon, a multinational enterprise is

> a parent company that controls a large
> cluster of corporations of various
> nationalities. The corporations that
> make up each cluster appear to have
> access to a common pool of human and
> financial resources and seem responsive
> to elements of a common strategy. Size
> is important as well; a cluster of this

sort with less than $100 million in
sales rarely merits much attention.
Moreover, the nature of the group's
activities outside its home country is
relevant, mere exporters, even exporters with well-established sales subsidiaries abroad, are unlikely to draw
much attention, and mere licensers of
technology are just as rarely mentioned. Finally, the enterprises involved generally have a certain amount
of geographical spread; a patent with
a stake in only a country or two outside its home base is not often found
on the list [of multinational enter-
prises].[20]

Four basic characteristics of the MNC can be discerned from this definition: size, central control,
geographical spread, and distribution by industry.
What, then, is an "international" corporation?
Charles Kindleberger sees an international corporation as one having "no country to which it owes
more loyalty than any other or any country where it
feels completely at home. It equalizes the return
on its investment capital in every country, after
adjustment for risk."[21] Jack Behram defines it as a

large [domestic] corporation which has
a substantial overseas investment in
operating subsidiaries or affiliates--
sometimes including licensees. A size-
able export volume out of total sales
would not indicate that a company was
"international." Nor does size make
a company "international."[22]

Obviously, there are marked differences, from the
way they are defined, between multinational and
international enterprises. The problem of definition is hardly minimized because a transnational
enterprise is defined a "an internationally owned
and/or [financially] controlled enterprise . . .
the capital of which is owned or controlled by economic agents of more than one nationality,[23] while

a global corporation "may be global, with such per-
vasive operations that it is beyond the effective
reach of the national policies of any country and,
in the absence of supranational policy, free to some
extent to make decisions in the interest of corporate
efficiency alone."[24]

Because of the confused state of the art, all
that can be said here is the terms multinational,
international, transnational, and global corporation
can be regarded as interchangeable. However, "multinational" will be used interchangeably with transnational" throughout this study. Accordingly, a
multinational corporation is a centrally controlled
business enterprise--manufacturing, mining, and
financial--which has operations in two or more countries. Implicit in this definition, which tallies
with Vernon's, are two characteristics: central
control under a common strategy and operations in
two or more countries. First, the headquarters of
the MNC is located in one country, usually a developed country, called the home state. A corollary
to this characteristic is that the MNC seeks to
maximize the profits not of its overseas subsidiaries but rather of the parent company. Thus, the
parent company may even be operating certain of its
subsidiaries at an "official" loss. Second, the
subsidiaries are to be found in other countries,
usually in the developing countries of Africa, Asia,
Latin America, the Caribbean, and the Middle East,
that is, the host states.

Semantics aside,[25] the term Third World is a
convenient euphemism for the countries generally
regarded as underdeveloped. They are the nonindus-
trial, technologically less-developed, and raw-
materials-producing countries of the international
economy's South.[26] Because the term North-South
suffers from the same deficiencies of oversimplification as the term East-West since it fails to dis-
tinguish between Northern countries such as the
United States and the Soviet Union, and contains
distortions resulting from the location of South
Asia, two-thirds of Africa, and most of Central
America in the "industrialized" Northern Hemisphere,
the term Third World refers to "the peripheral
countries of Africa, Asia, the Middle East, Latin

America, and the Caribbean whose economies have been conditioned by the development and expansion of other economies," core societies to "which they have been subjected or appended."[27]

Finally, "expropriation" is used in this book in its widest sense to include all forms of the state's taking private property for public use, in time of peace, war, or national emergency. As here used, an "expropriatory" measure is any measure that has the effect of

1. unilaterally terminating or modifying concession agreements or state's contracts (with aliens);
2. effectively taking over control or management of alien-owned enterprises, thus effectively impairing operations of such enterprises and forcing the enterprises to cease operations; and
3. establishing a state (public) monopoly in strategic sectors of the economy such as banking, insurance, power, and telecommunications.

The term expropriation, however, does not include the state's taking of public property belonging to a foreign sovereign, inasmuch as such property is covered by state immunity under international law. Accordingly, the terms expropriation and nationalization will be used interchangeably throughout this study.

NOTES

1. Akinsanya, The Expropriation of Multinational Property in the Third World, pp. 77-114; Pinelo, pp. 110-57; Theodore Moran, "The Politics of Economic Nationalism and the Evolution of Concession Agreements," American Journal of International Law 66 (1972): 216-19; Vernon, "Long-Run Trends in Concession Contracts," Proceedings of the American Society of International Law (1967): 81-89; Joan E. Spero, The Politics of International Economics Relations (New York: St. Martin's Press, 1977), pp. 191-214; David H. Blake and Robert Walters, The Politics of Global Economic Relations (Englewood Cliffs, N.J.: Prentice-Hall, 1976).

2. See Akinsanya, "Host-Governments' Responses to Foreign Economic Control: The Experiences of Selected African Countries," International and Comparative Law Quarterly 30 (1981): 769-90.

3. See Akinsanya, Expropriation, pp. 16-48.

4. See Ian Brownlie, Principles of Public International Law (Oxford, England: Clarendon Press, 1973), p. 524, n. 3; Daniel S. Blanchard, "The Threat to U.S. Private Investment in Latin America," Journal of International Law and Economics 5 (1971): 230.

5. U.S., White House, "Policy Statement on Economic Assistance and Investment Security in Developing Nations," International Legal Materials 11 (1972): 241.

6. Akinsanya, Expropriation, pp. 25-48; 208-23.

7. Charles H. Hyde, "Confiscatory Expropriation," American Journal of International Law 32 (1938): 759-65; Philip M. Brown, "Mexican Land Laws," American Journal of International Law 21 (1927): 294-98.

8. See Loftus E. Becker, "Just Compensation in Expropriation Cases: Decline and Partial Recovery," Proceedings of the American Society of International Law (1959); 336-44.

9. See Government of Canada, "Policies of Governments Toward Foreign Direct Investment," in Controlling Multinational Enterprises, pp. 169-80; Isaiah A. Litvak and Christopher J. Maule, "Nationalisation in the Caribbean Bauxite Industry," International Affairs 51 (1975): 50-51; Government of Canada, Foreign Direct Investment in Canada (Gray Report) (Ottawa: Government of Canada, 1972).

10. Lord Hartley W. Shawcross, "The Problems of Foreign Investment in International Law," Hague Recueil des Cours 1 (1961): 342.

11. Morris, Lavipour, and Sauvant, "Politics of Nationalization," pp. 131-33; Akinsanya, Expropriation, pp. 140-47.

12. See Frederic S. Pearson, "Foreign Military Intervention and Changes in United States Overseas Business Activity," Paper read at the

Annual Meeting of the International Studies Association, February 25-27, 1976, Royal York, Toronto, Canada.

13. U.S. Department of State, International Communications Agency, "Nationalism and the Multinational Corporation--An Interview With Samuel Pisar," Dialogue 6 (1973): 64.

14. Ibid., p. 65.

15. The terms OECD and EEC stand for the Organization for Economic Cooperation and Development and the European Economic Community, respectively.

16. See James F. Petras, Morris Morley, and Steven Smith, The Nationalization of Venezuelan Oil (New York: Praeger, 1977); Paul E. Sigmund, Multinationals in Latin America: The Politics of Nationalization (Madison: University of Wisconsin Press, 1980); George M. Ingram, Expropriation of U.S. Property in South America: Nationalization of Oil and Copper Companies in Peru, Bolivia and Chile (New York: Praeger, 1974); Adalberto J. Pinelo, The Multinational Corporation as a Force in Latin American Politics: A Case Study of the International Petroleum Company in Peru (New York: Praeger, 1973); Abdul A. Said and Luiz R. Simmons, The New Sovereigns (Englewood Cliffs, N.J.: Prentice-Hall, 1975), pp. 44-67; 77-107; 139-59.

17. See David E. Apter, "Charters, Cartels, and Multinationals--Some Colonial and Imperial Questions," in The Multinational Corporation and Social Change, ed. David E. Apter and Louis W. Goodman (New York: Praeger, 1976), pp. 1-39; Charles Wilson, The History of Unilever (London: Cassell, 1954); Yoshihiro Tsurumi, "The Multinational Spread of Japanese Firms and Asian Neighbors' Reactions," in The Multinational Corporation and Social Change, pp. 118-47; Vernon, Sovereignty at Bay: The Multinational Spread of U.S. Enterprises (New York: Basic Books, 1971); Mira Wilkins, The Emergence of Multinational Enterprise: American Business Abroad from the Colonial Era to 1914 (Cambridge, Mass.: Harvard University Press, 1974); Howard V. Perlmutter, "The Tortuous Evolution of the Multinational Corporation," Columbia Journal of World Business 4 (1969): 11.

18. See Akinsanya, Expropriation, pp. 208-23.

19. United Nations, Multinational Corporations in World Development, pp. 118-21.

20. Vernon, p. 4.

21. Charles P. Kindleberger, American Business Abroad: Six Lectures on Direct Investment (New Haven, Conn.: Yale University Press, 1969), p. 180.

22. Jack N. Behrman, "Multinational Corporations, Transnational Interests and National Sovereignty," Columbia Journal of World Business 4 (1969): 2 (emphasis in original).

23. United Nations, Multinational Corporations in World Development, p. 121.

24. Ibid.

25. See Allen H. Merriam, "Semantic Implications of the Term Third World," International Studies Notes 6 (1979): 12-15.

26. Akinsanya, p. 10.

27. Ibid.

=== 3.
===

Multinationals and
the Development
(or Underdevelopment) of
the Third World

During the past two decades or so, one of the
major arguments in the literature on international
political economy has centered on the role of MNCs
and direct foreign investments in less developed
countries (LDCs). On one side are those who see the
multinational corporations as

> making possible the use of total world
> resources with the maximum of efficiency
> and the minimum of waste and whose pres-
> ence is vital for the rapid growth and
> development of all economies, especially
> the LDCs.[1]

Because MNCs take a global view of research, marketing, and production, they represent "the transcen-
dence of politics in the interest of world peace and
development." Therefore, in the interest of "world
efficiency and welfare," the nation-states control
over "economic affairs is giving way as it should,
to the multinational corporation and eventually to
other international institutions better suited to a
highly interdependent world economy of which the
multinational corporation is the predominant expression."[2]

On the other side are those who see MNCs as
the most important aspect of the imperialist penetration, indeed, the most important aspect of the

imperialist exploitation of Third World countries,
"heightening their dependency and deepening the process of dependent development."[3] According to this
school, the MNC is an

> instrument of the international class
> struggle supplanting the bourgeois
> nation-state precisely because it is a
> more efficient means by which the capi-
> talist economies can dominate and ex-
> ploit the less-developed countries.[4]

In his contribution in the Bhagwati volume,[5] the
late Stephen Hymer analyzes the rise and importance
of MNCs in terms of two economic laws of development:
The Law of Increasing Firm Size and the Law of Uneven Development. According to Hymer, The Law of
Increasing Firm Size is the tendency since the Industrial Revolution for firms to increase in size "from
the workshop to the factory to the national corporation to the multi-divisional corporation and now to
the multinational corporation."[6] The Law of Uneven
Development, Hymer continues, is the tendency for
the world economy to produce poverty as well as
wealth, underdevelopment, and development. The implications of these laws of development are clear:

> A regime of North Atlantic Multi-
> national Corporations would tend to
> produce a hierarchical division of
> labor between geographical regions
> corresponding to the vertical divi-
> sion of labor within the firm. It
> would tend to centralize high-level
> decision-making occupations in a few
> key cities in the advanced countries,
> surrounded by a number of regional
> sub-capitals, and confine the rest of
> the world to lower levels of activity
> and income, i.e. to the status of
> towns and villages in a new Imperial
> system. Income, status, authority,
> and consumption patterns would radiate
> out from these centers along a declin-
> ing curve, and the existing pattern

> of inequality and dependency would be
> perpetuated. The pattern would be
> complex, but the basic relationship
> between different countries would be
> one of superior and subordinate, head
> office and branch office.[7]

The case of the radicals or Marxists against MNCs,
which is well put, indeed, well-represented in the
Bhagwati volume, is premised on three grounds. In
the first place, because of "internal contradictions"
in the U.S. "capitalistic" system or any "capitalistic" system for that matter, large business entities
(i.e., MNCs) are forced or compelled to establish
subsidiaries overseas.[8] This doctrine of "institutional necessity" for direct foreign investment,[9]
which is very fundamental to the Marxist theory of
imperialism, tallies with Hobson's "liberal theory
of imperialism,"[10] namely, that the search for foreign investment outlets is a "function of the law of
the falling rate of profit, which is due in turn to
the accumulation of surplus capital in mature capitalist economies."[11] Second, the foreign policy of the
United States is a reflection of the "expansionist"
interests of the dominant bourgeois class. Third,
and more important, a primary goal of this dominant
bourgeois class is "to eliminate all obstacles (e.g.,
the nation-state) to corporate expansionism and to
increase at the expense of less developed countries."[12] It is small wonder, therefore, that the
struggle among "mature capitalist economies" for
outlets for their surplus capital is seen as the
raison d'être for imperialism (search for colonies)
and international crises (such as World Wars I and II
and the Vietnam War) while the underdevelopment of
developing countries of the Third World is attributed
to the corporate drive for power and profit.
　　Interposed between the "liberal" and Marxist
conceptions of MNCs but closer to the liberal view
is a school that holds the view that "within a modified framework and working with an agreed set of
guidelines and rules," the MNC, "through its ownership of and control over technology, capital and
marketing skills, can make a unique contribution to
the development effort."[13] In essence, the MNC

reflects a contemporary form of the
economic expansion of particular
nation-states. In other words, only
particular nation-states have been on
the defensive. . . . Indeed, some
nation-states, especially the United
States, have been on the economic of-
fensive, expanding at the expense of
other nation-states.[14]

Consequently, Kari Levitt, in Silent Surrender,[15]
calls "for a strengthening of Canadian nationalism
and a counter-offensive against these corporations
and the nation-states which stand behind them,"[16]
particularly the United States.[17] Because the MNC
is seen and regarded as an instrument of expansion
of particular nation-states that seek to compromise
the sovereignty of developing countries, both Marxists and nationalists "have risen in defense of the
nation-state . . . to protect weaker people against
economic exploitation, political dependence and cultural inundation."[18]

THE CONTRIBUTIONS OF MULTINATIONAL
CORPORATIONS: BANE OR BLESSING?

It is critical to an understanding of the impact of MNCs in developing countries to examine its
characteristics. Broadly defined, an MNC is a company (or corporation) with its parent headquarters
located in one country (i.e., home state) and subsidiary operations in two or more countries (i.e.,
host states). Accordingly, an MNC is characterized
by a parent company and a cluster of subsidiaries
(affiliates) in a number of countries with a common
pool of managerial, financial, and technical resources. To be sure, a unique characteristic of the
MNC is that it sees the world as a single economic
unit and, therefore, plans, organizes, and manages
on a global scale. Put differently, the parent company "operates the whole in terms of a coordinated
global strategy . . . in order to achieve its long-
term goal of corporate growth."[19] Richard Barnet
and Ronald Muller have noted:

> The power of the global corporation
> derives from its unique capacity to
> use finance, technology and advanced
> marketing skills to integrate produc-
> tion on a worldwide scale and to real-
> ize the ancient capitalist dream of
> One Great Market.[20]

In fact, some scholars have used the extent of centralization of policy and integration of key operations among subsidiaries to determine the multina-
tionality or otherwise of a corporation.[21] According to Christopher Tugendhat, it is the parent company (headquarters), first, that evolves corporate
strategy; second, it decides on the location of new
investment; third, it allocates export markets and
research programs to various branch offices (subsidiaries); above all, it also decides the prices that
should be charged on intrafirm exchanges (transfer
prices). On the other hand, the branch offices (subsidiaries) operate under the discipline and within
the framework of a common global strategy and a common global control.[22] In essence, through vertical
integration and centralization of decision making,
the head office (parent company) perpetuates its
monopoly position with respect to technology, access
to capital and markets, and so on.

Multinationals are responsible for most direct
foreign investments (DFIs). However, the measure of
such investments is more limited than the total flow
of resources from MNCs. In general, DFI refers to
the flow of equity and loan capital from a parent
company to an affiliate. But even in this limited
sense of the flow of financial resources (including
reinvested profits), the measure certainly under-
states the size of flows for which the parent company
is responsible. For example, a loan to a branch office from a home-country bank (such as Bank of
America or First National City Bank of New York)
would not be included in DFI although the transaction may well depend on the reputation or formal
guarantee of the head office. Additionally, no account is taken of the flow of other resources from
the head office to the branch office, namely, technology, management services, and marketing services.

As Harry Johnson rightly noted, "the essence of direct foreign investment is the transmission to the 'host' country of a 'package' of capital, managerial skill and technical knowledge."[23] In fact, various studies have shown that an increasing proportion of the operations of MNCs in developing countries takes forms that are quite unrelated to financial flows from parent offices to branch offices but nevertheless imply some degree of control by the parent (foreign) company.[24] Consequently, a distinction must and should be made between portfolio investment and DFI.

Undoubtedly, portfolio capital flows and DFI constitute the two major forms of private foreign capital flows. Portfolio investment refers to or involves the purchase or acquisition of securities issued by foreign institutions without any control over or participation in their management. To be sure, much of the international capital flows of the nineteenth century--between two-thirds and three-quarters--was in the form of portfolio capital flows or bonds. On the other hand, DFI entails the establishment of a foreign subsidiary or the takeover of a foreign firm (which could be a subsidiary of an MNC) or a local firm. Thus, while a measure of central control by the parent company is an essential definition of DFI, its primary goal is managerial control of a production unit in a foreign country. It has been observed:

> It is the ownership of capital that
> buys the foreign firms the power to
> exercise control over operations. In
> turn, the extent to which they are
> prepared to transfer technology and
> skills may depend largely on the de-
> gree of control over operations which
> they can exercise. . . . The foreign
> firm must find production abroad pref-
> erable to any other means of operat-
> ing in the markets abroad, such as
> servicing the foreign markets by ex-
> ports or by selling the technology it
> possesses. But given the fact that
> there are imperfections in the markets

for goods and services and factors,
foreign direct investment may be the
preferred alternative. The fact that
the foreign firm possesses a monopoly
over technology renders the market
for such technology imperfect. The
best means of exploiting such a monopoly would be by setting up a production facility abroad.[26]

To be sure, the main distinguishing feature of DFI,
indeed, a feature that sets it apart from portfolio
investment, is the exercise of control over the
decision-making process of the "investor entity by
the investing entity,"[27] although it should be noted
that the control exercised by the foreign firm over
the decision-making process depends on the extent of
its equity participation, particularly in relation
to other shareholders. Thus,

a 30 percent ownership of equity by
the foreign entity, with no other
single shareholder holding more than
10 percent of total equity, is likely
to afford a more significant element
of control than a 49 percent share-
holding, where the remaining shares
are held by one enterprise.[28]

While a measure of control by the parent company is
an essential definition of DFI, its primary goal is
managerial control of a production unit in a foreign
country. This, then, explains why MNCs should be
distinguished from corporations that are, for example, neither involved nor engaged in international
production.
    For Hymer, giant corporations engaged in inter-
national transactions are not a new phenomenon:

They were a characteristic form of
the mercantilist period when large
joint-stock companies, e.g. The Hud-
son's Bay Company, The Royal African
Company, The East India Company . . .

organized long-distance trade with
America, Africa and Asia. But neither
these firms nor the large mining and
plantation enterprises in the production sector, were the forerunners of
the multinational corporation.[29]

The forerunners of contemporary MNCs did not begin
to develop until the end of the nineteenth century.
According to one source,[30] U.S. corporations began
to expand abroad as early as the 1890s; this process,
the source added, was accelerated in the interwar
period. Although the growth of U.S.-based MNCs was
slower in the 1930s, Latin America proved to be very
attractive to private investors in the 1930s. However, following World War II, and particularly in
the 1950s, a period that witnessed large-scale DFI
in the majority of developing countries, especially
in extractive and manufacturing industries, the mag-
nitude, direction, and character of U.S. DFI changed.
In the first place, while Latin America accounted
for the bulk of U.S. DFI before World War II, Canada, Western Europe, and other developed market
economies absorbed much of U.S. DFI after the war.[31]
Because DFI entails the "exercise of control over
decision-making process of the investor entity by
the investing entity,"[32] it was small wonder therefore that U.S. DFI has excited political concern in
Canada and Western Europe.[33] Second, whereas U.S.
DFI in 1946 stood at $7 billion, it had risen to
nearly $80 billion by 1970. Third, while direct in-
vestment in the extractive and traditional manufacturing industries has remained strong, a large portion of postwar U.S. DFI has gone into advanced manufacturing industries; additionally, another large
portion ($20 billion), which is in petroleum, repre-
sents about 40 percent of U.S. DFI in developing
countries.[34]

In essence, what distinguishes the contemporary
MNC from its forerunners is "not only its size and
the scope of its operations but also its structure,
organisation and its view of the world economy and
its role in the development of that economy."[35]
Therefore, a central characteristic of MNCs is the
predominance of large-sized firms. According to the

1980 _Fortune_ list of the world's 50 largest industrial companies, the five largest MNCs (and these
include Exxon, Royal Dutch/Shell Group, Mobil, General Motors, and Texaco) have annual sales that
stood at $288 billion while the total sales of the
50 have grown to $1.2 trillion--greater than the
gross national product of any investor state except
the United States.[36] To be sure, the world's largest MNC at the time of writing, namely, Exxon, has
an annual sales of $103.1 billion while Standard Oil
(Ohio), which took the fiftieth place on the _Fortune_
list, has annual sales of $11 billion. It is hardly
surprising, therefore, that Raymond Vernon maintains
that a corporation "with less than $100 million in
sales rarely merits much attention."[37] More significant, a study by the United Nations reveals that
"nearly 200 multinational corporations, among the
largest in the world, have affiliates in twenty or
more countries."[38] The study, which surveyed the
world's 650 largest industrial corporations, almost
all of which are MNCs, found:[39]

1. That about 54 percent (358) of these corporations
   are United States-based, including 60 percent
   (127) of the 211 corporations with sales over $1
   billion;
2. That the major home states of other MNCs are
   Japan, France, Canada, Sweden, the United Kingdom,
   and the Federal Republic of Germany;
3. That these seven countries (namely, the United
   States, Japan, France, Canada, Sweden, the United
   Kingdom, and the Federal Republic of Germany) account for 600 (i.e., 92.3 percent) of these 650
   MNCs;
4. That the number of U.S. affiliates in all countries between 1950 and 1966 increased from 7,000
   to 23,000 while the 1960s also have witnessed a
   rapid growth of Japanese, French, and German MNCs
   compared with less dramatic growth in case of
   U.K.-based MNCs; and
5. That seven of the world's 10 largest MNCs are
   based in the United States (see Table 3.1).

Obviously, the very _size_ of these corporations as
compared with other economic entities, including the

TABLE 3.1

The World's 20 Largest Industrial Companies by Rank,
Nationality, Sales, and Net Income 1980

Rank	Company	Nationality	Sales ($ thousand)	Net Income ($ thousand)
1	Exxon	USA	103,142,834	5,650,090
2	Royal Dutch/ Shell Group	Neth./UK	77,114,243	5,174,282
3	Mobil	USA	59,510,000	3,272,000
4	General Motors[a]	USA	57,728,000	762,500
5	Texaco	USA	51,195,830	2,642,542
6	British Petroleum	UK	48,035,941	3,337,121
7	Standard Oil of California	USA	40,479,000	2,401,000
8	Ford Motor[a]	USA	37,085,000	1,543,300
9	ENI[b]	Italy	27,186,939	98,046
10	Gulf Oil	USA	26,483,000[c]	1,407,000
11	IBM	USA	26,213,000	3,562,000
12	Standard Oil (Indiana)	USA	26,133,080	1,915,314
13	Fiat	Italy	25,155,000	N.A.
14	General Electric	USA	24,959,000	1,514,000
15	Francaise des Petroles	France	23,940,355	946,772
16	Atlantic Richfield	USA	23,744,302	1,651,423
17	Unilever	UK/Neth.	23,607,516	658,820
18	Shell Oil[d]	USA	19,830,000	1,542,000
19	Renault[b]	France	18,979,278	160,165
20	Petroles de Venezuela	Venezuela	18,818,931	3,450,921

[a]When Fortune's ranking of the world's 50 largest industrial companies appeared seven years ago, General Motors, Ford, and Chrysler (USA) clustered comfortably among the top five. The trio, unfortunately, have not aged well. In 1980, General Motors and Ford suffered some $2.8 billion in losses while Chrysler, which had slipped to the fortieth place in 1979, finally dropped off the Fortune list.

[b]Government-owned. Ente Nazionale Idrocarburi (ENI) is a holding company with the following companies in the group: Agip, Snam, Agip Nucleare, Anic, Snamprogetti, Saipem, Nuovo Pignone, Lanerossi, Sofid, Inoc.

[c]Fortune estimate.

[d]Shell Oil is a majority-owned (60 percent) subsidiary of Royal Dutch/Shell Group.

N.A. Not available.

Source: Fortune (New York), August 10, 1981, p. 205.

economies of many nations, suggests an important
source of power. Indeed, the sheer wealth of some
of these corporations, as demonstrated in Table 3.1,
makes a prima facie case for considering them significant actors in the international system. Since
they are predominantly based in the industrialized
"First World," they are not infrequently perceived
as agents of neocolonialism through the nationalis-
tic eyes of the emergent states of the Third World.

To be sure, the importance of these economic
characteristics (sales and net income) is shown in
Table 3.2, which intersperses billion-dollar-or-more
MNCs (in terms of sales) with 100 nation-states
ranked by the size of their gross national products
(GNPs).

From Table 3.2, it is obvious that General
Motors and Exxon outranked all but 22 nation-states.
More significant, while the top 50 entries (in the
table) show that MNCs account for only nine (i.e.,
18 percent) of the next 50 entries, 32 are MNCs,
namely, 64 percent.

Closely related to their large size is the
predominantly oligopolistic character of MNCs. More
often than not, the markets in which they operate
are dominated by few buyers or sellers. Frequently,
they are also characterized by the importance of
technological innovation, massive advertising, and
product differentiation, which reinforces or sus-
tains their oligopolistic nature.

A central characteristic of an MNC is that it
seeks to maximize the profits of the parent company
rather than any of its affiliates, although this may
mean operating certain of its affiliates at an "official" loss. This is quite possible, given the environment in which MNCs operate. First, there is a
dearth of well-qualified government officials to examine and investigate whether commercial and business laws are being complied with by MNCs or local
firms. Second, the very laws themselves, and taxation practices, more often than not are antiquated
or have remained unrevised for too long (in the
statute book) to take cognizance of the major changes
in the origins of economic power. Third, "whereas
we normally think of the institutions of organized
labor in advanced countries as a countervailing

TABLE 3.2

Countries (lowercased) and Multinational Corporations (uppercased)
Ranked According to Size of Gross National Product 1978

Rank	Entity	Size of GNP ($ billion)	Rank	Entity	Size of GNP ($ billion)
1	United States	2,117.89	51	Algeria	22.29
2	Soviet Union	965.52	52	Colombia	21.79
3	Japan	836.16	53	Thailand	21.79
4	Fed. Rep. of Germany	587.70	54	IBM	21.08
5	France	439.97	55	GENERAL ELECTRIC	19.65
6	People's Rep. of China	424.62	56	Portugal	19.54
7	United Kingdom	281.09	57	Libya	18.96
8	Italy	218.32	58	UNILEVER	18.89
9	Canada	216.09	59	GULF OIL	18.07
10	Brazil	187.19	60	Kuwait	18.04
11	Spain	128,92	61	Pakistan	17.53
12	Poland	128.33	62	CHRYSLER	16.34
13	Netherlands	117.19	63	Egypt	15.52
14	Australia	113.83	64	Israel	15.30
15	India	112.66	65	New Zealand	15.27
16	German Dem. Rep.	95.49	66	ITT	15.27
17	Belgium	89.52	67	Chile	15.18
18	Sweden	84.75	68	PHILIPS' GLOEILAM PENFABRIEKEN	15.12
19	Mexico	84.15	69	STANDARD OIL (INDIANA)	14.96
20	Switzerland	76.05	70	Malaysia	14.54
21	Czechoslovakia	71.32	71	Hong Kong	14.05
22	Saudi Arabia	63.31	72	SIEMENS	13.86
23	GENERAL MOTORS	63.22	73	VOLKSWAGEN	13.33
24	EXXON	60.33			

25	Austria	52.72	74	TOYOTA MOTOR	12.77
26	Yugoslavia	52.34	75	RENAULT[a]	12.72
27	Turkey	51.75	76	Morocco	12.61
28	Denmark	50.41	77	ENI[a]	12.57
29	Argentina	50.25	78	North Korea	12.53
30	Indonesia	48.82	79	FRANCAISE DES PETROLES	12.51
31	Nigeria	45.72	80	Peru	12.44
32	ROYAL DUTCH/SHELL GR.	44.04	81	ATLANTIC RICHFIELD	12.30
33	FORD MOTOR	42.78	82	DAIMLER-BENZ	12.09
34	South Korea	42.46	83	HOECHST	12.07
35	South Africa	40.94	84	United Arab Emirates	11.44
36	Venezuela	40.71	85	BAYER	11.39
37	Norway	38.50	86	Ireland	11.21
38	Rumania	38.17	87	SHELL OIL	11.06
39	Hungary	36.86	88	U.S. STEEL	11.05
40	MOBIL	34.74	89	NESTLE	11.00
41	Finland	32.38	90	BASF	10.73
42	Greece	30.53	91	PEUGEOT[b]	10.62
43	TEXACO	28.61	92	E.I. DUPONT de NEMOURS	10.58
44	Bulgaria	28.45	93	MATSUSHITA ELEC. INDUSTRIAL	10.02
45	BRITISH PETROLEUM	27.41	94	NISSAN MOTOR	9.95
46	Taiwan	23.93	95	NIPPON STEEL	9.52
47	Philippines	23.25	96	WESTERN ELECTRIC	9.52
48	STANDARD OIL OF CALIFORNIA	23.23	97	CONTINENTAL OIL	9.46
49	NATIONAL IRANIAN OIL	22.79	98	MITSUBISHI HEAVY INDUSTRIES	9.20
50	Iraq	22.72	99	THYSSEN	9.18
			100	HITACHI	9.15

aGovernment-owned.
bName changed from Peugeot-Citroen on June 26, 1980.

Source: Charles W. Kegley, Jr., and Eugene R. Wittkopf, World Politics: Trend and Transformation. New York: St. Martin's Press, 1981, pp. 134-35 (Table 5.3).

force or check upon the power of the corporation, this is not the case in most LDCs where organized labor is either weak or absent."[40] Fourth, and more important, MNCs offer bribes to local officials with a view to inducing them "to do or omit to do something in violation"[41] of their lawful duties. Therefore, because the basic objective of the MNC is the maximization of global profits, it is almost certain, indeed inevitable, that conflicts will arise between host governments (which seek to maximize tax revenues and minimize tax-dodging) and MNCs' local subsidiaries (operating under the discipline and within the framework of a common global strategy and a common global control). The relations between the host government and a local subsidiary of an MNC (in the natural resource sector) are certain to be confrontational because of a changing balance of power in favor of the host government and because of host government's determination to increase its share of its profits in the development and exploitation of the country's nonrenewable natural resources.[42] To be sure, because the parent company sees the world as a single economic unit, and therefore plans, organizes, and manages on a global scale, the operations of the branch office (subsidiary) "may give rise to a structure of inputs, outputs, costs, prices, and profits that is consistent with neither the needs of the host state nor the desires of its government."[43]

A further central characteristic of MNCs is that they are generally the product of developed market economies. A large proportion of contemporary MNCs are located in the industrialized countries of the North, that is, the First World. As shown in Table 3.1, seven of the world's ten largest MNCs are based in the United States. Furthermore, from a United Nations study on foreign subsidiaries of contemporary MNCs by the end of 1969, the United States alone accounts for 35.5 percent of the total number of foreign subsidiaries, followed by the United Kingdom (26.1 percent), the Federal Republic of Germany (10.7 percent), and France (7.4 percent). Together these four countries account for 79.7 percent of the total, as shown in Table 3.3. To be sure, the concentration of MNCs in the industrialized

TABLE 3.3

Multinational Corporations of Selected Developed Market Economies:
Parent Companies and Subsidiaries by Home State 1968-69

Home State	Total Parent		Parent Companies with Subsidiaries in				Subsidiaries	
	Number	%	1 Country	2-9 Countries	10-19 Countries	Over 20 Countries	Minimum Number[a]	%
United States	2,468	33.9	1,228	949	216	75	9,691	35.5
United Kingdom	1,692	23.3	725	809	108	50	7,116	26.1
Federal Republic of Germany	954	13.1	448	452	43	11	2,916	10.7
France	538	7.4	211	275	42	10	2,023	7.4
Switzerland	447	6.1	213	202	26	6	1,456	5.3
Netherlands	268	3.7	92	149	20	7	1,118	4.1
Sweden	255	3.5	93	129	24	9	1,159	4.2
Belgium	235	3.2	137	88	8	2	594	2.2
Denmark	128	1.8	54	69	4	1	354	1.3
Italy	120	1.7	57	54	3	6	459	1.7
Norway	94	1.3	54	36	4	--	220	0.8
Austria	39	0.5	21	16	2	--	105	0.4
Luxembourg	18	0.2	10	7	1	--	55	0.2
Spain	15	0.2	11	4	--	--	26	0.1
Portugal	5	0.1	3	2	--	--	8	--
Total	7,276	100.0	3,357	3,241	501	177	27,300	100.0

[a]"Minimum number of subsidiaries" refers to the number of "links" between parent companies and host states. Two or more subsidiaries of a particular multinational corporation in a given foreign country are counted as one link.

Source: United Nations, Multinational Corporations in World Development, p. 138.

First World had become more pronounced by 1977, as one can see from Table 3.4, indicating that nearly 10,400 MNCs (all based in 19 First World countries) have at least one affiliate in one or more foreign countries (i.e., host states). Table 3.4 indicates that three countries (the United States, the United Kingdom, and the Federal Republic of Germany) account for 55.77 percent of these corporations, with the United States alone accounting for 26.83 percent. As noted in Chapter 1, the concentration of British investments in the former British colonies (i.e., in Africa, Asia, and the Western Hemisphere) or the concentration of U.S. investments in the Western Hemisphere and Asia or the dominance of Japanese investments in Asia reflect past colonial or semicolonial relationships.[44]

More significant, the degree of concentration of MNCs in the developed market economies is nowhere more demonstrated than in the distribution of the stock of DFI as measured by book value. Although the nonavailability of statistical information on MNCs in many Third World countries obscures the overall picture, available data show that of a total estimated stock of DFI of some $165 billion by the end of 1971, most of which is owned by MNCs, the U.S. share stands at 52 percent while the United Kingdom, France, and the Federal Republic of Germany account for 14.5, 5.8, and 4.4 percent, respectively (see Table 3.5). Additionally, the size of subsidiaries varies with the sector and the area of operation, although some changes seem to have occurred in this pattern in the past two decades.

In the first place, in the natural resources sector--a sector which has evoked strong passions among Third World radical groups which watch their vital and irreplaceable natural resources being extracted for the benefit of MNCs (which operate them) and their home states--subsidiaries appear to be 300 to 400 percent larger than those in the manufacturing sector. Second, in the petroleum and service trade sectors, the average size of subsidiaries is somewhat somewhat larger in the nonindustrialized Third World than in the industrialized First World. Finally, in the manufacturing sector, the size of foreign subsidiaries of MNCs in Third World countries

TABLE 3.4

Multinational Corporations with One or More Affiliates by Number
of Host Countries and Third World Host Regions 1977

Location of Parent Companies	Number of Parent Companies with Affiliates in One or More Countries in the Third World	Number of Parent Companies with Affiliates in the Third World				
		Western Hemisphere Only	Africa Only	Asia Only	In More than One of the Three Regions	Total
United States	2,783	522	53	130	492	1,197
United Kingdom	1,598	97	102	176	264	639
Federal Republic of Germany	1,404	134	29	57	96	316
Switzerland	852	48	6	11	44	109
Netherlands	600	28	10	18	48	104
France	564	36	125	19	66	246
Canada	432	77	9	12	23	121
Japan	380	46	5	77	97	225
Belgium	320	16	49	2	23	90
Australia	323	11	1	150	19	181
Italy	249	23	9	7	19	58
Sweden	258	27	3	5	28	63
New Zealand	167	2	--	55	1	58
Denmark	132	7	4	4	7	22
Norway	116	4	--	5	6	15
Spain	79	22	4	3	5	34
Austria	54	3	1	5	2	11
Finland	52	4	2	--	1	7
Portugal	10	2	3	1	--	6
Total	10,373	1,109	415	737	1,241	3,502

Source: United Nations Commission on Transnational Corporations, Supplementary Material
on the Issue of Defining Transnational Corporations, Publication no. E/C.10/58, March 23, 1979,
pp. 8, 11.

TABLE 3.5

Stock of Direct Foreign Investment (Book Value)
Held by Major Countries 1971[a]

| Country | 1971[b] | |
	$ million	% Share
United States	86,001	52.0
United Kingdom	24,019	14.5
France	9,540	5.8
Federal Republic of Germany	7,276	4.4
Switzerland	6,760	4.1
Canada	5,930	3.6
Japan	4,480	2.7
Netherlands	3,580	2.2
Sweden[c]	3,450	2.1
Italy	3,350	2.0
Belgium	3,250	2.0
Australia	610	0.4
Portugal	320	0.2
Denmark	310	0.2
Norway	90	0.0
Austria	40	0.0
Others[d]	6,000	3.6
Total	165,000	100.0

Note: Totals do not add due to rounding.

[a]According to the Organization for Economic Cooperation and Development, "by the stock of foreign investment
. . . is understood the net book value to the direct investor of affiliates (subsidiaries, branches, and associates) in LDCs. . . . Governments of Development Assistance Committee member countries decline all responsibility for the accuracy of the estimates of the Secretariat
which in some cases are known to differ from confidential
information available to the national authorities. . . .
Any analysis of detailed data in the paper should therefore be done with the utmost caution."

[b]Estimated (except for the United States, the United
Kingdom, the Federal Republic of Germany, Japan, and
Sweden) by applying the average growth rate of the United
States, the United Kingdom, and the Federal Republic of
Germany between 1966 and 1971.

[c]The figures for Sweden are for 1970, and they are
in current prices for total assets of majority-owned manufacturing industries.

[d]Estimated, including developing countries.

Source: United Nations, Multinational Corporations
in World Development, pp. 139-40.

is only half that in the developed market economies whereas in the public utilities sector (whose control by aliens not unnaturally raises issues of security and sovereignty),[45] the size is almost double.

As for changes in this pattern of investment, it should be noted, first, that while the size of U.S. subsidiaries in the developed market economies increased by 200 percent between 1950 and 1966, the increase in Japan was more than fourfold and almost threefold in the EEC. Second, no increase in the average size of U.S. subsidiaries (except in Africa) and U.K. subsidiaries was recorded in the Third World. This development may well be attributed to the fact that "affiliates in developing countries often serve the local markets only, especially in the case of import-substituting manufactures, while the relatively larger affiliates in developed countries frequently serve bigger regional as well as national markets."[46]

We have been examining some characteristics of the MNC. The question then arises: To what can we attribute the power of the MNC? Undoubtedly, a key to the power of the MNC lies in the ownership of capital in a major way since this entails power of control over decision making that offers several degrees of freedom to the MNC. As noted by Constantine Vaitsos,

> The application of centralised control in decision making by transnational enterprises . . . transforms them into one of the most important non-market forces in the world economy. This is a result of their ability to shape the demand facing their products and to influence their economic environment through central planning and the exercise of their power.[47]

To be sure, a structure of trade and production controlled by the parent companies of MNCs, more often than not, enables decisions on the location of physical output (and, of course, their consequences) to be

divorced from the question of the output's evaluation through administrative price-setting. This, in
turn, affects generation and distribution of income
within and between countries. In fact, the pricing
of such goods and services traded among subsidiaries
constitutes a critical element in business behavior;
it relates to such wide-ranging objectives as:

1. global tax minimisation or tax
   dodging;
2. reduction of tariff payments for
   goods imported by subsidiaries and
   increase of tariffs and/or price
   levels for those produced by them
   in the host-State;
3. maintenance of market captivity
   and price barriers of entry against
   competitors;
4. hedging against changes in currency values;
5. reduction of political and business risk from high rates of declared profitability that might be
   susceptible to host-government's
   reactions; and
6. trade union pressures and antitrust actions.[48]

Needless to say, these channels of effective income
remission that such intrafirm trade permits and
allows, more often than not, result in significant
and unacceptable financial losses for the host government.
    However, a key to the power of the MNC lies
not only in the ownership of capital in a major way
but also

> in its ownership and control of knowl-
> edge, broadly defined to include the
> technology of production, organisa-
> tional skills and market skills. . . .
> Often the "soft" technology that the
> TNC [transnational corporation] pos-
> sesses (marketing, purchasing, organi-
> sation, training, overall management,

finance, etc.) may be more important
than the "hard" technology embodied
in machinery and equipment.[49]

Indeed, such advantages imply economic power, and
access to them commands a price. It is small wonder,
therefore, that some scholars have argued that the
essential characteristic of the MNC is the "creation,
commercialisation and oligopolisation of relevant
applied knowledge"[50] rather than the ownership of
fixed assets or financial resources.

It would bear repeating here that MNCs are responsible for most DFIs. However, as indicated earlier in this chapter, the measure of such investments is more limited than the total flow of resources from MNCs. In general, DFIs refer to the
flow of equity and loan capital from the parent company to its foreign wholly or majority-owned subsidiary. More often than not, account is not taken
of the flow of such other resources as technology,
management services, and marketing services from the
head office to the branch office.

Aside from this fundamental problem, two other
problems arise when attempting to measure direct investment originating from the developed market economies as a group. As it is rightly pointed out by
Isaiah Frank,[51] the first problem is related to the
yardstick for determining what constitutes DFI as
opposed to portfolio investment. Since it is agreed
that it is the ownership of capital in a major way
that buys the foreign firm "the power to exercise
control over operations," the problem, as it is noted
by Frank, is "to give quantitative expression to
this condition [i.e., measure of central control] in
terms of the required minimum percentage of equity
ownership."[52] The point of the matter is that there
is no uniformity of practice among investor states
while any fixed threshold for equity is arbitrary.

A second problem relates to the distortions in
converting national data into a single currency (such
as the U.S. dollar) under conditions of inflation
and fluctuating exchange rates of the type experi-
enced during the 1970s. Therefore, the distorting
effects of exchange rate fluctuations should always
be taken into consideration.[53]

Furthermore, and perhaps more fundamental, while the United States publishes comprehensive data on DFIs in the Third World, data on DFIs by other investor states are generally and simply not available in the same detail or in comparable forms.

SIZE AND GROWTH OF PRIVATE FOREIGN CAPITAL FLOWS

Share of Direct Foreign Investment in Capital Flows

Data on types of capital flows from the developed market economies to the developing countries as well as the percentage share of each type of capital flow, especially the share of direct foreign investment in the total capital flows, are indicated in Tables 3.6 to 3.8.

Several points emerge from a reading of Table 3.6. First, official development assistance accounts for more than 50 percent (i.e., 58 percent) of the total capital flows to the developing countries while DFI accounts for nearly 50 percent of all private capital flows (i.e., 23 percent) during the period under review. Second, portfolio capital and export credits account for 19 percent of total capital flows. They have obviously grown much faster than other types of capital flows. Third, while official development assistance increased two-and-a-half times, export credits increased six times and portfolio flows grew eightfold over the period 1956-71.

While Table 3.7 shows the types of capital flows to the developing countries as well as the percentage share of each type over the period 1960-78, Table 3.8 reveals that DFI accounts for 19.7 percent of the total capital flows to the developing countries between 1960 and 1965, while the figures for the periods 1966-71 and 1972-78 stood at 21.6 percent and 18.7 percent, respectively, meaning that the share of DFI in total private foreign capital flows has been declining steadily. The reason for this development can be seen in the increasing and easy access of Third World countries to the international capital markets, although it must be noted

TABLE 3.6

Capital Flows from Development Assistance Committee Countries to Developing Countries 1956-71
($ million)

| | Private Capital Flows | | | | | | | | Official Flows | | Total |
| | 1 | | 2 | | 3 | | 4 | | 5 | | 6 |
Year	Total Private Capital Flows	% of Total	Direct Investment	% of Total	Portfolio and Bank Lending	% of Total	Export Credits	% of Total	Grants and Net Loans	% of Total	
1956	2,998	47.9	2,350	37.6	190	3.0	458	7.3	3,260	52.1	6,258
1957	3,779	49.5	2,724	35.7	601	7.9	454	5.9	3,856	50.5	7,635
1958	2,917	39.9	1,970	27.0	733	10.0	214	2.9	4,387	60.0	7,304
1959	2,820	39.5	1,782	25.0	691	9.7	347	4.9	4,311	60.4	7,131
1960	3,150	38.8	1,767	21.8	837	10.3	546	6.7	4,965	61.2	8,115
1961	3,106	33.6	1,829	19.8	704	7.6	573	6.2	6,143	66.4	9,249
1962	2,453	29.1	1,495	17.7	386	4.6	572	6.8	5,984	70.9	8,437
1963	2,557	29.8	1,603	18.7	296	3.5	660	7.7	6,015	70.2	8,572
1964	3,729	38.7	1,572	16.3	1,298	13.5	859	8.9	5,916	61.4	9,645
1965	4,121	39.9	2,468	23.9	902	8.7	751	7.3	6,199	60.0	10,320
1966	3,959	38.1	2,179	21.0	555	6.3	1,124	10.8	6,431	61.9	10,390
1967	4,381	38.3	2,105	18.4	1,269	11.1	1,007	8.8	7,060	61.7	11,441
1968	6,377	47.5	3,043	22.7	1,738	12.9	1,596	11.9	7,047	52.5	13,425
1969	6,587	47.7	2,910	21.2	1,630	11.8	2,047	14.9	7,192	52.2	13,779
1970	7,019	46.8	3,557	23.7	1,230	8.3	2,211	14.7	7,984	53.2	15,003
1971	8,399	48.3	4,087	23.5	1,510	8.7	2,802	16.1	8,997	51.7	17,395
1956-71	68,352	42.0	37,441	23.0	14,691	9.0	16,221	10.0	95,749	58.0	164,099

Source: Grant L. Reuber et al., Private Foreign Investment in Development (London: Oxford University Press, 1973), p. 5.

TABLE 3.7

Capital Flows[a] from Industrial Countries[b] to Developing Countries 1960-78
($ million)

Type	Average 1960-65	Average 1966-71	1972	1973	1974	1975	1976	1977	1978
Official Devel. Assistance	5,494	6,663	8,538	9,378	11,317	13,585	13,734	14,696	18,308
Other Official Flows	379	773	1,546	2,463	2,183	3,024	3,295	3,319	4,000[c]
Private Flows	3,186	6,020	8,333	9,458	7,330	22,152	20,872	29,988	32,820[c]
Direct Investment	1,789	2,090	4,234	4,719	1,124	10,494	7,824	8,792	9,470[c]
Bilateral Portfolio	536	818	1,984	3,286	3,795	5,313	5,166	10,454	11,350[c]
Multilateral Portfolio	201	513	667	257	-70	2,278	3,059	2,642	2,000[c]
Export Credits	660	1,794	1,448	1,196	2,481	4,067	4,823	8,100	10,000[c]
Grants by Private Voluntary Agencies	N.A.	N.A.	1,036	1,364	1,217	1,342	1,357	1,489	1,500[c]
Total Flows[d]	9,059	13,456	19,453	22,663	22,047	40,103	39,260	49,492	56,628[c]

N.A. Not available.

[a] Gross disbursements less amortization receipts on earlier lendings. The figures include flows to multilateral agencies.

[b] These include Australia, Austria, Belgium, Canada, Denmark, France, the Federal Republic of Germany, Italy, Japan, the Netherlands, New Zealand, Norway, Sweden, Switzerland, the United Kingdom, and the United States. Also included is the EEC Commission.

[c] Estimates.

[d] Figures prior to 1972 exclude New Zealand.

Source: Isiah Frank, Foreign Enterprise in Developing Countries. Baltimore, Md.: Johns Hopkins University Press, 1980, p. 10.

TABLE 3.8

Share of Direct Foreign Investment
in Total Private Foreign Capital
Flows to Developing Countries 1960-78

Direct Foreign Investment (in percent)	1960-65	1966-71	1972-78
Total Private Foreign Capital Flow	56.2	48.2	35.6
Total Net Flow	19.7	21.6	18.7

Source: Isiah Frank, Foreign Enterprise in Developing Countries. Baltimore, Md.: Johns Hopkins University Press, 1980, p. 12.

here that very few such countries--notably, Brazil, Mexico, and Argentina, indeed, the same developing countries that are able to attract much DFI (i.e., from MNCs)--have been able to borrow from the world capital markets. According to one study,[54] only three Third World countries outside Europe, namely, Israel, Mexico, and Argentina, were able to float bonds totaling more than $100 million on the international capital markets between 1964 and 1968.

Extent of Direct Foreign Investment

It can be recalled from Table 3.5 that of a total estimated stock of DFI of some $165 billion by the end of 1971, the U.S. share stands at 52 percent while the United Kingdom, France, and the Federal Republic of Germany account for 14.5, 5.8, and 4.4 percent, respectively. According to Table 3.9 the stock of DFI in developing countries stood at over $85 billion. Although this represented more than a 200-percent increase between 1967 and 1977, it should be noted, as rightly pointed out by Frank, that "the

TABLE 3.9

Stock (Book Value) and Flow of Direct Foreign Investment in Developing Countries
(Year-End 1967 and Year-End 1977)
($ million)

Country	Stock Year-End 1967	Flow 1968-72	Flow 1973-77	Stock Year-End 1977	Stock Year-End 1967 %	Flow 1968-72 %	Flow 1973-77 %	Stock Year-End 1977 %
Australia	101	354	428	883	0.3	2.1	1.3	1.0
Austria	7	12	71	90	*	0.1	0.2	0.1
Belgium	692	160	378	1,230	2.0	0.9	1.1	1.4
Canada	1,477	433	1,438	3,348	4.2	2.5	4.4	3.9
Denmark	31	49	102	182	0.1	0.3	0.3	0.2
Federal Republic of Germany	1,198	1,703	3,915	6,816	3.4	10.0	11.9	8.0
France	2,980	1,253	1,310	5,543	8.5	7.3	4.0	6.5
Italy	879	860	871	2,610	2.5	5.0	2.6	3.1
Japan	702	923	4,037	5,662	2.0	5.4	12.3	6.7
Netherlands	1,789	889	1,291	3,969	5.1	5.2	3.9	4.7
Norway	12	52	104	169	*	0.3	0.3	0.2
Sweden	189	198	404	791	0.5	1.2	1.2	0.9
Switzerland	695	321	854	1,870	2.0	1.9	2.6	2.2
United Kingdom	6,804	1,535	3,779	12,118	19.4	9.0	11.5	14.2
United States	17,448	8,369	13,949	39,766	49.8	48.9	42.5	46.8
Total	35,004	17,111	32,932	85,047	100.0	100.0	100.0	100.0

*Negligible or less than 0.1 percent.
Source: Isiah Frank, Foreign Enterprise in Developing Countries. Baltimore, Md.: Johns Hopkins University Press, 1980, p. 13.

extent of the real increase is inflated by both
price increases and the depreciation of the dollar
in relation to the currencies of the other major investing countries."[55] More important, the period
reveals dramatic increases in the shares of Japan
(from 2.0 to 6.7 percent of the total) and the Federal Republic of Germany (from 3.4 to 8.0 percent of
the total) and slight increases in the shares of
Australia and Sweden; the same period witnessed substantial declines in the shares of the United States
(from 49.8 to 46.8 percent), the United Kingdom (from
19.4 to 14.2 percent), and France (from 8.5 to 6.5
percent).

While Table 3.9 indicates the stock of DFI in
all developing countries by the end of 1977, particularly the percentage share of each investor state,
Table 3.10 shows the roles played by these investor
states in selected host countries. As noted in Chapter 1, Table 3.10 shows the dominance of U.S. investments in Latin America as a region. In Brazil, for
example, the U.S. share of DFI in 1971 stood at 37.7
percent, and this dropped by 5.5 percent five years
later. This is in contrast with Western Europe and
Japan, whose combined share stood at 40.5 percent in
1971 and increased by 8 percent five years later.
Looking at DFI in Asia as a region, it is obvious
that the preponderance of Japanese investments in
Indonesia, South Korea, and Thailand is comparable
to that of U.S. investments in such Latin American
countries as Colombia, Mexico, and Panama. However,
while the share of U.S. investments in most Latin
American countries (especially Brazil, Venezuela,
Peru, Argentina) seems to be on the decline (because
of the politics of economic nationalism), the share
of Japanese investments in most Asian countries continues to be on the increase. And, in India and
Nigeria, like other Anglophone African countries,
the predominance of U.S. investments is evident although the trend in most Anglophone countries in
Africa and Asia is toward joint ventures between U.K.
investors and host governments or nationals of host
states.[56]

TABLE 3.10

Stock of Direct Foreign Investment in Selected Developing Countries by Country of Origin and Selected Years

	Latin America									Africa	
	Argentina	Brazil		Colombia		Mexico		Panama		Nigeria	
	1973	1971	1976	1971	1975	1971	1975	1969	1974	1968	1973
Total Value of Stock ($ m)	2,274	2,911	9,005	503	632	2,997	4,736	214	534	999	1,999
Distribution of Stock (%)											
United States	39.5	37.7	32.2	55.9	48.1	80.9	68.7	90.8	86.3	19.8	29.2
Canada	3.9	10.1	5.3	10.1	10.1	1.7	2.3	N.A.	N.A.	--	--
Western Europe										18.9[e]	19.6[e]
Federal Republic of Germany	4.5	11.4	12.4	2.4	2.5	2.8	2/3	N.A.	N.A.	--	--
France	8.5	4.5	3.6	3.4	4.3	1.7	1.0	N.A.	N.A.	--	--
Italy	1.1	1.1	0.9	N.A.	N.A.	1.6	0.5	N.A.	N.A.	--	--
Netherlands	6.3	1.2	2.6	3.0	3.5	1.1	2.3	N.A.	N.A.	--	--
Spain	0.4	N.S.	N.S.	N.A.	N.A.	0.8	0.1	N.A.	N.A.	--	--
Sweden	2.0	2.0	2.4	N.A.	N.A.	1.2	1.1	N.A.	N.A.	--	--
Switzerland	9.1	6.6	10.9	2.8	4.6	2.8	3.0	2.5	2.3	--	--
United Kingdom	12.0	9.4	4.7	2.0	2.2	3.0	5.6	2.6	3.2	56.3	44.2
Japan	0.3	4.3	11.2	0.1	0.6	0.7	1.3	N.A.	N.A.	--	--
Australia	--	--	--	--	--	N.A.	N.A.	N.A.	N.A.	--	--
Argentina	N.S.	0.3	0.2	N.A.	N.A.	N.A.	N.A.	N.A.	N.A.	--	--
Brazil	0.4	N.S.	N.S.	0.1	0.3	N.A.	N.A.	N.A.	N.A.	--	--
Hong Kong	--	--	--	--	--	--	--	--	--	--	--
Philippines	--	--	--	--	--	--	--	--	--	--	--
Singapore	--	--	--	--	--	--	--	--	--	--	--
South Korea	--	--	--	--	--	--	--	--	--	--	--
Panama	3.5	2.8	3.1	7.2	8.3	N.S.	2.5	N.S.	N.S.	--	--
Others[f]	8.2	8.8	10.4	15.0	15.5	1.9	9.3	4.0	8.1	5.9	7.0
Total	100.0	100.0	100.0	100.0	100.0	100.0	100.0	100.0	100.0	100.0	100.0

	Asia												
	Hong Kong		India	Indonesia[b]		South Korea		Philippines		Singapore[c]		Thailand[d]	
	1971	1976	1974	1971	1976	1973	1975	1973	1976	1971	1976	1969	1975
Total Value of Stock ($ m)	759	1,952	1,683	1,831	6,362	582	927	146	513	543	1,523	70	175
Distribution of Stock (%)													
United States	53.5	47.2	12.9	25.2	6.7	21.5	17.4	64.2	47.9	31.8	32.9	26.5	14.0
Canada	N.A.	N.A.	6.2	N.A.	N.A.	N.A.	N.A.	0.3	7.8	N.A.	N.A.	N.A.	N.A.
Western Europe													
Federal Republic of													
Germany	0.8	1.0	3.6	0.9	2.7	0.7	0.6	0.2	0.3	1.3	3.0	--	--
France	N.A.	1.2	N.A.	N.A.	N.A.	0.6	0.6	N.A.	N.A.	N.A.	N.A.		
Italy	N.A.	N.A.	N.A.	N.A.	N.A.	0.2	N.A.	N.A.	N.A.	N.A.	N.A.		
Netherlands	2.3	1.2	3.0	2.0	2.5	1.1	6.2	N.A.	N.A.	17.5	14.0	11.9[e]	5.8[e]
Spain	--	--	--	--	--	--	--	--	--	--	--	--	--
Sweden	N.A.	N.A.	3.6	N.A.	N.A.	N.A.	N.A.	--	--	N.A.	N.A.		
Switzerland	1.8	2.2	5.5	N.A.	N.A.	N.A.	N.A.	0.8	1.8	18.6	14.8	4.7	2.0
United Kingdom	11.3	8.2	60.8	N.A.	N.A.	0.8	N.A.	16.4	5.8	6.8	14.0	36.6	41.0
Japan	22.4	15.4	2.0	29.7	36.9	70.7	66.5	9.7	24.2	N.A.	N.A.	1.0	0.3
Australia	4.5	5.2	N.A.	5.0	2.6	N.A.	N.A.	0.3	2.5	--	--	--	--
Argentina	--	--	--	--	--	--	--	--	--	--	--	--	--
Brazil	--	--	--	--	--	--	--	--	--	--	--	--	--
Hong Kong	N.S.	N.S.	N.A.	6.3	10.3	0.8	0.6	1.3	1.8	N.A.	N.A.	N.A.	N.A.
Philippines	0.3	0.8	N.A.	14.3	4.2	N.A.	N.A.	N.S.	N.S.	N.A.	N.A.	0.3	0.8
Singapore	1.1	3.1	N.A.	2.6	1.8	N.A.	N.A.	N.A.	N.A.	N.S.	N.S.	N.A.	N.A.
South Korea	N.A.	N.A.	N.A.	2.5	0.9	N.S.	N.S.	N.A.	N.A.	N.A.	N.A.	N.A.	N.A.
Panama	N.A.	N.A.	1.4	N.A.	N.A.	0.9	2.5	0.2	0.4	N.A.	N.A.	N.A.	N.A.
Others[f]	1.1	10.5	4.0	11.0	31.4	3.5	5.4	6.6	7.5	23.9	21.0	4.4	14.7
Total	100.0	100.0	100.0	100.0	100.0	100.0	100.0	100.0	100.0	100.0	100.0	100.0	100.0

N.A. Not available.

N.S. Not significant.

aExcludes investment in the petroleum sector.

bApproved projects only.

cInvestment in manufacturing only.

dRegistered capital of alien firms.

eTotal stock for all Western European countries.

fIncludes developed and developing countries of origin for which separate data are not available.

Source: United Nations, Transnational Corporations in World Development: A Reexamination. New York: United Nations, 1978, Annex III, Table III-49, pp. 256-58.

Pattern of Investment:
Regional/Sectoral Distribution

As shown in Table 3.6, DFI accounts for nearly 55 percent of all private capital flows to the
Third World between 1956 and 1971. Available data
show that DFI flows among the developed market economies have been much higher than such flows to the
developing countries since the mid-1950s. The reason can partly be attributed to the growing uncertainty surrounding DFI in most Third World countries,
particularly those in Africa and the Middle East.
For example, between 1970 and 1971 as well as between 1972 and 1978, DFI flows to the developing
countries averaged $3.8 billion and $6.7 billion,
respectively. Between 1970 and 1971, DFI flows to
the developed market economies are estimated to have
trebled. In fact, between 1972 and 1978 when DFI
flows to the Third World averaged $6.7 billion, this
figure represented just under 19 percent of DFI
flows in the world.
As to the regional distribution of DFI to the
Third World, Table 3.11 shows that Latin America accounts for almost 37 percent of DFI between 1969 and
1976 and about 45 percent at the end of 1976, thus
clearly emerging as the dominant region of the Third
World attracting or receiving DFI. Again, as noted
above, Brazil is the only Latin American country,
indeed, the only Third World country, that has received a lion's share of DFI in the Third World,
namely, 15.8 percent. Trailing behind Brazil, among
Third World recipients of DFI (in terms of volume),
are Mexico, Indonesia, Venezuela, and Nigeria. Compared with Latin America, which accounted for $40
billion of the stock of DFI in the Third World,
while the share of the Middle East stood at only
$4.1 billion, the combined totals of Brazil, Mexico,
and Indonesia stood at $19.33 billion. The reason
for this can be found in the growing uncertainty
surrounding the investment climate in the Middle
East, particularly as several countries in the region, and these include Iraq, Saudi Arabia, and
Kuwait, have expropriated foreign-owned oil interests
or acquired majority equity interests in major
foreign-owned oil corporations.[57]

Finally, the sectoral distribution of DFI in the Third World shows that it is heavily concentrated in two sectors, namely, the petroleum and mining sectors. Whereas 29 percent of the total DFI in the developed market economies (DMEs) was in petroleum, only 33 percent of total DFI in the Third World was in this sector at the end of 1967. Manufacturing in the DMEs accounted for 29.1 percent, mining and smelting for 10.7 percent, while the share of agriculture and public utilities (and other sectors) stood at 6.2 and 20.9 percent, respectively.[58] In fact, at the end of 1966, the sectoral distribution of DFI in the Third World stood as follows: petroleum 39.7 percent; mining and smelting 9.3 percent; manufacturing 26.9 percent; others 24.1 percent. There seems to be an asymmetry in the sectoral distribution of DFI in the DMEs and the developing countries. Whereas 50 percent of the stock of DFI in the Third World is in the extractive sector and a little more than 25 percent in manufacturing, about 50 percent (49.7 percent at the end of 1966) of the stock of DFI in DMEs is in manufacturing while bout 30 percent (28.8 percent) is in the extractive sector.

Let us now examine the variations in DFI between different sectors in the Third World. As Table 3.12 demonstrates very clearly, the Middle East tops the list in the petroleum sector, accounting for almost 90 percent of the total investment, followed by Africa with 39.4 percent. When it comes to manufacturing, the Western Hemisphere and Asia have a combined total of 67.1 percent, with Africa and the Middle East accounting for 24.9, while Asia tops the list in agriculture, thanks to rubber and tea plantations in Malaysia and India, respectively.

However, one significant characteristic of DFI in the Third World is its concentration in a few countries in each of the major regions. According to one United Nations study,

Only a few developing countries have a stock of direct investment of more than $1 billion. Thus, Argentina, Brazil, India, Mexico, Nigeria, Venezuela and certain Caribbean islands,

TABLE 3.11[a]

Regional Distribution of Direct Foreign Investment Flows (1969–76) and Estimated Stock[b] (Year-End 1976) from Developed Market Economies[c] To Developing Countries by Selected Capital-Importing Countries[d]

Region/ Country	Flows ($ million)								1969-76	% of Total[e]	Stock ($ million)	% of Total[e]
	1969	1970	1971	1972	1973	1974	1975	1976				
Europe	168	303	224	424	652	895	810	369	3845	8.8	6745	9.2
Greece	5	10	9	14	88	143	43	46	348	0.8	946	1.3
Spain	105	240	127	366	509	668	578	235	2828	6.5	4605	6.3
Turkey	-1	4	1	1	26	24	47	-5	97	0.2	495	0.7
Africa	638	802	587	656	202	275	948	928	5033	11.5	11629	15.9
Algeria	85	80	1	41	40	8	29	44	328	0.8	394	0.5
Libya	152	283	104	151	-193	-3	-576	263	181	0.4	893	1.2
Morocco	-f	5	4	7	5	-26	5	1	1	--	301	0.4
Angola	4	2	2	2	8	7	--	-1	24	0.1	99	0.1
Zaire	15	6	6	10	18	52	9	238	354	0.8	1088	1.5
Gabon	--	1	--	--	11	13	47	7	78	0.2	627	0.9
Ghana	22	7	-4	6	8	14	7	-2	58	0.1	298	0.4
Ivory Coast	1	-3	--	-1	4	1	6	30	38	0.1	450	0.6
Liberia	-2	73	-36	23	78	57	180	83	456	1.0	883	1.2
Nigeria	66	61	48	76	71	88	472	-152	730	1.7	2748	3.8
Zimbabwe	23	19	22	23	30	33	25	--	175	0.4	300	0.4
Zambia	9	10	8	22	17	14	32	1	113	0.3	201	0.3
Latin America and the Caribbean	1195 (1185)g	1510 (1441)	1391 (1514)	1558 (1463)	3207 (2629)	4677 (2668)	4307 (3365)	2846 (1756)	20691 (16021)	36.7	40027 (32787)	(44.8)
Jamaica	-3	13	13	-7	5	3	32	-79	-36	-0.1	891	1.2
Mexico	196	137	79	181	252	480	393	-166	1552	3.6	4634	6.3
Panama	154	195	221	18	222	14	340	128	1292	3.0	2378	3.3
Trinidad & Tobago	2	7	-3	6	-7	10	3	1	19	--	1201	1.6
West Indies	37	14	17	27	25	110	1	4	235	0.5	744	1.0
Argentina	114	84	123	70	92	35	54	210	782	1.8	2210	3.0
Brazil	225	294	371	629	1257	1307	1457	1366	69C6	15.8	10466	14.3
Chile	-80	-29	-24	-102	-10	-43	-128	4	-412	-0.9	404	0.6
Colombia	53	4	72	-7	12	38	49	6	227	0.5	1206	1.6
Peru	35	-9	11	45	87	457	327	159	1112	2.5	1859	2.5
Venezuela	43	51	-11	-1	-101	-240	265	-360	-354	-0.8	3640	5.0

Middle East	106	-67	169	466	878	-314	1536	1109	3863	8.9	4090	-5.6
Iran	40	15	23	4	36	-614	495	-109	-110	-0.3	1091	1.5
Iraq	--	-1	--	--	-7	-9	-45	1	-61	-0.1	121	0.2
Kuwait	41	26	--	--	--	--	--	-1	66	0.2	649	0.9
Saudi Arabia	4	7	8	4	1	6	32	44	106	0.2	694	0.9
Asia and Oceania	551	779	912	855	1813	1699	3382	1780	11771	(26.9)	17891	(24.5)
					(1810)[f]	(1697)	(3379)	(1770)	(11753)		(17881)	
India	40	42	47	19	41	52	85	19	345	0.8	2419	3.3
Pakistan	5	4	--	-1	--	--	6	-1	13	--	749	1.0
Hong Kong	23	26	31	58	143	81	215	79	633	1.5	1379	1.9
Indonesia	48	49	117	90	348	182	1289	746	2869	6.6	4246	5.8
South Korea	5	14	32	67	261	81	51	83	594	1.4	1033	1.4
Malaysia	6	37	32	65	139	123	73	51	526	1.2	2351	3.2
Philippines	70	-3	17	14	60	140	117	152	567	1.3	1372	1.9
Singapore	9	16	22	46	105	92	70	42	402	0.9	1742	2.4
Thailand	17	14	8	21	20	44	19	16	159	0.4	346	0.5
Papua New Guinea	42	130	47	86	112	73	-2	49	537	1.2	749	1.0
Gross Total[h]	2919	3544	3633	4474	6717	7874	11506	7649	48316		80382	
Tax-Haven Countries[i]	10	69	-123	95	581	2011	945	1100	4688		7250	
Net Total[e]	2909	3475	3756	4379	6136	5863	10561	6549	43628	100.0	73132	100.0

[a] The data in this table for 1973 and 1974 do not tally with those on total DFI in Table 3.7 because this table does not take account of major recomputations of the U.S. data for the years reflected in revised OECD data including those in Table 3.7.

[b] Items may not add to totals because of rounding and incomplete country listing.

[c] See Table 3.7, note b, for list of countries.

[d] Includes reinvested earnings.

[e] Excludes tax-haven countries.

[f] Flows of less than ± $500,000.

[g] Figures in parentheses are those excluding tax-haven countries.

[h] Includes unspecified total.

[i] Bahamas, Bermuda, Netherlands Antilles, and New Hebrides.

Sources: Y. Billerbeck and Y. Yasugi, Private Direct Investment in Developing Countries, World Bank Staff Paper No. 348 (Washington, D.C.: International Bank for Reconstruction and Development, July 1979), p. 70; Isiah Frank, Foreign Enterprise in Developing Countries (Baltimore, Md.: Johns Hopkins University Press, 1980), pp. 18-19.

TABLE 3.12

Sectoral Distribution of Stock of Direct Foreign Investment
in Developing Countries Year-End 1967

Industrial Sector	Africa		Western Hemisphere[a]		Asia and Oceania		Middle East	
	$ million	%	$ million	%	$ million	%	$ million	%
Petroleum	2,597.6	39.4	4,485.5	24.3	1,102.3	22.1	2,776.4	89.5
Manufacturing	1,236.4	18.8	6,652.7	36.1	1,547.1	31.0	190.3	6.1
Mining	1,279.8	19.4	2,016.1	10.9	252.5	5.1	6.0	0.2
Trade	398.2	6.0	1,668.3	9.0	504.4	10.1	30.0	1.0
Agriculture	496.8	7.5	607.4	3.3	939.1	18.8	2.5	0.1
Public Utilities	66.3	1.0	1,370.7	7.4	123.0	2.4	10.5	0.3
Others	516.0	8.9	1,648.6	9.0	522.5	10.5	87.0	2.8
Total	6,591.1	100.0	18,449.3	100.0	4,991.5	100.0	3,102.7	100.0

[a]Including the Caribbean.

Source: United Nations, Multinational Corporations in World Development, Publication no. E.73.II.A.11, p. 177.

84

account for 43 percent of the total
stock of investment in developing
countries, which is roughly the same
proportion as that of their combined
gross domestic product to the estimated total for all developing countries.[59]

And, according to OECD estimates for the end of 1967,
in 13 other Third World countries the stock of DFI
stood between $500 million and $1 billion, accounting for nearly another 30 percent of the total stock
of DFI in the Third World. To be sure, in Algeria,
Libya, Nigeria, Zambia, Jamaica, Netherlands Antilles, Trinidad and Tobago, Peru, Venezuela, Iran,
Kuwait, and Saudi Arabia, the stock of investment in
the extractive sector, decidedly the dominant sector, exceeds $200 million. In several other coun-
tries, manufacturing is the dominant sector; for example, more than $200 million went into manufactur-
ing in Argentina, Brazil, India, Mexico, and the
Philippines. And, in India and Malaysia, investment
in agriculture stood at more than $200 million.
    But things have changed since the 1960s. Ac-
cording to Grant Reuber and others,[60] the book value
of DFI in the Third World at the end of 1970 stood
at approximately $40 billion, which represents about
25 percent of the world's total DFI. Just over 30
percent of this is in manufacturing while petroleum
accounts for 33.3 percent, mining 10.3 percent, and
others (including agriculture, shipping, trade, banking, and tourism) account for 24.9 percent as shown
in Table 3.13.
    In essence, the extractive sector, quantita-
tively, was the most important sector by the end of
1970. However, by the early 1970s, investment in
manufacturing accounted for approximately 50 percent
of total DFI.[61] The shift in the pattern of investment, namely, from the extractive sector to the manufacturing sector, has been influenced by the growing
assertiveness of many Third World countries to exercise greater control over the exploitation of their
vital, and nonrenewable natural resources in the
later 1960s and the early 1970s. This assertiveness
has found expressions in several United Nations

TABLE 3.13

Regional and Sectoral Distribution of Direct Foreign Investment in Developing Countries Year-End 1970

	Industrial Sector					Percent
	Petroleum	Mining	Manufacturing	Others	Total	
Latin America						
$ billion	4.8	2.1	7.5	5.4	19.8	50.8
Percent	24.2	10.6	37.9	27.3	100.0	
Europe						
$ billion	0.4	0.1	1.5	0.5	2.5	6.4
Percent	16.0	4.0	60.0	20.0	100.0	
Middle East						
$ billion	3.2	--	0.2	0.1	3.5	9.0
Percent	91.4	--	5.7	2.9	100.0	
Africa						
$ billion	3.3	1.4	1.3	1.6	7.6	19.5
Percent	43.4	18.4	17.1	21.1	100.0	
Asia						
$ billion	1.3	0.4	1.8	2.1	5.6	14.4
Percent	23.2	7.1	32.1	37.5	100.0	
Total						
$ billion	13.0	4.0	12.3	9.7	39.0	100.0
Percent	33.3	10.3	31.5	24.9	100.0	

Source: Grant L. Reuber et al., Private Foreign Investment in Development (Oxford, England: Oxford University Press, 1973), Appendix A.

General Assembly Resolutions on Permanent Sovereignty
Over Natural Resources.[62] For example, Article 2 of
the UNGA Resolution 3281 (XXIX) of December 12, 1974,
(Charter of Economic Rights and Duties of States) has
this much to say:

> 2(1) Every State has and shall freely
> exercise full permanent sover-
> eignty, including possession; use
> and disposal, over all its wealth,
> natural resources and economic
> activities.
> (2) Every State has the right:
> (a) To regulate and exercise au-
> thority over foreign investment
> within its national jurisdiction
> in accordance with its laws and
> regulations and in conformity
> with its national objectives and
> priorities. No State shall be
> compelled to grant preferential
> treatment to foreign investment;
> (b) To regulate and supervise the
> activities of transnational cor-
> porations within its national
> jurisdiction and take measures to
> ensure that such activities com-
> ply with its laws, rules and regu-
> lations and conform with its eco-
> nomic and social policies. Trans-
> national corporations shall not
> intervene in the internal affairs
> of a host State . . .;
> (c) To nationalize, expropriate
> or transfer ownership of foreign
> property, in which case appropri-
> ate compensation should be paid
> by the State adopting such mea-
> sures, taking into account its
> relevant laws and regulations and
> all circumstances that the State
> considers pertinent.[63]

Although the United Nations General Assembly resolutions have recommendatory and moral force rather than

legal force, resolutions dealing with legal matters constitute strong evidence of state practice, and the principles embodied in such resolutions may well acquire the character of customary international law.[64]

Because of changing political and economic circumstances in the Third World--indeed, because the balance of power has changed in favor of the host government vis-à-vis the MNCs--many MNCs that are sensitive to the new waves of economic nationalism have developed new strategies (such as joint ventures and technical cooperation agreements) to retain control of their operations while giving the appearance of host government's participation in the operations of their local subsidiaries. MNCs have entered into joint ventures with the host government; although they may, and they do have minority equity interests in such ventures, by concluding management contracts with the host government, "the headquarters of the former parent companies still exercise de facto control over joint-ventures in which they are 'technically,' and patently, junior partners."[65]

But why do MNCs establish affiliates in the Third World? The reasons are not very hard to seek. The establishment of an MNC's subsidiaries in the developing countries can be attributed to the following factors:[66]

1. the desire to protect markets initially developed by exports and threatened by trade barriers;
2. the incentives initially provided by the host government, such as tax-free holiday; free convertibility of currency; unrestricted repatriation of profits and dividends; exemption from import and custom duties on essential goods;
3. availability of cheap labor and need to have access to "strategic" raw materials (especially in respect of U.S. multinationals in South Africa);
4. oligopolistic competition in world markets, namely the tendency for multinational corporations to match direct investment by their rivals in particular markets;
5. the dynamics of the international markets for their products, meaning that once a multinational corporation faces a decline in its technological

advantage in its existing markets, it would expand to new markets where it can retain its competitive advantage;

6. the necessity to grow in order to maintain or increase market shares; in fact, no pioneer corporation that wished to preserve its lead in market
shares and consequently in profits can afford to
abandon that market to the latecomers;

7. the protection of the local markets following import substitution industrialization program embarked upon by the host state.

Above all, MNCs locate subsidiaries abroad, especially in developing countries, because of the threat,
actual or potential, of local competition. More
significant, the establishment of subsidiaries
abroad was, for MNCs, an institutional necessity.

  It would appear that the factors motivating
the establishment of foreign subsidiaries of MNCs
and the economic characteristics of these subsidiaries depend on the activity in which the MNC is engaged. For example, MNCs engaged in the manufacture
and subsequent export of components are primarily
interested in labor cost differentials and such incentives as are offered by the host government. As
David Colman and Frederick Nixson have noted, MNCs
increasingly

> are identifying specific unskilled
> labour-intensive activities or pro-
> cesses within their overall manufac-
> turing operations and transferring
> these parts of the production process
> to LDCs, where cheap labour more than
> offsets the transport costs incurred.[67]

The countries frequently mentioned are Hong Kong,
Mexico, India, Singapore, South Korea, Taiwan, and
Thailand. More significant,

> data are flown from the USA to the
> West Indies and South East Asia for
> punching upon tape by low-wage key
> punch operators and the tapes flown
> back to the USA; loose ammunition is

sent to Mexico for loading into magazines by cheap local labour.[68]

What comments can one make on this "strategy" of industrial development, that is, the export of labor-intensive components? First, the MNC is only transferring labor-intensive technology and exporting components rather than finished products. Second, apart from the revenue and employment generated, the host state does not derive any other benefits. Third, little capital, if any, has been invested by the MNC; if anything, whatever capital is invested is footloose or mobile, and more significant, "unskilled labor is not given any real training, technological spin-off is likely to be minimal and dependence on the TNCs [transnational corporations] for inputs, markets, decisions affecting output, etc. is complete."[69] Fourth, this strategy obviously and certainly reinforces the position of developing countries as suppliers of cheap labor to the DMEs.

An examination of the contributions of MNCs to the development (or underdevelopment) of Third World countries compels one to make these observations. In the first place, it is difficult to generalize about the effects of MNCs on employment, technology, labor skills and so on because of the variety of activities in which they engage, namely, primary production for export; import-substituting manufacturing; manufacturing for export; banking and finance; and other service activities. To be sure, in attempting to discern the impact the MNC has on any single aspect of economic life, one has to run the world twice: first, the ways thing actually went and, second, the ways things might have gone had the MNC, as an institution, not existed. For example, it is not enough to say that 40,000 jobs have been created or destroyed in, say, Nigeria by the activities of MNCs. We know (or think we know) what happened to employment. We need to know what would have happened without the MNC. Would 40,000 jobs have been created or destroyed anyway? Put differently, would employment trends have been any different without the multinational? If not, then clearly there are no MNC effects to worry about and, certainly, there is no need to formulate policies to deal specifically with them.

Second, and more fundamental, there are great differences in the size of these MNCs--differences that invariably are associated with their national origins, differences in the degree in which they tend to compete with each other, and the differences in the attitudes of their executives. And, third, it cannot be assumed that the contributions of a subsidiary of a U.S.-based MNC in the Federal Republic of Germany to that economy are similar to the contributions of that subsidiary in Chile to the Chilean economy.

Because many readers may not be intimately familiar with the operations of MNCs in the Third World and/or the political economy of Third World countries, a particular breakdown has been chosen for the remainder of the discussion in this chapter that should be sufficiently intelligible to the expert and the dilettante alike. For example, it is often said, indeed, claimed,

1. that multinational corporations bring the much-needed, and scarce finance capital with which they create additional facilities for the host states;
2. that MNCs alleviate balance of payment deficits of their host states not only through finance capital they bring along but also through import-substitution as well as their increased exports relative to local firms which, it has been argued, are less efficient than MNCs; and,
3. that they transfer to Third World countries modern technology including the managerial skills that go with its operation, and by creating new production facilities, they create more jobs, thus, help in stemming potential political discontent arising from unemployment among urban youths.

In essence, MNCs are the engines of development in the Third World. Certainly a case has been made for DFI in the Third World. Before proceeding to consider the contributions of MNCs to the development of Third World countries, let us examine the institutional conditions as well as the economic structure of Third World economies using Ronald Muller's classic study of the impact of MNCs on Third World development as a guide.[70]

BASIS OF POWER OF MULTINATIONAL CORPORATIONS

The Institutional Setting

It has been noted elsewhere in this chapter that it was and is possible for the MNC to maximize the profits of the parent company rather than that of its branch offices (subsidiaries), given the environment in which MNCs operate and thrive, namely, because Third World countries are less developed or underdeveloped. And, in an institutional context, less developed meant: (1) that there is a dearth of well-qualified government officials to ensure that business or commercial laws are faithfully executed; (2) that these laws themselves as well as taxation practices are archaic or have remained in the statute books for too long to take cognizance of changing situations; and (3) that organized labor is nonexistent or, at best, weak. What these implied is that there is no effective check on the power of the MNC in the Third World as opposed to what obtains in the industrialized North.

The Structure of Technology

Undoubtedly, there are a number of strategies that developing countries can follow in their pursuit of industrial development. But basically, it is essentially a choice between producing goods for export (export-led growth) and producing goods for the domestic market (import substitution). However, a developing country pursuing a policy of import-substituting industrialization has a number of options: (1) it can use its foreign exchange earnings to import investment goods (i.e., looms), raw materials, fuels, etc. to manufacture consumer goods; (2) it can use its foreign exchange earnings to import capital goods (machine tools) to make investment goods (looms) which in turn produce consumer goods (cloth) and to make intermediate goods and develop domestic raw material supplies; or (3) it can use its foreign exchange earnings to import capital goods (machine tools) to make capital goods (machine tools).

An examination of the development strategies of Third World countries has revealed that while a majority of them have pursued variation 1 of the import-substituting industrialization strategy, the more advanced, semi-industrialized countries have

pursued variation 2. Whether Third World countries
are pursuing what has been referred to as outward-
looking development strategies or are pursuing variation 1 or have moved on to variation 2 is not as
significant as being entirely dependent on foreign
technology. What dependence on foreign sources of
technology has meant is that, first, it permits the
establishment of oligopoly power; second, it re-
stricts or retards the development of local competition and, indeed, the growth of a local business
elite and local enterprise; and, third, it permits
an astonishing rate of profits, the greater majority
of which leaves the host state through many devices,
legal and illegal. The point to emphasize here is
that once such a process starts, it becomes, as Muller
observed, "cumulative and self-perpetuating."[71]

The Structure of Finance

An examination of the financial structure of
Third World countries has led one to question the
widely held view that the MNC is "basically an example of a long-run capital movement from capital rich
to capital poor regions."[72] To be sure, MNCs

> often actually don't bring in very
> much capital, frequently only 25 per-
> cent of the investment is in the form
> of foreign equity, with 50 percent or
> more made up of loans obtained at
> favored rates in the local money mar-
> kets.[73]

What is significant for the present discussion is
that MNC subsidiaries operating in capital-poor countries borrow from the local financial institutions,
and, more often than not, with "the credit rating
and financial resources backup of the entire global
network of the parent MNC of which they are a part."[74]
Two consequences flow from this process. First,
local firms, usually with poor credit ratings and
poor financial resources backup, would not be able
to generate the much-needed finance capital for their
own operations. Second, since the local financial
institutions want to minimize risks, and in any

event have limited loan capital relative to demand, they will inevitably and certainly show a lending pattern biased toward MNC subsidiaries. This is particularly so if the local financial institutions are affiliates of a so-called private multinational bank such as the Bank of America, Standard Bank, Barclays Bank, or the First National Bank of Chicago.

Undoubtedly, these banks play a powerful role in the financial structure of the Third World where, in many instances, they control up to 50 percent of the private deposits of a country. For example, the leading banks in Nigeria not only in terms of turn-over but also in terms of profits (after tax) are the United Bank of Africa (an affiliate of the British-French Bank) and the First Bank of Nigeria (an affiliate of Standard Bank). What is significant about these banks is that they prefer lending to such MNC subsidiaries as the United Africa Company of Nigeria and Compagnie Francaise de L'Afrique Oc-cidentale (Nigeria) Limited for the same reasons as do locally controlled banks.

However, there is much more at stake in such a lending operation. In the first place, the world-wide parent networks of banks and corporations are not two distinct entities. In fact, there are inter-locking interests of common ownership, management, and technical personnel in the groups controlling banks and corporations. As a recent study reveals, the 13 largest U.S.-based MNCs "maintain close rela-tions with each other as well as other TNCs [trans-national corporations] in South Africa through their boards of directors and banking ties."[75] Put dif-ferently, subsidiaries of U.S.-based MNCs and multi-national banks in South Africa have direct contacts with each other through interlocking directorships.[76] Second, whatever the consequences of these inter-locking directorships, there is "the well-established fact of near-perfect correlation between the world-wide expansion of MNCs and the commensurate expan-sion by multinational banks."[77]

MULTINATIONAL CORPORATIONS: RESOURCE UTILIZATION AND DEVELOPMENT

Now to an examination of the contribution of MNCs to resource utilization and development. It is usually assumed that MNCs are engines of development. Indeed, it has been claimed by proponents of DFIs, and these include scholars and organizations such as the Council of Americas and the International Chamber of Commerce, that MNCs contribute resources that are generally not available or insufficiently available, namely, capital, technology, and marketing skills. Additionally, it has been argued that MNCs create jobs, alleviate balance-of-payments deficits of their host states, and, more significant, they are able to use their resources more efficiently than local firms, thus maximizing their contribution to the developmental efforts.

These claims or arguments have been questioned increasingly in recent years not only by Third World scholars and leaders but also by Western scholars. It would be recalled that Orlando Letelier, Chile's Ambassador to the United States during the administration of President Salvador Allende Gossens, declared unequivocally when asked whether Allende's policies were not hurting DFIs in Chile:

> In general terms, we have been export-ing capital, not importing it . . . between 1950 and 1967 . . . $450 mil-lion flowed into Chile as direct in-vestment. Now deduct depreciation for such investments during that period, which the companies took back out of the country, and the net figure would be only $257 million. In the same period, the outflow of profits and dividends just on investments was $1.056 billion, about four times the net investment.[78]

Reinforcing Letelier's view, Barnet and Muller have observed:

> When the global corporations proclaim themselves engines of development, we can judge their claims only if we know what development track they are on. A mechanical definition of development based on growth rates is obscene in a

world in which most people go to sleep
hungry. A development model like
Brazil's, in which the stock market
booms and two-thirds of the population
is condemned to an early death by poverty, hunger, and disease, is a cari-
cature of progress.[79]

What Letelier and Barnet and Muller are saying, in
effect, is, first, that MNCs are vehicles through
which capital is transferred from capital-poor to
capital-rich regions and, second, that, overall,
MNCs are not engines of development in the Third
World as claimed by MNCs and proponents of DFI. The
next section will assess various aspects of the impact of MNCs on the development of Third World countries.

Multinational Corporations as Sources of Finance

Because Third World countries are generally
held to be capital deficient, it is usually assumed
that the very act of DFI by an MNC results directly
or indirectly in a capital transfer from a capital-
rich to a capital-poor country. Put simply, the
simple view of DFI through MNCs is that what is invested in country A (capital importing) cannot be invested in country B (capital exporting) at the same
time. Thus, by investing abroad, MNCs do not invest
at home and, thus, help economic growth in host
states and hinder it in home states. Hence, Robert
Gilpin has maintained that MNC capital exports allow
the domestic economy to atrophy. Consequently, he
proposes a government effort at stimulating new domestic investment in the United States, specifically
by means of stepped-up research and development,
opening up new profit opportunities to reduce incentives to invest abroad.[80]
When Gilpin maintains that U.S.-based MNCs invest abroad because of easy sources of profit, the
inference that can be drawn from this assertion is
that the rate of return on the invested capital is
much higher in the host states than in the United

States--otherwise the MNCs would not have undertaken
the foreign investment in the first place. However,
while it may be true that DFI hurts potential output
in home states, this damage is unlikely to be as
great as it appears because the repatriated earnings
have to be deducted from any net loss. Again, while
MNC capital inflows benefit potential output in host
states, some of this, which seems to have been ignored, has to be given up to service the imported
capital.

But suppose the MNC investment had not been
made? One possibility is that somebody else, perhaps the government, would have undertaken the investment anyway and the net contribution of DFI to
the capital base as well as to growth in the host
state is zero. Or nothing would have happened, in
which case, DFI would have been credited with the
full contribution. In essence, it is difficult to
tell whether DFI adds to or supplants local investment in host states. As Richard Caves and Grant
Reuber noted:

> Whether or not [DFI] supplements or
> possibly even stimulates local invest-
> ment opportunities can only be deduced
> by summing up the net effect of for-
> eign competition on local investment
> plans throughout the economy.[81]

To be sure, what if MNC capital spending in a particular country involves no fusions at all? Put
differently, suppose the capital is borrowed locally
by the local subsidiary of a foreign-based MNC? The
fact is that several studies on the global investment activities of MNCs do not generally support the
claim that the very act of an MNC's DFI results
directly or indirectly in a capital transfer from a
capital-rich to a capital-poor country.

A study commissioned by the United Nations,
and carried out by Fernando Fajnzylber, revealed the
following:

1. That MNCs operating in Latin America
largely make use of local loan capital
to finance their operations;

2. That banks generally prefer lending
   to MNCs subsidiaries than local
   firms for reasons not unconnected
   with the "credit rating and financial resources back-up" of the
   parent companies;
3. That subsidiaries of United States-
   based MNCs in Latin America between 1957 and 1965 financed 83
   percent of their operations from
   local sources;
4. That United States-based MNCs repatriated, on the average, 79 percent of their net profits to United
   States stockholders between 1960
   and 1968;
5. That 38 percent of the financial
   resources used by United States'
   manufacturing corporations in Latin
   America comes from reinvested earnings; while the figure for the
   manufacturing sector was low, it
   was increasing, going from 42 percent to 52 percent in the period
   1960-1964 and 1965-1968; and,
6. That the net outflow of finance
   capital from Latin America by
   United States-based MNCs is certainly greater if we add to these
   figures the fact that an estimated
   46 percent of MNCs' investment
   funds in Latin America went into
   the acquisition of local firms.[82]

Other studies have tended to reinforce the view that
MNCs are, in fact, not the major suppliers of finance
capital to the so-called capital-poor countries.
    First, studies by Aldo Ferer and the Chilean
government under President Eduardo Frei (1963-70)
have shown that about 78 percent of the operations
of U.S. manufacturing subsidiaries in Latin America
were financed out of local loan capital, and, specifically, that MNC subsidiaries in Chile preempt
financing because they can borrow twice as much on
their inventories and capital assets as can local

firms and at the same time scarce financing is re-
tailed in the form of consumer debt at exorbitant
interest. Second, according to Barnet and Muller,
some 52 percent of all profits of U.S. manufacturing
subsidiaries were repatriated between 1965 and 1968,
meaning that for every dollar of net profit earned,
52 cents left the country although 78 percent of the
resources or funds used to finance the operations of
these subsidiaries were generated locally. More
significant, the capital outflow resulting from the
operations of U.S. mining, petroleum, and smelting
subsidiaries is "even worse. Each dollar of net
profit is based on an investment that was 83 percent
financed from local savings; yet only 21 percent of
the profit remains in the local economy."[83] This
conclusion seems to tally with the positions taken
by two other Latin American scholars that the percentage of reinvested earnings by U.S. subsidiaries
in the extractive sector in Latin America as compared with that obtained in the manufacturing sector
is deplorably low. According to Fred Rippy, U.S.
direct investments in Latin America during the first
half of the twentieth century had earned high rates
of return. To him, dividends paid by some small
mining companies in Mexico were fantastic--one paid
an annual average dividend of 124.5 percent from
1908 to 1928 and another paid an annual average dividend of 945.8 percent from 1903 to 1927--meaning
that the large mining and petroleum companies made
"excessive" profits on their investments. Again, in
Venezuela, the Creole Petroleum Company (a subsidiary
of Standard Oil Company of New Jersey) paid an annual
average dividend of 31.8 percent on its common stock
from 1938 to 1951 while the International Petroleum
Company (a subsidiary of Standard Oil) in Peru and
Colombia paid an annual average dividend of over 40
percent from 1921 to 1950.[84]

Furthermore, Vaitsos quotes U.S. Senate sources
indicating that "less than 15 percent of the total
financing needs of U.S.-based manufacturing subsidiaries abroad originated from U.S. sources."[85] According to him, this

    15 percent is an overestimate of the ac-
    tual financial contribution in view of

the common practices of capitalising
intangibles and second hand machinery,
the reevaluation of assets affecting
equity accounts, etc.[86]

Consequently, the term <u>foreign investment</u>, for him,
is inaccurate; indeed, it is a misnomer. A more
correct term, he maintained, "would be 'foreign controlled firms' financed basically from local savings."[87] A study by Gert Rosenthal and carried out
under the auspices of the Adlai Stevenson Institute
of International Affairs, Chicago and the Permanent
Secretariat of the Central American Common Market
shows:

1. That foreign firms in Guatemala's
   manufacturing sector absorbed year-
   ly up to 38 percent of total annual
   local bank loans to the manufacturing sector in the period 1965-1969;
2. That the annual figure in the public utilities sector ranged from 75
   percent to 100 percent;
3. That the figure for all sectors
   ranged from 11 percent to 15 percent.[88]

The study also reveals the extent of foreign exchange
drain associated with MNC subsidiaries' operating in
the Central American Common Market area, namely,
that while net capital inflows increased by 344 percent between 1960 and 1971, total reported remittances went up by 982 percent during the same period.
And, on the use of local savings, the study has this
much to say: "In short, the foreign firm is financed
wholly or in part through internal [local] savings,
and not with additional external financing."
    Supporting this general conclusion are Paul
Streeten and Sanjaya Lall, who found in Colombia
that short-term loans "in many cases . . . provide
the bulk of local financing for foreign investors."
In a United Nations study of 159 firms (12 locally
owned, 45 foreign-owned, 64 majority foreign-owned,
and 38 with less than 50 percent foreign equity) in
six countries (Colombia, India, Iran, Jamaica, Kenya,

and Malaysia), Streeten and Lall found that for over
40 percent of the sampled firms, "It would be cheaper
for the host economy to substitute its own capital
for the existing foreign capital."[89] In summary,
they note: "We may be justified in concluding that
they [global operations] do not offer any marked
financial benefits to the host economies."[90]

　　More damaging to the claims that MNCs transfer
scarce finance from the so-called capital-rich regions of the North to the so-called capital-poor regions of the South is the recent study by Isaiah
Frank, which reveals the following:

1. That MNCs, with very few exceptions, raise their
   finance capital from local sources either by permitting equity participation (by some local firms/
   foreign investors) or through public subscription;
2. That extractive firms appear to rely least on
   local financing because most developing nations
   do not have capital markets capable of providing
   the huge capital outlay required for extractive
   operations while the service-sector firms, with
   the possible exception of the insurance industry,
   raise both equity and loan capital from local
   sources; and,
3. That while U.S. and German manufacturing subsidiaries are less inclined to seek local equity financing, British, Japanese, French, and Australian
   manufacturing firms generally prefer local equity
   participation or prefer to borrow as much local
   capital as possible.[91]

It is basic from the present analysis about the
sources of finance capital for MNC subsidiaries that
"reinvested earnings," sometimes called "retained
earnings," are an important source of finance for
the MNC. The point to emphasize here is that these
"retained earnings" are largely generated from local
sources. Undoubtedly, a potential addition to local
savings, "reinvested earnings" are under the control
of the MNC and can be repatriated. In essence, the
use of local loan capital by foreign firms, indeed,
the draining of local financial markets by MNCs for
their own ends, notwithstanding the reasons advanced
for using local sources of finance,[92] has meant that

local firms cannot adequately and effectively finance their own operations.

Where MNCs do not drain local loan capital to finance their operations, they buy, in many cases, already established local firms rather than establish new productive facilities. A study by the Harvard Business School of the 187 largest U.S.-based MNCs accounting for some 70 percent of total U.S. DFI in Latin America shows that between 1958 and 1967, U.S. subsidiaries used a substantial part of their investment in acquiring existing local firms. To be sure, about 50 percent of all U.S. manufacturing subsidiaries established during this period were "takeovers" of existing industry. This finding tallies with the position held by Vernon (also of the Harvard Business School) who contends that almost a third of MNC subsidiaries in the Third World have been established through the acquisition or purchase of existing local firms. Undoubtedly, it is sound business judgment to buy an already operating plant rather than take the risk of building a new one. However, changing ownership does not necessarily increase productive facilities needed for development, because the previous owners may decide to consume or export the proceeds of the sale rather than invest them in other sectors of the economy. It is small wonder, then, that developing countries "tend to frown on such acquisitions, regarding them as alienating the domestic economy without providing offsetting benefits and in some cases, as being intended to reduce competition and increase the dominant position of the foreign affiliate."[93]

These problems can be resolved by the host government taking certain measures. First, it can forbid an MNC subsidiary from using local loan capital to finance its operations. While this measure itself is not foolproof, it can put a ceiling on what percentage of its finance capital can be drawn from local financial institutions, including the so-called private multinational banks. In Japan and Canada, the governments have taken measures to forbid local borrowing by wholly owned MNC subsidiaries, and in the Andean Common Market countries, local borrowing is permitted provided the enterprise has majority local equity participation. Second, the

government can impose restrictions on foreign firm
attempts to acquire existing local firms. Such measures have been taken by many DMEs such as Japan,
Canada, Australia, Sweden, and Norway. In fact,
takeovers are forbidden by law in these countries.

Multinational Corporations: Financial
Transfers and the Balance of Payments

       We have now come to an evaluation of the im-
pact of MNCs on the balance of payments of Third
World countries, which is no less complex a task
than an evaluation of the impact of other economic
variables. Indeed, if the evaluation concentrates
only on the capital flow of direct investment, the
net effect on the host state is undoubtedly positive.
We have seen earlier in this chapter that the stock
of DFI by the end of 1977 in the Third World stood
at over $85 billion. If the earnings generated by
past investments that accrue to the foreign subsidiaries are deducted from that flow, the net flow is
generally negative for Third World host countries.
Between 1965 and 1970, as shown in Table 3.14, the
net DFI inflow into 43 developing countries was 30
percent of the investment income outflow, and if the
oil-producing countries in the sample are excluded,
inflow was 68 percent of outflow. In fact, available data show that between 1964 and 1968, the United
States and the United Kingdom (representing 80 percent of total DFI) received approximately $5.8 bil-
lion from developing countries (in investment income)
and paid $3.2 billion (in capital flow). Undoubted-
ly, the excess of this outflow over inflow is a familiar source of tension between MNCs and host Third
World countries, and such tension is particularly
likely to occur in cases where an MNC has operated
in the host country over an extended period of time
and where the outflow of investment income increasingly exceeds the inflow of new capital.
       Put differently, while the initial act of an
MNC's DFI (assuming that the capital comes from foreign rather than local sources) implies a capital
inflow, and consequently, a credit item in the
balance-of-payments accounts, a stream of profits,

TABLE 3.14

Selected Third World Countries: Inflow of Direct Foreign Investment and
Outflow of Income on Accumulated Past Direct Foreign Investment 1965-70[a]

Type of Transaction	$ million					
	1965	1966	1967	1968	1969	1970
Inflow	1,342.4	1,215.4	1,074.0	1,372.0	1,513.5	1,612.7
Outflow	3,186.6	4,063.9	4,246.2	4,982.6	5,155.8	5,341.8
Balance	-1,843.7	-2,848.5	-3,172.2	-3,610.6	-3,642.2	-3,729.1
Non-Oil-Producing Countries						
Inflow	906.8	841.4	689.0	975.0	1,127.6	1,290.7
Outflow	940.9	1,247.9	1,380.2	1,588.6	1,720.8	1,678.8
Balance	-34.1	-406.5	-691.2	-613.6	-593.2	-388.1
Oil-Producing Countries						
Inflow	435.6	374.0	385.0	397.0	386.0	322.0
Outflow	2,245.2	2,816.0	2,886.0	3,394.0	3,435.0	3,663.0
Balance	-1,809.6	-2,442.0	-2,481.0	-2,997.0	-3,049.0	-3,341.0

[a]All statistics—inflows and outflows—are expressed in gross figures.

Source: United Nations, Multinational Corporations in World Development, Publication no.
E.73.II.A.11, p. 193 (Table 42).

interest/dividend/royalty payments that are generated by the investment and repatriated abroad through several devices, some of them illegal, cannot but have adverse effects on the balance of payments of the host state.

We can now examine the financial policies and objectives pursued by MNCs; this exercise is all the more necessary if we are to do a serious evaluation of the impact of MNCs on the balance of payments of Third World countries. It will be recalled that a central characteristic of an MNC is that it seeks to maximize the profits of the parent company rather than of any of its subsidiaries. Certainly, this objective, namely, maximization of global profits, is bound to conflict with the objectives of the host government. The host government will, among other objectives, want the MNC: (1) to create as many jobs as possible to absorb an increasingly large number of unemployed urban school graduates; (2) to provide the maximum tax revenues; (3) to save foreign exchange through import-substitution industrialization or to generate foreign exchange earnings through additional exports; and (4) to reinvest its high profits in the host economy rather than repatriate them, and thus help improve the balance-of-payments position. In asking the MNC to reinvest its profits, it is assumed that the host government is not unaware of what has come to be known as the "Streeten Dilemma," namely, that reinvestment of such profits may eventually lead to the domination and control of the economy by aliens. Additionally, the host government may attempt to control the transfer of funds between the local MNC subsidiary and any other affiliate of the parent through the use of foreign exchange regulations, tax regulations, and direct controls. These objectives are perfectly legitimate, and, prima facie, they are a lawful exercise of powers of government.

On the other hand, the MNC will want to maximize its transfer of funds from the host state to minimize global tax payments, foreign exchange risks, or any other risks (such as the possibility of expropriation, nationalization, "intervention," war/revolution, or abrogation of contractual arrangements) that it may face. Just as host state measures aimed at ensuring that MNCs' operations yield the maximum tax revenues for the government are legitimate, the minimization of the overall amount of tax that the multinational pays on its global operations is equally legitimate, and the MNC will devise a variety of methods to achieve this objective, namely, dividend, interest, and royalty payments; capital transfers; and payments for goods, services, and knowledge. However, the most powerful weapon that the MNC has in circumventing host state measures aimed at regulating or controlling all forms of illegal transfer of funds is the use (or abuse) of transfer pricing.

What, then, are transfer prices? When MNCs buy from and sell to their own subsidiaries, they establish prices that have nothing to do with market prices. Colman and Nixson have noted:

> Transfer prices (sometimes referred to as accounting prices) are the prices charged on transactions that take place within the TNC and they can deviate to a considerable extent from market prices (so-called arms-length prices).[94]

For example, if an automobile manufacturing corporation with operations in several countries wishes to export from one of its wholly owned subsidiaries in one country to a wholly owned distributing company in another country, for tax reasons all it does is to direct the exporting subsidiary to undervalue its exports. The results of the intrafirm transaction are twofold: The MNC maximizes its global profits while the host state loses not only tax revenues but also the foreign exchange that it would have received had there been an arm's-length transaction between independent buyers and sellers. Again, if an MNC wishes to transfer funds from a particular country, albeit illegally, it can raise the prices charged for imports to the subsidiary and lower the prices paid for exports from the subsidiary.

Now to some concrete examples. Litton Industries (a U.S.-based MNC) was indicted in the 1970s for undervaluing imports from its Mexican subsidiary to avoid some $216,000 in customs duties while an-

other U.S. corporation with similar satellite operations in Mexico made a $3 million out-of-court settle-
ment for falsified invoices. To be sure, a memorandum of the U.S. Senate Investigations Sub-Committee
not only revealed how U.S. grain corporations manipu-
lated transfer prices to obtain big subsidies costing
U.S. taxpayers some $333 million, but also the memo-
randum noted how transfer-pricing manipulation
worked:

> We have information that one company
> [Cargill] sold wheat to its wholly-
> owned South American affiliate [Tradex-
> Panama]. The company collected the
> subsidy when it showed proof of ship-
> ment to its affiliate.
>   The affiliate then sold the
> wheat to another affiliate in Geneva
> which thereupon made a final sale for
> $2.20 (a bushel) or 10 cents above the
> American price. . . . As far as we
> can tell, the wheat never left the
> ship on which it was originally loaded,
> and all transfers were mere paper
> transfers. This practice was repeated
> numerous times.[95]

In all these cases, it is the developing host state
that gets cheated while the MNC maximizes its global
profits.
    But what reasons can we adduce for transfer
pricing other than profit maximization and tax minimization? According to Sanjaya Hall, they include:

1. the minimization of liabilities in a weak currency;
2. the existence of quantitative restrictions on
   profit remittances;
3. the existence of multiple exchange rate systems;
4. the possibility of pressures against high profits
   earned by MNCs and demands by local employees for
   higher wages;
5. the deprivation of local shareholders and their
   desire to have their share of profits in foreign
   currency; and

6. the existence of a generous tax system in the
   home state allowing deferral of tax on foreign
   earnings and a credit for foreign taxes; for example, the U.S. Internal Revenue Code.[96]

However, it has been claimed that the more blatant
forms of transfer-price manipulation are no longer
possible. This view is not shared by all for two
reasons. First, most Third World governments simply
do not have the personnel with sufficient expertise
and experience to investigate all possible transfer-
price abuses and engage in arm's-length negotiations
with MNC subsidiaries. Second, basic policies and
decisions on transfer pricing of the MNC are made at
the headquarters with little or no discretion allowed the branch office (affiliate). As Barnet and
Muller observed, quoting the treasurer of an MNC:

> Even where we have sophisticated local
> management, both long-term and short-
> term financing is determined in San
> Francisco and not just left to the dis-
> cretion of the local management. . . .
> I don't say that our companies don't
> have any leeway. . . . But someone
> along the line has to say "this is
> what we do," and that's San Francisco.[97]

Some DMEs (such as Australia, Canada, and the United
Kingdom) are also at the mercy of MNC transfer-price
manipulations; they are only better equipped than
most Third World countries in dealing with this
problem.[98]

Consequently, it has been said that an indis-
pensable aid to most Third World governments, namely,
in dealing with this problem, "is the training of
personnel who can understand the internal functions
of transnational enterprises, administer the policies
and be able to negotiate with foreign factor suppliers."[99] Hopefully, one of the major functions of
the United Nations Centre on Transnational Corporations created in late 1975 is to establish a comprehensive information system covering "priority areas
where information gaps are most pressing," such as
transfer pricing and taxation, restrictive business

practices, market concentrations, sources of finance, alternative forms of management control, and political activities of MNCs. To be sure, the founders of the center had hoped that it would not only provide advisory services to Third World governments but also provide technical assistance and train personnel from the Third World who would be able to negotiate effectively and efficiently with MNC subsidiaries.

However, even if the center is able to provide the services enumerated above--indeed, if developing countries have the personnel with sufficient expertise and experience to investigate all possible transfer price abuses--most Third World governments would still find it difficult if not impossible to deal with certain types of transfer-price abuse. Undoubtedly, it is difficult to discover the market or arm's-length price of a particular product with which to compare the transfer price; in fact, a comparable product may not exist when MNCs are producing non-standardized products, and, as James Hanson argued, rightly too:

> Finding adequate substitutes for arms-length prices is difficult in a dynamic world of changing cost functions, altered trade patterns and relocations of production for individual tradeable goods, coupled with continually changing product mixes for individual units of multinational corporations.[100]

There is another technique, a modern version of the eighteenth-century triangular trade, by which the parent company underprices exports or overprices imports to a tax-haven (such as the Bahamas) and then reexports the goods at their market value or even at an inflated price to another subsidiary in the country where they are to be sold. This is possible since, as indicated in Chapter 1, between 24 and 35 percent of transactions (imports and exports) by U.S- or U.K.-based MNCs were conducted on an intrafirm basis,[101] indeed, under circumstances in which price can be and is controlled by the headquarters because the MNC is trading with itself. To date, U.S. sub-

sidiaries in Latin America have been consistent in
underpricing their exports, on the average charging
40 percent less than prices charged by local enterprises since 75 percent of these exports were intrafirm in nature. In fact, not only do MNCs, through
intrafirm deliveries, underprice their exports, they
also overprice their imports.

A detailed study by Vaitsos of import overpricing, as shown in Table 3.15, reveals the following average overpricing: (1) 155 percent in the
pharmaceutical industry; (2) 40 percent in the rubber
industry; (3) 25.5 percent in the chemical industry;
and (4) 16-60 percent in the electronic industry.
He arrived at this conclusion by comparing prices
charged by a large number of MNC subsidiaries in
these industries with established world prices. More
revealing in the Vaitsos' study is the import price
of certain popular drugs produced by U.S. subsidiaries with the price charged in their home state.
According to Vaitsos, the prices of such tranquiliz-
ers as Valium and Librium in Colombia were, respectively, 82 and 65 percent higher than the established
world markets while the price charged for tetracyline
(an antibiotic) was almost ten times the U.S. price.[102]
A Bogotá newspaper, El Espectador, quoting an official investigation, stated in February 1970 that
chlordiazepoxide (Librium), a drug used in the treatment of mental illness, was overpriced by 6,500 percent.[103] Additionally, and for the period 1966-70,
the average import overpricing by U.S. pharmaceutical
subsidiaries in Colombia was 87 percent. As for the
electronics industry, the price charged for transis-
tors was 11 times the U.S. price. And, another study
by Vaitsos on the Ecuadorian electronics industry
shows that of 29 imported products that were price-
marked in relation to Colombian prices, seven were
overpriced by up to 75 percent, while six were overpriced by about 200 percent, and 16 were imported at
comparable prices. Needless to say, these sharp
business practices were confirmed by studies on
transfer pricing in several Third World countries
such as Chile, Peru, Argentina, Brazil, Mexico, Iran,
Pakistan, Nigeria, and the Philippines. For example,
overpricing of imports in Chile ranges from 30 percent to over 700 percent; in Peru, it ranges from 50

TABLE 3.15

Overpricing of Imported Intermediate Parts by Foreign
Ownership Structure: Colombia 1968
(percent)

Ownership Structure	Pharmaceutical Industry			Rubber Industry			Chemical Industry			Electronics Industry		
	b	c	d[a]	b	c	d	b	c	d	b	c	d
Foreign Owned	50	25	155	33	60	40	30	12	25.5	40	90	16-60
Joint Ventures	N.A.	N.A.	N.A.	N.A.	N.A.	N.A.	45	37	20.2	50	90	6-50

N.A. Not available.

[a]Individual firm data are as follows (in percent): #1: 253.6; #2: 133.7; #3: 132.8; #4: 306.2; #5: 483; #6: 39.5; #7: 179.4; #8: 79.1; #9: 58.3; #10: 73.8; #11: 475.4; #12: 374.7; #13: 177.5; #14: 164.8; #15: 60.4; #16: 476.9; #17: 34.4.

[b]Approximate percentage of sales of sample firms relative to total sales of firms with a similar ownership structure.

[c]Total volume of imports sampled and evaluated as a percentage of the firm's total imports.

[d]weighted average of overpricing of evaluated imports.

Source: Constantine V. Vaitsos, "Interaffiliate Charges by Transnational Corporations and Inter-Country Income Distribution," Ph.D. dissertation, Harvard University, 1972, p. 48.

percent to 300 percent; and in Ecuador, from 75 percent to 200 percent.[104] Incidentally, these three countries (Chile, Peru, and Ecuador) are members of the Andean Common Market, others being Colombia and Bolivia.

What these somewhat normal intrafirm transactions have meant for Third World countries with per-capita income as low as $300 per year were losses for the host governments not only in terms of foreign exchange earnings but also in terms of tax revenues. On the other hand, they have meant for MNCs maximization of global profits. For example, over-pricing in the Colombian pharmaceutical industry in 1968 alone cost the Colombian government $30 million ($20 million in foreign exchange and $10 million in tax revenues). To be sure, an examination of the transfer-price mechanism undertaken by the Colombian Planning Office for 1968 and the Import Control Board for 1967-70 for a wide range of pharmaceutical products saved the country $3.3 million annually in the pharmaceutical sector out of a total import bill of $15 million.[105]

More important, triangular trade is just one more example of the basic conflict in outlook, goals, and interest between the MNC and poor Third World countries trying to solve fundamental problems of inequality, poverty, and unemployment. But those who make a case for DFI, and these include Harry Johnson and Jack Behrman, have argued, and quite frankly, that the purpose of the MNC "is not to transform the economy by exploiting its potentialities--especially its human potentialities--for development, but to exploit the existing situation to its own profit by utilization of the knowledge it already possesses, at minimum cost at adaptation and adjustment to itself."[106] Johnson has put the issue more forcefully:

> Misunderstanding, confusion and acri-
> mony . . . are likely to be enhanced
> by the popular failure to appreciate
> two facts about the multinational en-
> terprise in the context of a develop-
> ing country. The first is that the
> profits of the enterprise are . . . a

return on its past investments in the
generation of productive knowledge;
they should not be regarded simply as
a return on the capital invested in
the particular local production facility. The second is that the enterprise is a competitive <u>profit-seeking
institution</u>, not a government with the
powers of taxation, and therefore cannot be expected to assume the responsibility for promoting the development
in the same way as a development plan
undertakes that responsibility.[107]

In essence the contribution of the MNC to development in the Third World is incidental to the purpose
of making profits.

Undoubtedly, the various strategies for maximizing an MNC's global profits give us a true picture of the profits actually earned by these enterprises in poor Third World countries. In order to
assess correctly the annual return on, for example,
U.S. investment in a Third World country, say, Brazil,
it is absolutely necessary to include in the calcula-
tion: (1) overpricing of imports and underpricing
of exports; (2) reported profits and royalties (i.e.,
to the home and host states); and (3) fees repatriated by the local subsidiaries to the parent companies.

This exercise readily calls to mind what has
been referred to as the suction-pump and high-profit
theses, namely, with respect of the former thesis,
that the MNC pumps out from the host economy in the
form of dividends and profits more than it puts in
by way of fresh capital inflows, and with respect of
the latter thesis, that the profits made by MNC subsidiaries tend to be higher than those made by comparable national or locally owned enterprises. Those
who defend the high profits made by MNCs' subsidiaries contend that the profits made by an MNC subsidiary are "to a substantial degree a return on its
past investments in the generation of productive
knowledge," and "should not be regarded simply as a
return on the capital invested" (see Note 107).
MacBean and Balasubramanyam have noted: "Whether or
not the profits earned by foreign firms are high

needs to be adjudged in terms of their contribution
to their economies of the countries in which they
operate."[108]   They added:

> A major contribution of FPI [foreign
> private investment] is in terms of the
> technology and skills that it imparts
> to the host countries. It would be
> hard to counter the argument that the
> so-called "profits" . . . are economi-
> cally justified as representing a re-
> turn on the scarce technology and
> skills these firms possess and as be-
> ing a fair reward for risk taking. The
> high profits they earn may thus repre-
> sent a return on the past investment
> they have made in the production,
> which does not appear on the firms'
> books as an addition to material capi-
> tal.[109]

According to a study by Vaitsos of 15 foreign-
owned pharmaceutical companies in Colombia in 1968,
while the annual rate of return on investment ranged
from 38.1 percent to 962.1 percent,[110] with an average effective return of 136.3 percent, these companies' average reported/declared profits to the
Colombian government for tax purposes was 6.7 percent. And, in the rubber industry, while the average
annual rate of return stood at 43 percent, the average reported profit to the local tax authorities was
16 percent. In Peru, studies carried out by Swedish
economists of 64 U.S. mining subsidiaries between
1967 and 1969 found out that while the "reported
profits" of these companies to the Peruvian authorities, presumably for tax purposes, stood at $60 mil-
lion, the "declared profits" to the U.S. authorities
stood at $102 million.[111]   To be sure, a Peruvian
Parliamentary Investigation of sharp accounting practices of Southern Peru Copper Corporation found out
that between 1960 and 1965, while Southern Peru's
reported profits to the U.S. Securities and Exchange
Commission stood at some $135 million, the reported
profits to the Peruvian government for tax purposes
stood at $69 million.[112]   Obviously, all these "re-

ported" or "declared" profits did not take account
of underpricing of exports by MNC subsidiaries.

While other studies on U.S. investments in
Latin America in the manufacturing sector have put
the minimum annual rate of return at nothing less
than 40 percent, a study commissioned by the United
Nations (see Table 3.16) puts the average annual returns on U.S. DFI in all sectors for developing countries as a whole and Africa in particular at 17.5
and 22.3 percent, respectively. In fact, the average annual rate of return on book value of capital
investment by U.S. wholly owned subsidiaries in the
Third World at the end of 1968 was 11 percent (excluding petroleum) while the figure for the DMEs
(which by the way have shown considerable resentment
over the domination of U.S. subsidiaries in the most
technologically advanced sectors of the economy)
stood at 9.6 percent (excluding petroleum). Comparable figures for U.K. DFIs are put at 9.8 percent
(for developing countries) and 9.3 percent for DMEs.
It should be noted that the figures of 11 percent
(for U.S. subsidiaries) and 9.8 percent (for U.K.
subsidiaries) refer only to profits. If we include
the royalties, rents, and service charges earned by
U.K. and U.S. subsidiaries, then the annual rate of
return could range between 14 and 20 percent. This
figure, albeit conservative, is substantially higher
than that earned by domestic capital in these countries. Nonetheless, this estimate does not take account of underpricing of exports, and, according to
Vaitsos, reported or declared profits by MNC subsidiaries accounted for 3.4 percent of effective returns;
royalties accounted for 14 percent while overpricing
accounted for 82.6 percent of effective returns.[113]

In concluding this section, we must examine
other ways in which the operations of MNCs have a
direct impact on the balance of payments of host
Third World states. Specifically, we are referring
to a number of payments for patents, licenses, brand
names and trade marks, management, and service fees
which, according to estimates made in 1971 by the
United Nations Conference on Trade and Development,
absorbs some 7.3 percent of the combined export earnings and amounted to 0.68 percent of the combined
gross domestic product of Argentina, Brazil, Colombia,

TABLE 3.16

Average Returns[a] on Book Value of United States and United Kingdom Direct Foreign Investments by Area 1965-68 (percent)

Area of Investment	United States Average		United Kingdom Average
	All Sectors	Excluding Petroleum	Excluding Petroleum
Developed Market Economies	7.9	9.6	9.3
United States	--	--	8.6
Canada	8.0	8.6	11.3
Europe[b]	7.1	10.0	7.9
Japan	14.2	20.2	--
Southern Hemisphere	9.7	12.0	9.5
Developing Countries	17.5	11.0	9.8
Western Hemisphere	12.1	11.1	8.7
Asia	34.7	11.7)	
Africa	22.3	7.7)	10.4
European developing countries	--	--)	--
Unallocated	8.5	11.6	--
Total	10.7	10.0	9.5

a Adjusted earnings (branch earnings + dividends + interest + reinvested earnings) over book value at year end.

b U.S. data include all European countries other than Eastern Europe. United Kingdom data include European developed countries as defined by OECD.

Source: United Nations, Multinational Corporations in World Development, Publication no. E.73.II.A.11, p. 187 (Table 37).

116

Mexico, Nigeria, and Sri Lanka.[114] For example, payments for patents, royalties, licenses, know-how, trademarks, management, and technical services made by Argentina (1969), Brazil (1966-68), Colombia (1966), Mexico (1968), Nigeria (1965), and Sri Lanka (1970) have been put at $127.7 million, $59.6 million, $26.7 million, $200 million, $33.8 million, and $9.3 million, respectively.[115] With specific reference to Brazil, a very recent study found out that between 1966 and 1976, Volkswagenberg repatriated $100 million in profits from its Brazilian affiliates and another $100 million in technical fees. In 1975 alone, technical and management fees paid by MNC affiliates in Brazil to their parents amounted to $223 million compared with $237 million in profit remittances.[116]

In fact, the total cost for payments (in respect of patents, royalties, licenses, know-how, trademarks, management, and technical services) to 13 developing countries, representing 65 percent of the total population and 56 percent of the total gross domestic product of developing countries, is estimated at approximately $1.5 billion, which amounts to more than half of the total flow of DFI to developing countries. These estimates, according to a United Nations study, are increasing at an annual rate of 20 percent and are absorbing an increasing proportion of the export earnings of developing countries. The study made one interesting observation:

> Estimates of royalties . . . may distort the true payments for know-how in various ways. The distortion may take the form of overpricing of intermediate products and capital goods, which are tied to the imports of technology, or the underpricing of exports to the suppliers of the technical know-how. Since royalties constitute only one of the channels of effective income remission, especially in the case of wholly-owned subsidiaries, changes in royalties do not necessarily imply changes in technology flows. They may

        simply reflect a readjustment in the
distribution of returns among the different channels of income remission as
a result of corporate strategy and
government policies.[117]

In any event, talking about global royalty payments
alone, estimates, which can be distorted by the possibilities of transfer pricing, have been put at anywhere between $3 billion and $5 billion annually.
Other payments made by MNC subsidiaries to their
headquarters include contributions to headquarters'
overhead expenditure, research and development, as
well as preinvestment expenses.
      From our examination of the impact of MNC oper-
ations on the balance of payments of a host country,
it is obvious that the devices employed by an MNC to
transfer funds from a host Third World country demonstrate, in our view, its flexibility of operation
and make meaningless the officially declared or reported profits on MNC operations in developing countries. To be sure, Dario Abad, a Colombian econo-
mist, pointing out the meaninglessness of officially
declared profits, has noted that the average reported
rate of return for foreign-owned manufacturing enterprises in Colombia between 1960 and 1968 was 6.4 percent. He found it "difficult to accept" that these
firms would continue to enter Colombia at this rate
of declared profitability while Colombian-owned firms
were showing higher rates of return and the interest
rate in financial markets ranged between 16 and 20
percent.[118] Also pointing out the meaninglessness
of officially declared profits on MNC operations in
the Third World, a study on Kenya has this much to
say:

        Foreign companies have a great deal of
        room to manoeuvre in transferring un-
        taxed surpluses and surpluses taxed at
        half the rate of profits tax out of
        Kenya. We consider that the amount of
        surpluses transferred in the form of
        dividends after taxation might be less
        than half the total surplus trans-
        ferred by foreign enterprises in the

manufacturing sector. The particular
manner in which these additional
transfers are carried out makes non-
sense of the regulation that the amount
remitted after tax must be proportion-
ate to the foreign share in equity
capital.[119]

What Abad and the International Labour Office study
seem to be saying is that the MNC pumps out of the
host economy in the form of profits and dividends
more than it puts in by way of fresh capital inflows.
This conclusion is shared by Rosenthal, who found
out that while net capital inflows in the Central
American Common Market countries between 1960 and
1971 increased by 344 percent, capital outflows rose
by 982 percent.[120]

True, the high profits made by MNC subsidiaries
in poor Third World countries have been defended as
justifiable compensation for risk taking as well as
representing a return on past investments in the
generation of productive knowledge. We believe, however, that these high profits are made at the expense of the people of those countries. Certainly,
many Third World governments are not unconcerned
about the impacts of MNCs' operations on their balance of payments. They have taken measures which,
they hope, will help in maximizing local retention
of profits. First, they have encouraged MNCs' subsidiaries to reinvest a larger proportion of their
profits in host economies. Second, they have out-
lawed 100 percent foreign equity participation in
certain sectors of the economy, otherwise known as
the "commanding heights" of the economy, namely,
banking, insurance, petroleum production and distribution, and public utilities (power, communication,
water, radio, and television). Third, foreign investors are directed, by law, to sell between 50 and
60 percent of their equity shares to local investors
or through public subscription. It must be emphasized here that joint ventures between foreign firms
and local investors or between MNC subsidiaries and
host states have not led to the maximization of local
retention of profits if majority equity participation by indigenes in joint ventures is not reflected

at the management and/or board levels or when host
governments, in acquiring majority equity interests
in MNC subsidiaries, conclude management or service
contracts with their junior partners.[121]

A state's directive that MNC subsidiaries
should endeavor to reinvest a greater proportion of
their profits locally would create more problems
than it would solve in alleviating the burden imposed on the balance of payments. This is because
reinvestment of high profits in the host economy may
lead to eventual domination and control by alien investors, whereas high profits earned by MNC subsidiaries, by extension, amount to monopolistic exploitation and a regressive transfer of wealth from capital-
poor (developing) to capital-rich (developed) countries. MacBean and Balasubramanyam have noted:

> If fresh foreign capital inflows do
> not exceed the rate of return on past
> capital the country will be faced with
> a balance-of-payments problem; if it
> does grow at a faster rate and since
> the rate of return on existing capital
> is greater than that on domestic capi-
> tal an increasing proportion of the
> country's capital will come to be owned
> by foreigners.[122]

To be sure, Streeten has put the dilemma faced by
Third World countries more forcefully:

> Either they permit or even encourage
> this growth of foreign capital, in
> which case they are faced with growing
> foreign ownership of their capital
> stock. Or else they limit this pro-
> cess of alienation, in which case a
> part of their export earnings will be
> mortgaged to remitting profits and re-
> patriating capital. It is small won-
> der that this ineluctable dilemma has
> led to ambivalence and hostility to-
> wards foreign investments.[123]

To sum up, it is impossible to quantify with any degree of accuracy or reliability the direct and in-

direct effects of MNCs' operations on the balance of
payments of host Third World countries. What is
clear, however, is that while the financial contribution turns out to be a financial drain--indeed,
while potential capital inflows were minimized--the
balance of payments outflows (i.e., capital outflows)
were accentuated not only through import overpricing
and export underpricing but also through high royalty payments and payments for patents, licenses,
brand names and trademarks, and management and service fees.

Multinational Corporations and Technology Contributions

Another important contribution to development
that MNCs often claim is the transfer of technology
to developing countries. According to conventional
development wisdom, MNCs can help close the ever-
increasing gap between the rich (industrialized)
North and the poor (largely agrarian) South by sharing their advanced technology with developing countries so as to help them increase their productivity,
on which rapid economic growth depends. To date,
technology is the key that unlocks the door to economic power and, by extension, political power.
Consequently, this section attempts to answer
the following questions:

1. What are the employment effects of MNCs' operations in developing countries? Specifically, do
   MNCs create jobs in Third World host states? Do
   they export jobs to Third World host states as
   alleged by the AFL-CIO and the sponsors of the
   Burke-Hartke Bill in the U.S. Congress? Do MNCs
   destroy jobs in Third World host states as contended by critical writers? Again, what is the
   relationship between MNCs' technology and income
   distribution in Third World host states?
2. Do the marketing practices of MNCs shape or distort local tastes and, thus, create a form of
   cultural dependency?
3. Does the MNC make a fundamentally important technological contribution to the development of

Third World countries? And, what are the costs
to Third World host states of the technology so
transferred to MNC subsidiaries by the parent
companies?

4. Do the operations of MNCs in Third World host
   states lead to dependent or independent development?

These questions will be answered in the order
in which they are asked, and our conclusion in this
chapter follows.

EMPLOYMENT EFFECTS OF MNCs OPERATIONS

Capital Intensity of MNCs Operations

The MNC today is perhaps the most controversial
phenomenon of the world economy. To its advocates,
the MNC is seen, indeed, regarded as the modern St.
George·fighting the dragon of economic underdevelopment, bestowing on Third World host states the benefits of technical and managerial skills and, more
important, creating more employment opportunities.
To its critics, and they are many, the MNC is seen,
and, indeed, regarded as the ogre of the world economy. But the more-often expressed criticism relates
to the capital intensity of MNCs' operations as well
as the wage policies pursued by MNCs. For example,
it has been argued by critical, not necessarily
Marxist scholars: (1) that MNCs transplant in Third
World states techniques that are perfected abroad
and are designed for capital-rich and labor-poor
economies and, consequently, inappropriate and ill-
suited for capital-poor and labor-rich Third World
countries; (2) that because most MNCs' operations
are capital-intensive, MNCs do not create or generate
much more employment opportunities than most domestic
enterprises; and (3) that MNCs generally tend to pay
higher wages than domestic enterprises, and therefore
MNCs' wage policies contribute to the unequal income
distribution in many Third World host states, indeed,
that MNCs' wage policies exacerbate the unequal income distribution in many Third World host states
and unwittingly·may well have contributed to the
polarization of social forces in many Third World
host states.

These claims have been challenged by neoconventional scholars who argue:

1. that MNCs transfer technology but nevertheless
   agree (with critical scholars) that the technology
   so transferred may <u>not</u> be appropriate to the needs
   of many Third World host states or that the appropriateness of the technology utilized varies
   from industry to industry;
2. that while most MNCs' operations generally tend
   to be more capital-intensive than many domestic
   enterprises, the generalizations of critical
   scholars, in their views, are in some ways <u>inaccu-
   rate</u> if only because some domestic enterprises are
   able to produce goods comparable to those of their
   multinational enterprises, and therefore, their
   operations tend to generate comparable employment;
   and,
3. that MNCs generally tend to pay higher wages than
   domestic enterprises but nevertheless contend
   that the income-distribution effects are almost
   impossible to determine.[124]

These issues obviously bear closer examination princi-
pally, and if only because, for an example, the employment effects of MNCs' operations depend, among
other factors, on the nature of the project, the
type of investment, the demands of the labor movement for uniformity of wage and fringe benefits for
similar jobs, as well as the harmonization of working conditions and public policy on labor relations.
    Undoubtedly, most developing countries of the
Third World are characterized by a high incidence of
unemployment. It is not surprising, therefore, that
the creation of employment opportunities constitutes
a cornerstone of government economic development
policies.[125] According to the authors of Nigeria's
Second National Development Plan 1970-74:

> Full employment of resources, espe-
> cially of the labour force, is the
> necessary policy objective for an
> economy dedicated to rapid growth and
> social harmony. The existence of ex-
> cess capacity means resource waste and

> lost economic opportunities which an
> economy like Nigerian can ill-afford.
> This is true not only of investment
> capacity, but also, even more strong-
> ly, of the nation's human resources.
> Commitment to a full employment policy
> implies that Government accepts re-
> sponsibility to create, on a continu-
> ing expanding basis, the appropriate
> socioeconomic environment for maximum
> utilisation of productive factors.[126]

It is small wonder, then, that the 1970-74 Second
National Development Plan envisaged the creation of
3.3 million jobs, largely in the small-scale nonagri-
culture industries.

Since Third World countries are generally said
to be capital poor and labor rich,[127] what, then,
are the employment effects of MNCs' operations in
Third World host states, particularly those that
have created a favorable climate for DFI?[128] Unfortunately, the results of studies of employment effects of MNCs' operations in many Third World countries are not as clear-cut and definitive as critical scholars would want us to believe. In essence,
studies of employment effects of MNCs' operations in
many Third World countries have shown mixed results.

As to whether DFI is more capital intensive
than domestic investment, thus creating fewer jobs,
Constantive Vaitsos has argued that "compared with
the rest of the manufacturing sector, foreign direct
investments in developing countries provide less direct labor utilization per unit of capital committed."[129] Specifically, Sanjaya Lall and Paul Streeten
contended that DFI tended to be more capital intensive than domestic investment, thus creating fewer
employment opportunities,[130] while Richard Jolly
noted that using capital-intensive techniques of
production in capital-poor countries will increase
the share of capital in value added and concentrate
the labor share in the hands of a small number of
skilled workers.[131] This explains, as Brian Wallace
noted recently, and rightly too, why

> in a relatively capital scarce country
> like Colombia, foreign plants pay higher

> wages and have a lower labor share of
> value added. Foreign plants' produc-
> tion may also be more likely to mirror
> the factor endowments of the investing
> country (where labour is relatively
> more scarce and capital more abundant
> than in the recipient country) and
> this may result in production tech-
> niques that emphasize high capital
> intensity and create relatively fewer
> jobs.[132]

Essentially, because the operations of MNCs are more
capital intensive than those of domestic enterprises,
MNCs tend not to generate much more employment opportunities than do domestic enterprises. To be sure,
a higher relative wage results in the selection of a
more capital-intensive production technique and a
lower level of employment. Obviously, this should
not be the case because scholars on the theory of
choice of production techniques for developing countries, drawing on orthodox static economic theory,
have taken the position that developing countries
"should select investment projects which utilised to
the full their plentiful factors (for example, labour)
and economised on scarce factors (for example, capital)."[133] Since Third World countries are generally
said to be labor rich, labor-intensive rather than
capital-intensive production techniques should be
adopted.

In a study of the impact of MNCs on the distribution of power and wealth in Colombia, Wallace examined whether indigenization or domestication or
Colombianization of DFI under Decree Law 1900 of
1973 would lead to the "creation of more employment
and, hence, a wider distribution of income (inasmuch
as remuneration of factories would be spread among
more workers)."[134] Comparing the ability of foreign
and domestic plants in 27 manufacturing industries
to generate employment per unit of capital (L/K) and
per unit of value added (L/Q), Wallace came to two
conclusions. First, domestic manufacturing plants
create or generate more employment than do foreign
plants per unit of output. Second, foreign plants
in the same industry generate less employment than
do domestic plants per unit of capital. Accordingly,
the domestication of DFIs in Colombia not only im-

proves the distribution of wealth and power if only
because foreign-owned enterprises have tended to
distribute "their remuneration to relatively fewer
employees than . . . domestic firms,"[135] it also affects the creation of employment in the Colombian
manufacturing sector. And, given the level of unemployment and underemployment in four of the country's
eight major cities,[136] it is apparent that the domestication of DFI in Colombia cannot be said to be
overemphasized. According to Albert Berry, the rate
of unemployment in Colombia's four major cities
(where foreign plants are more concentrated geographically than are local plants) in 1969 stood at
10-12 percent;[137] in fact, the share of manufacturing in the total labor force has grown from a little
over 3 percent in the mid-1920s to about 6 percent
by 1970.[138] This situation certainly explains why
the Inter Agency Team of the International Labour
Office on Colombia lamented in these words:

> Without rapid growth in the industrial
> sector, the Colombian economy will not
> be able to solve the employment prob-
> lem. . . . It is manufacturing that
> will have to provide the increasing
> exports needed for a sustained growth
> of employment and it is only in this
> sector that the battle to free the
> Colombian economy from excessive de-
> pendence on imports of capital and in-
> termediate goods can in the end be won.
> More specifically, the manufacturing
> sector will have to absorb a bigger
> proportion of the labour force, and
> this means that its rate of expansion
> must be much faster than during recent
> years, and that the number of jobs it
> creates per unit of investment must be
> higher.[139]

Unfortunately and as Richard Barnet and Ronald Muller
observed, "the one characteristic of global corporate
technology . . . is that it destroys jobs"[140] in
Third World countries that "abound in human resources," simply because the sort of technology

exported by MNCs to such countries is "capital intensive and labor saving."[141] And, Wallace has concluded:

> Foreign plants had a higher capital
> intensity (K/L) in 21 of the 27 indus-
> tries for which a comparison was made.
> This difference was significant at the
> .002 level for a one-tailed test. This
> supports the view that foreign plants
> generate less employment per unit of
> capital than do domestic plants in the
> same industry.[142]

However, Wallace's observation was by no means representative of other studies on the employment-generation effects of the operations of foreign enterprises vis-à-vis domestic enterprises. Other studies on the employment effects of MNCs' operations in Third World countries including Colombia have shown mixed results.

Still on Colombia, while a Central Bank study noted that DFI was <u>substantially</u> more capital intensive than was domestic investment,[143] which is the conclusion reached by Konrad Matter, who has argued that industries dominated by foreign-owned enterprises are unable to create many jobs because they are capital intensive,[144] a comparative study of the performance of foreign and domestic enterprises in Latin America by Livio De Carvalho found that domestic enterprises of similar size with foreign enterprises are also capital intensive and, therefore, generate comparable employment.[145] Albert Berry, who shares the views expressed by Wallace, Matter, and in the Central Bank study, attributes the capital intensity of the operations of foreign enterprises in Colombia not only to the size of such enterprises but also to the production techniques (namely, technologies) borrowed from DMEs that have high capital/labor ratios.[146] As Wallace neatly puts it: "To the extent that foreign firms are somewhat larger than domestic ones, they might be expected to create less employment."[147]

As noted above, studies of employment effects of MNCs in other Third World countries have shown

mixed results. Olukunle Iyanda's study of Nigeria
(with Joseph Bello) found that MNCs used more capital
per employee than do domestic enterprises. As they
put it, "for the MNEs, the average capital per employee is N 4,468.1 while the corresponding figure
for indigenous companies is N 1,305.4."[148] Thus,
they concluded that while an MNC is "generally larger
in terms of employment, domestic enterprises seem to
be more labour-intensive" and, consequently, "may
generate, relatively, more employment opportunities
than the MNEs."[149] With respect to Thailand, Indonesia, India, Mexico, and the Philippines, the position taken by Tambunlertchai, Wells, Agarwal, and
Mason, respectively, is that foreign enterprises are
more capital intensive than are domestic enterprises.[150] Quoting evidence from a number of sur-
veys indicating the relatively greater capital intensity of MNCs, Barnet and Muller lamented that "even
the construction industry, once an important source
of employment for poor countries at a rapid stage of
rapid industrialisation, will no longer absorb as
many new workers as formerly because cranes, bull-
dozers, and other laborsaving machinery are being
substituted for labour."[151] Again, although the
mechanization of agriculture in Latin America has
"dramatically increased crop yields . . . it has not
absorbed labor."[152]

However, a study carried out by the International Labour Office on Kenya found that when industry was taken into account, domestic enterprises
were slightly more capital intensive than were foreign enterprises.[153] Specifically, the ILO report
maintained that foreign enterprises are more likely
to be more labor intensive in those manufacturing
sectors where foreign and domestic capital compete:
"Although they are short of supervisors, they can re-
cruit them more easily than locally owned firms (and
possibly use their supervisors more productively,
through better management)."[154]

A similar conclusion, namely that foreign enterprises do not always tend to be more capital intensive than domestic enterprises are, has been
reached by Forsyth and Solomon with respect to
Ghana.[155] And as to whether foreign enterprises employ more capital-intensive technology than domestic

enterprises do, while Thomas Biersteker's illuminating study of Nigeria found foreign enterprises to be
slightly more capital intensive in the textile industries, it found no significant differences in the
saw-milling and cement industries. According to
him, MNCs in the textile industry employed slightly
more capital-intensive technology than did their domestic competitors, regardless of their size; in the
cement industry, MNCs employed more capital per employee until 1968 when the pattern was reversed; and,
in the saw-milling industry, MNCs were more capital
intensive in seven of the ten years surveyed. In essence, "although multinational enterprises generally
tend to employ more capital-intensive technologies
than domestic firms in the same sector in the same
year, only in the textile industry is the difference
statistically significant over the ten-year period
1963-1972."[156] He added:

> The data suggest that the relationship
> between firm ownership and capital in-
> tensity of production is sectorally
> specific in Nigeria. Hence the gen-
> eralizations of both critical and neo-
> conventional schools are in some ways
> inaccurate. . . . Unemployment has
> probably increased because of multi-
> national investment in the textile in-
> dustry. But it has not necessarily
> increased in the cement or saw mill-
> ing industries.[157]

It seems in order to conclude that available evidence
on whether MNCs employ more capital-intensive technologies than do domestic enterprises in producing
similar products is somewhat ambiguous.
    Let us now examine the employment potential of
DFI in natural resource-based industries. True,
plantation industries such as coffee, tobacco, sisal,
and tea are relatively labor intensive; in fact, it
is difficult to foresee the annual plucking of two
leaves and a bud in the tea industry being replaced
by mechanical devices. However, extractive industries not only tend to be relatively capital intensive but also offer more scope for mechnical innova-

tions. To be sure, rapid advances have occurred in mining technology, resulting in widespread displacement of labor by technology.

A case in point is the Nigerian oil industry. That the oil industry has contributed immensely to the Nigerian economy, there is no doubt. These contributions include: (1) creation of employment opportunities and the availability of training opportunities for Nigerians; (2) local expenditure on goods and services; (3) contributions to government revenues, gross domestic product, and foreign exchange reserves; and (4) supply of energy to industry and commerce.[158]

For the moment, we are concerned with the first contribution. One of the major contributions of the oil industry to the Nigerian economy is the creation of employment opportunities. Initially, Nigerians were employed in such nonbasic activities as the building of roads and bridges, the clearing of drilling locations, transportation of materials and equipment, and the building of staff housing and recreational facilities. And, as the industry's training programs progressed (such as on-the-job training for employees, overseas training for employees, and scholarship awards tenable in higher institutions such as the Universities of Lagos, Ibadan, and Ife), Nigerians began to be employed in seismic and drilling operations and as supervisory and management staff. From all available data, employment of Nigerians by the oil industry stood at over 5,000 while employment by enterprises dependent on the oil industry stood at over 15,000. In fact, direct employment by the oil industry is unlikely to increase significantly in the future because the industry, by its nature, tends to employ capital-intensive techniques, as illustrated by the size of the capital-labor ratio in the industry. For example, if one relates the Naira value of the industry's net capital investment to the staff complement in 1972, one would obtain an indicator of capital intensity that stood at N 13,433.74. This contrasts with a figure of N 541.81 for other nonoil industries. This means that for every employee on the payroll, the oil industry made a net capital investment of N 13,434.00 during 1972. More important, when we relate the value of the stock of capital to the number of employees on the payroll and we define a unit of labor as one man-year, and the stock of capital assets is valued in Naira, we would then be able to indicate some sort of index of capital intensity for the industry.[159] See Table 3.17. It is basic that the Nigerian oil industry has not done as well as the construction, manufacturing, building, and agriculture industries.

TABLE 3.17

Index of Capital Intensity for the
Nigerian Oil Industry 1970-73

As at end of	Capital Stock (₦ thousand)	Labor (Man-Years)	Capital/ Labor Ratio
1970	562,057	7,629	73,674
1971	701,321	4,544	154,340
1972	638,477	5,003	127,619
1973	652,882	5,269	123,910

Source: S. B. Falegan and G. O. Okah, "The Contribution of Petroleum to Nigeria's Economy," p. 174.

In essence, the very high capital-labor ratio in the oil industry means that growth in oil operations is reflected in the expansion of capital investment and not in the generation or relative expansion of employment. However, while MNCs' operations in the extractive sector are capital intensive and, therefore, do not generate much employment, they are likely to have a much more favorable impact on the creation of labor skills. So because MNCs employ capital-intensive techniques, their demand for skilled labor is likely to be high; and since MNCs tend to pay higher wages than domestic enterprises do, MNCs' operations are, therefore, likely to accentuate income inequality in the host economy.

More important, the consumption pattern of skilled
workers, most of whom may be expatriates and very
few indigenes, is foreign-oriented, thus leading to
a distortion of domestic tastes and creating a form
of cultural dependency. However, the indirect
employment-generation effects of MNCs' operations in
the plantation industries seem to be greater than in
the extractive industries. First, a high proportion
of the outlays made by plantation industries is certain to generate demand in the host economies. To
be sure, plantation industries, because they are
relatively labor intensive, tend to generate a substantial demand for food and other basic consumer
goods. Furthermore, plantation industries generate
employment in industries processing and packing the
plantation products. The indirect employment-generation effects of MNCs' operations seem to be greater
in the plantation industries than in the extractive
industries because the extractive industries are
relatively capital intensive, meaning that the demand for skilled labor is likely to be high. Nevertheless, there were some important demand effects
created by the needs of the extractive industries
for nonlabor inputs. While demands for transport
services and electricity in the copper industry do
permit industrial growth in these sectors, their employment effects are usually not very high. However,
in the oil industry, the demand effects for construction, drilling, and other technical services and,
consequently, their employment effects, are relatively high. For example, by 1973, 29 major construction
and 67 service companies that had a combined turn-
over of ₦ 138.7 million and had over 6,000 employees
(as can be seen from Table 3.18) existed mainly to
service the Nigerian oil companies. In fact, the
service companies have consistently employed more
workers than do the oil companies themselves. To be
sure, for every 100 workers employed by the oil companies, the service companies, on the average, have
employed 116 workers.

TABLE 3.18

Direct and Indirect Employment of Multinational
Corporation Operations in the Nigerian Oil Industry

Employers	1971-72	1972-73	1973-74
Oil Companies	4,544	5,003	5,272
Service Companies	5,531	5,656	6,011

Source: S. B. Falegan and G. O. Okah, "The Contribution of Petroleum to Nigeria's Economy," p. 179.

Since employment creation may and can be used
as a redistributive mechanism, particularly as unemployment is demoralizing and political dangers arise
from widespread unemployment, why, then, do MNCs
transfer inappropriate, capital-intensive technologies to Third World countries? A major reason for
transferring capital-intensive technology is that it
is precisely through its ownership and/or control of
this technology (which is part of the investment
package) or knowledge that the MNC can earn monopoly
or "excess" profits in the host country. Indeed,
the ownership or control of technology or knowledge
is the real key to the power of the MNC. Second,
the limited domestic markets, which are characteristic of Third World countries, and other factors such
as their varying stages of development and heteroge-
neity do not offer sufficient incentives for MNCs to
develop separate technologies for every market within
which they operate. More important, it would be preposterous to expect profit-maximizing and cost-
minimizing MNCs to experiment with new technologies.
As the Development Assistance Committee of the OECD
puts it, the path of least resistance, for most foreign investors, lies in duplicating developed country systems of manufacture or construction, obviously

the result of decades of innovation, for the purpose
of substituting more and more intricate, automatic,
and hard-to-maintain capital equipment for more and
more expensive labor.[160] Asserting that MNCs are
not altogether insensitive to the developmental
needs and aspirations of Third World host states,
Alasdair MacBean and V. Balasubramanyam noted, very
forcefully:

> The foreign firms' reluctance to ex-
> periment with technologies and prod-
> ucts appropriate to the factor endow-
> ments, income levels and local condi-
> tions of the developing countries may
> be entirely rational on economic
> grounds. It is less expensive to
> transfer abroad a tested and tried
> technique than invest in a new tech-
> nique. Moreover, no two developing
> countries are alike in terms of their
> resource endowments and socio-economic
> characteristics. The foreign firms
> may be hard put to design differing
> techniques to suit the differing eco-
> nomic climates in which they oper-
> ate.[161]

Third, perhaps the developing countries of the
Third World are to be blamed for the capital-intensive nature of the MNCs' operations. Because of
their excessive enthusiasm or obsession for industrialization, most governments in the Third World
may have, albeit unwittingly, encouraged MNCs to employ more capital-intensive techniques, particularly
in the manufacturing sector. By way of encouragement, they have offered MNCs such incentives as generous depreciation allowances, lower tax rates for
designated industries, tax holidays for new and "priority" industries, concessionary tariff rates on imports of machinery and equipment, and overvalued exchange rates.[162] These measures meant granting a
subsidy on the use of capital; indeed, such policies
have not only encouraged further employment of capital in what are already capital-intensive industries
but have also guided DFI toward relatively capital-

intensive operations. To date, because most governments in Third World countries insist on MNCs using
the latest and more capital-intensive techniques,
and because MNCs want to be regarded as "good" corporate citizens, MNCs, not unnaturally, bow to these
pressures.

Fourth, expenditures on research and development (R and D), a significant portion of which is
quite often borne by governments, are largely concentrated in the DMEs. According to a United Nations
study, only 6 percent of R and D by U.S.-based MNCs
in the 1960s was spent outside the United States.[163]
Consequently, the emerging products and processes
tend to be increasingly inappropriate. In any event,
given MNC dominance of technological development, it
is only fair to conclude that the little scientific
or technological research taking place within Third
World countries is more likely to be geared to the
needs or interests of MNCs than toward the needs of
domestic (i.e., Third World host state) productive
sectors.[164] Other reasons why MNCs employ capital-
intensive techniques in their operations in the
Third World can be briefly stated:[165]

1. MNCs transfer to Third World countries technologies with which their managers and technicians
   are familiar. In fact, it may well be that MNC
   management may not be able to operate other technologies or simply that other technologies do not
   exist.
2. For the MNC, what determines the choice of techniques of production is global factor availability
   rather than domestic factor availability. The
   multinational corporation has access to capital
   from various sources including international capital markets. Therefore, it is only rational for
   the MNC to employ capital-intensive techniques
   even in labor-rich Third World countries.
3. The claim that labor is abundant in Third World
   host states is questionable and deceptive because
   wages may be "high" in relation to the productivity of the labor force; this problem is compounded
   by the "distorted" factor prices in these countries, meaning that there is even less incentive
   for the development of labor-intensive techniques.

4. The qualitative aspects of the labor force are very significant; indeed, the composition of available labor force in many Third World countries is very fundamental in that it affects the choice of techniques of production. More significant, and as Streeten argued, and quite rightly, the interests of the MNC lie "in minimising labour relations with a foreign labour force, which may be unskilled, underfed, unhealthy, unreliable, undisciplined and perhaps hostile, and dealings with which may give rise to political difficulties."[166]

5. Labor-intensive techniques, if anything, are associated with small scales of production whereas the multinational corporation typically produces on a large scale, and incidentally, it is that scale which determines the efficient factor intensity.

To sum up, perhaps the arguments for employing capital-intensive techniques in MNCs' operations in Third World host states are really arguments for modern techniques, namely, "techniques which are first of all mechanised and possess the advantages of the influence of machine-spaced operations on the productivity of labour, techniques giving a high and consistent quality of output and using easily available spare parts."[167]

Employee Compensation and Effects on Income Distribution

The operation of MNCs in the labor markets of Third World countries has aroused considerable interest among scholars in the comparison of wage payments made by MNCs' subsidiaries and domestic enterprises. For example, it has been argued that MNCs pay higher wages than do domestic enterprises, and therefore MNCs contribute to uneven income distribution, namely, domestic inequality and a widening of the elite-mass gap. While neoconventional scholars agree with critical scholars that MNCs pay higher wages than do domestic enterprises and encourage the development of compradors (whose interests and activities are not at variance with their own), they contend that

MNCs do not exacerbate domestic inequalities, which
they suggest more often than not are the outcome of
government policies or the general process of industrialization.[168] There is some element of truth in
these claims. For the moment, we would make comparisons between the employee compensation of MNC subsidiaries and domestic enterprises, and later explore
some hypotheses about the extent to which MNCs have
contributed to domestic inequalities through their
operations in the labor market.

Ideally, one would wish to compare the wages
(including fringe benefits) received by employees of
MNC subsidiaries and domestic enterprises since
wages are certainly a portion of the financial payments to employees. Others include housing and related benefits, transportation (official cars or car-
basic allowances), vacation, and medical benefits.
Ideally, one would wish to compare the wages received by employees performing identical tasks in
foreign/domestic enterprises and countries. Difficulties arise not only in evaluating the comparabil-
ity of jobs in particular occupations but also in
calculating the value of nonmonetary (fringe) benefits received in addition to wages. Furthermore,
when wages received by employees in different coun-
tres are being considered, there is the additional
problem of converting them into a common unit of
measurement. True, exchange rates are often used
for this purpose. However, such rates do not always
or accurately reflect the real value of money of
different countries.[169] Obviously, detailed statistics on consumption patterns and prices would need
to consider this, as it was rightly observed in a
study by the International Labour Office.[170] More
fundamental, lack of data, particularly with regard
to MNCs' operations in Third World countries, definitely means that exact comparisons cannot be made.
Consequently, conclusions based on such limited data
must be treated with caution.

Despite these problems, several studies have
attempted to establish the differences in the wages
received by employees of MNC subsidiaries and domestic enterprises. First, reference must be made to a
study carried out by the International Labour Office,
which found that foreign-owned enterprises paid higher

wages than domestic enterprises in Argentina, Brazil, Chile, Colombia, India, Korea, Mexico, Pakistan, and the Philippines.[171] Similar conclusions were reached by Wells, Mason, Sourrouille, Diaz-Alejandro, Langdon, Jo, Papandreou, Sabolo and Trajtenberg, Possas, and Dunning in respect of Indonesia, the Philippines, Mexico, Argentina, Colombia, Kenya, Canada, and the United Kingdom.[172] With respect to Mexico, Canada, and the United Kingdom, an analysis by Dunning of a sample of 500 U.S.-based MNC subsidiaries in the United Kingdom in 1973 showed that the U.S. subsidiaries have tended to pay higher wages than domestic enterprises, and in Mexico and Canada they have tended to pay significantly more, considering the differences in employment structure.[173] Mason's comparative study of foreign and domestic enterprises in Mexico and the Philippines found that MNC subsidiaries paid significantly higher wages to five out of six categories of their employees than do domestic enterprises, while Fajnzylber's study of Mexico found that foreign enterprises paid wages that were 1.7 times higher than domestic enterprises paid in the same sector.[174] In Latin America, subsidiaries of U.S.-based MNCs paid annual wages that were between 1.4 and 2.1 times higher than those of domestic enterprises, while in India and Pakistan the ratios were 2.4 and 2.6, respectively.

To be more specific, a study of 12 MNC subsidiaries in Nigeria sampled by Iyanda and Bello showed: (1) that domestic enterprises paid less wages to their employees than did MNC subsidiaries; (2) that while MNC subsidiaries paid an average of ₦ 3,024.7 per employee, domestic enterprises paid ₦ 606.7 per employee; and (3) that MNC subsidiaries offer higher job security and other fringe benefits than do domestic enterprises.[175]

Biersteker's study is more illuminating. While his conclusion accords with conclusions reached by other scholars, the following observations are germane:

1. that during the ten-year period surveyed, 1963-72, MNC subsidiaries paid on the average $692 per employee compared with $521 paid per employee by domestic enterprises;

2. that MNC subsidiaries operating in textile, cement, and saw-milling industries pay higher wages than domestic enterprises, while MNC subsidiaries in sugar-refining industry pay lower wages than domestic enterprises for most of the years surveyed;

3. that MNCs paid on the average higher wages than domestic enterprises within each of the wage groups considered. Specifically, MNCs pay expatrite employees an average of $7,305 compared with $4,990 paid by domestic enterprises; second, MNCs pay Nigerian professionals $2,775 per year compared with $2,610 paid by domestic enterprises; third, MNCs pay their clerical staff an average of $868 compared with $770 paid by domestic enterprises; and fourth, MNCs pay skilled and unskilled workers an average of $420 compared with $367 paid by domestic enterprises;

4. that while MNCs pay higher wages than domestic enterprises for most industries, most wage groups and most of the period under survey, in most cases the differences between the average wages paid by MNCs and domestic enterprises are very slight and not statistically significant; and

5. that MNCs, in general, provide more in terms of housing, transportation, medical benefits, and more important, job security, than domestic enterprises, a conclusion also reached by Iranda and Bello.[176]

In essence, Iyanda and Bello as well as Biersteker and information elicited from our colleagues, relations, and former students (who are employed by MNC subsidiaries in Nigeria and Nigerian companies) tend to suport the widely held view by critical scholars that MNCs tend to pay higher wages than domestic enterprises do.

However, studies carried out by Wallace, Cohen, and Tambunlertchai with respect of Colombia, Singapore and Taiwan, and Thailand, respectively, have shown mixed results. Tambunlertchai's study[177] of foreign and domestic enterprises in Thailand found that foreign enterprises, overall, paid higher wages than did domestic enterprises but concluded that domestic enterprises paid higher wages to Thai workers than did foreign enterprises. A similar conclusion was reached by Cohen, who found that domestic enterprises in Singapore paid higher wages than did foreign enterprises, while no clear pattern emerged in Taiwan.[178]

Wallace's study of 421 manufacturing plants (not enterprises) in Colombia, which were aggregated into 27 industrial groupings as in Biersteker's study, is more illuminating. According to him, foreign plants paid significantly higher wages to all categories of employees than did domestic plants. However, analysis of the 27 industrial groupings sampled by Wallace reveals the following:

1. that in only _four_ did domestic plants pay higher wages to all personnel;
2. that in only _four_ did domestic plants pay more to foreign managers, _presumably_ than Colombian managers;
3. that in only _two_ did domestic plants pay more to Colombian managers, _presumably_ than foreign managers;
4. that in only _four_ did domestic plants pay more to clerical staff; and,
5. that in only _five_ did domestic plants pay more to unskilled workers.[179]

In essence, while foreign plants, overall, paid significantly higher wages to all categories of employees than did domestic plants, in terms of distribution of remuneration, the comparison of foreign and domestic plants presents a mixed picture.

Undoubtedly, the rapidly expanding use of capital-intensive technology by MNCs in their operations in Third World countries has contributed to unequal distribution of the national income because those who receive the income generated by these capital resources are the owners of these resources, namely, foreign-owned enterprises and their shareholders or a small group of domestic capitalists who already receive more than 40 percent of the country's income. The fact is: (1) that income distribution tends to be highly unequal where a small group of people own capital and a larger proportion of income is generated from capital-intensive rather than

labor-intensive techniques and (2) that income distribution tends to be more unequal over time where
there "is a relative change in technology towards
labor-saving techniques and . . . capitalist legal
institutions are not modified via, for example,
more progressive tax rates to keep pace with this
change."[180] Consequently, what would improve income
distribution in Third World countries hosting MNCs'
operations is increasing employment possibilities
for the poorest 40 percent of the population, progressive taxation that would reduce substantially
the incomes of the wealthy, and the introduction of
social security and/or unemployment insurance.

We have now come to an examination of an issue
that has generated much controversy among scholars
of the political economy of Third World countries,
namely, the effects of MNC operations on income distribution within Third World host states. We have
asserted above, first, that MNCs tend to employ more
capital-intensive techniques than do domestic enterprises, and, therefore, MNCs or foreign enterprises
in general neither create nor generate much more employment opportunities than do domestic enterprises;
second, overall MNCs or foreign enterprises pay
higher salaries/wages to their employees than do
domestic enterprises. These views seem to be shared
by radical and liberal/neoconventional schools. The
point of departure between the two schools of thought
is the interpretation of the effects of MNCs' wage
policies. Simply put, while critics of MNCs and
foreign-owned enterprises argue that wide disparities in the wages/salaries and fringe benefits paid
by MNCs and domestic enterprises to their employees
have not only contributed to the development or
emergence of local allies, so-called compradors, but
also have contributed to the widening of the elite-
mass gap, apologists of MNCs contend that it is not
clear whether such a gap widens, adding that it is
difficult to ascertain the effects of MNCs.

Let us examine how these arguments relate to
Nigeria. Those who argue that MNCs contribute to
the widening elite-mass gap contend, very forcefully,
first, that MNCs pay their employees higher salaries
and generous fringe benefits than do domestic enterprises, ostensibly because they require the "sta-

bilization" of domestic manpower;[181] second, the
payment of high salaries (for example, according to
Iyanda and Bello, MNC subsidiaries in Nigeria paid
an average of ₦ 3,024.7 per employee, compared with
₦ 606.7 paid by domestic enterprises per employee)
by MNCs widens the gap between their employees and
the rest of the domestic labor force; and, third,
that since the public and private sectors in Nigeria
compete for scarce high-level manpower resources,
the payment of high salaries by MNCs as well as the
offer of generous fringe benefits to their employees
would certainly lead to an "inflationary wage increase spiral" between the public sector and a private sector, dominated by MNCs and foreign-owned enterprises. To be sure, according to a recent study,
"periodic public service review commissions are established by the government to evaluate civil service wages and bring them into line with those offered by multinationals. Once the civil service
wage scales are adjusted upward, multinationals re-
spond with equal or greater increases that reestab-
lish them as the highest-paying employer in the domestic labor market, and the inflationary spiral
continues."[182]

The fact that needs to be emphasized at this
point is that such a spiral has developed in Nigeria,
a country where, because of the competition for
scarce high-level manpower resources between the
public and private sectors, foreign-owned enterprises, particularly MNCs' subsidiaries, are the
highest-paying employers in the domestic labor market, and where an examination of Nigerian public
service review commissions in the postindependence
period[183] reveals concerted attempts by the government to make salaries in the public service including the parastatals competitive with salaries in the
private sector, which is still dominated by foreign
business in spite of the Nigerian Enterprises Promotion Decrees (Acts) of 1972 and 1977.[184]

It seems fair to say from our observations
above that foreign-owned enterprises, particularly
MNC subsidiaries, by paying higher salaries/wages to
their employees than other employers of labor in
both the public and private sectors and by awarding
salaries that matched and usually exceeded salary

increases made in the public sector, may well have, albeit unwittingly, ensured a steady increase in the income of the wage sector. However, it is not at all clear if increasing income disparities in Nigeria can be attributed solely to the wage policies of MNCs' subsidiaries. In fact, it is possible to argue, indeed claim, that income in the wage sector as a whole is becoming more equally distributed. Between 1959 and 1971 (the year the Adebo Wages and Salaries Commission recommended an across-the-board increase in the salaries of public servants)[185] the pay differentials between the highest and lowest paid public servants had fallen down from a ratio of 28:1 to 16:1 while the wage/salary increases for the highest and lowest paid public servants stood at 10 percent and 71-133 percent, respectively.[186] Three years later, the recommendations of the Udoji Public Service Review Commission reduced the gap between the highest and lowest paid public servants from 16:1 to 10:1. And, with respect to the private sector,[187] the gap between the highest and lowest paid employees fell from 23:1 in 1963 to 15:1 in 1972. In essence, "it could be argued that the lower-income groups have no grounds to complain. Taken in absolute terms, however, there is much sense in arguing that the 'gap' between the two groups has in fact widened."[188]

With respect to the average income in the wage and nonwage sectors, available data show that the ratio of wage to nonwage income in Nigeria in 1967 stood at 6:1.[189] Four years later, the Adebo Commission increased the base salary of public servants (Table 3.19) and the income of the wage sector as a whole. More significant, the base public service salary of the Adebo Commission Report was doubled by the Udoji Commission in 1974, namely, three years later. No consideration was given to the nonwage/salary earners and peasant farmers (who as a class constitute some 75 percent of the total population) in the wake of the Adebo and Udoji Commission Reports. While statistics with respect to the distribution of average income in the wage and nonwage sectors in the post-Udoji period are not available, it is proper to assume that the 6:1 ratio of wage to nonwage incomes estimated by Ojetunde Aboyade in

1967 has probably increased several times in the wake of the recommendations of the Adebo and Udoji Commissions.

TABLE 3.19

Adebo Award by Salary Groups

Group Salary Level (₦)	% Distribution of Public Service Personnel	Award (₦)	As % of Preaward Salary
400 or below	40	72	30
Over 400	35	120	30
Over 1,000	15	240	24
Over 2,000	6	360	18
Over 4,000	3	480	12
Over 5,000	1	600	12

Source: Federal Republic of Nigeria, Second and Final Report of the Wages and Salaries Review Commission (Lagos: Federal Ministry of Information, 1971), p. 84.

In essence, the net result of the payment of higher salaries to a tiny minority of employees in the public and private sectors is the creation of many types of social inequalities in Nigeria, thus making it much more impossible to realize a "just and egalitarian society,"[189] while paying Chief Executives of Public Corporations and State-Owned Companies (such as the Central Bank of Nigeria, Nigerian Ports Authority) annual salaries ranging between ₦ 15,000 and ₦ 28,000 in a country where per-capita income ranges between ₦ 50 and ₦ 100 is not only to widen the urban-rural imbalance and, by extension, elite-mass gap but also to create more frustration and alienation among rural dwellers who constitute more than 75 percent of the total population. Simply put, DFI exacerbates inequality while the payment of fat salaries in countries where the per-capita income is deplorably low is to widen the urban-rural imbalance and, by extension, the elite-mass gap.

What possible explanations can we give for the significantly greater remuneration paid by foreign-owned enterprises, particularly MNC subsidiaries in Third World countries? It is possible that foreign enterprises pay high salaries either as a result of trade union pressures for parity in wages and conditions of service or in order to reduce criticisms of their operations. Second, foreign enterprises pay high salaries to attract and maintain a loyal and stable labor force. Third, because MNCs and the government compete for scarce high-level manpower resources, MNCs, not unnaturally, have to offer high salaries and generous fringe benefits. Finally, and as the Nigerian experience shows, MNCs offer their employees higher salaries to make them competitive with salaries in the public sector.

MNCs AND CONSUMPTION PATTERNS IN HOST STATES

We have examined the employment effects of MNC operations in developing countries. Another aspect of MNC operations in developing countries is the subject of our inquiry in this section, namely, the extent to which MNCs encourage inappropriate consumption patterns through product differentiation (or innovation), advertising, and marketing techniques as well as the use of competitive advantages that are characteristic of oligopolistic industries.

As is expected, the extent to which MNCs have encouraged inappropriate consumption patterns in Third World countries and created a form of cultural dependency in these countries has generated much controversy between critics and advocates of MNC operations in developing countries. According to critics of MNC operations, MNCs encourage inappropriate consumption patterns through product differentiation (or innovation), advertising, and marketing techniques as well as the use of competitive advantages. To be sure, MNCs encourage inappropriate consumption patterns because their products have a lower substantive value and a higher price than those made by domestic enterprises. Second, MNCs, it is argued by critics of their Third World opera-

tions, often encourage the consumption of substitutes or processed variants for preexistent products
(product replacement) or they introduce highly priced
products (with cosmetic and marketing changes) to
replace indigenous products. Unfortunately for poor
Third World countries, these highly priced products
have a lower substantive value than the indigenous
products that they have replaced in the domestic market. Third, critics of MNC operations argue that
MNCs create tastes for products with no preexisting
substitutes; additionally, they employ advertising
and marketing techniques to create a market for a
product with a higher price and questionable substantive value. In fact, an essential element of MNC
power, it is argued by critics of MNC operations in
developing countries, is their ability to create demands and/or mold tastes.

It is small wonder, then, that such expensive
products of DMEs as automobiles (such as Cadillacs,
Honda Preludes, Rovers, Mustangs, Firebirds, and
Lincoln Continentals), pharmaceuticals, electronic
goods (such as stereo sets and video cassette recorders), soft drinks (such as Coca-Cola, Pepsi-Cola,
Sprite, and Seven-Up), cigarettes, watches, and cam-
eras are being increasingly consumed by the middle-
and upper-income groups of developing countries, undoubtedly groups who constitute a tiny fraction of
the population. While these items constitute a
heavy drain on scarce foreign exchange since they
are frequently imported, even the lower-income groups
(the Wretched of the Earth) consume the sophisticated
and brand-differentiated products of the MNCs that
may be cheaper than the products of domestic enterprises, thanks to the powerful influence of advertising on television, radio, and print media (newspapers, billboards, hand-outs, and so on).

There is no doubt that advertising, on which
MNCs invest much expenditure in developed and developing countries, has stimulated demands and molded
tastes for MNCs' products in poor-income developing
countries, particularly among the middle- and upper-
income groups. According to Barnet and Muller,
"stimulating consumption in low-income countries and
accommodating local tastes to globally distributed
products" through advertising "is crucial to the de-

velopment of an ever-expanding Global Shopping Centre. . . . Telling poor people about products they have the money to buy right now, such as Coca-Cola and ITT's Twinkies . . . opens up new horizons. How, the World Managers argue, can the transfer of the consumption ideology, which had so much to do with the expansion of the U.S. economy, be bad for poor countries?"[190] As to the impact of advertising in creating demands and molding tastes for MNC products, it seems to be agreed by practitioners and scholars: (1) that a by-product of advertising campaigns is to give families without the bare necessities of life a spurious feeling of being middle-class and (2) that advertising creates a psychological dependence. For example, according to Evangelina Garcia, the housewife in Venezuela "measures her happiness by whether she has a refrigerator . . . before, a woman's happiness was to have children, depend on her husband, even to have goods but not to show them."[191]

Sharing Garcia's views, namely, that one's sense of self-esteem is determined by what one buys, are Peter Drucker and Albert Stridsberg. While Drucker noted that "the factory girl or the salesgirl in Lima or Bombay (or the Harlem ghetto) wants a lipstick. . . . There is no purchase that gives her as much true value for a few cents,"[192] Stridsberg advised that we rid ourselves of

> the conventional range of ideas about
> what will minister to the poor man's
> physical needs. The psychological
> significance of his spending his money
> on a transistor radio may be more im-
> portant than the physical benefit gen-
> erated by spending the same money for
> basic foodstuffs.[193]

Emphasizing the impact of advertising in creating or stimulating demands and molding tastes of poor-income developing countries, particularly among the lower-income groups, Barnet and Muller contended, and quite frankly, that the "advertiser is like a friend who tells you about all the wonderful things in the world that you didn't even know existed."[194]

Barnet and Muller demonstrated how MNCs, through advertising, have created demands for their products (such as baby foods and soft drinks)--which are more expensive than preexisting products--and molded the dietary habits of some poor-income Third World countries, particularly among the lower-income groups. They recall doctors in rural Mexican villages reporting that it is the practice "for a family to sell the few eggs and chickens it raises to buy Coke for the father while the children waste away for lack of protein."[195] Furthermore, studies by Joaquin Cravioto and Albert Stridsberg show how Mexican peasants buy white bread (rich in protein and vitamins) as a substitute for tortillas (rich in calcium) and Coca-Cola/Pepsi-Cola in place of locally produced cola. With respect to Bangladesh, studies by J. K. Roy show that poor families buy highly priced baby foods instead of the much cheaper cow's milk, and in the Caribbean, "nurses are employed by companies to get the names of new mothers at the hospital and then to 'race' to the women's homes to give them free samples and related advertising."[196]

The position taken by Barnet and Muller, Cravioto, Stridsberg, and Roy, namely, that MNCs encourage inappropriate consumption patterns in developing countries, seems to be shared by Biersteker and from our findings of the marketing practices of some food and pharmaceutical companies operating in Nigeria, notably, Food Specialities (Nigeria) Limited, Nestle, and Glaxo (Nigeria) Limited. On the introduction of powdered baby formulas (such as Nan, Farlac, and Farlene) into the Nigerian market, Biersteker has this much to say:

Nigerian consumers have been confronted with a barrage of advertising extolling the virtues of using powdered baby formulas in place of breast-feeding. The advertising has emphasized that use of the formulas is more modern than breast-feeding and illustrate this point by portraying upwardly mobile professional women using the product for their newborn children. The product has clearly taken on the qualities of a status symbol.[197]

Several advertisements (ranging from a quarter-page to a half-page) have appeared in the country's newspapers in respect of Farlene, Nan, and Farlac, to mention but a few of these powdered baby formulas. Two of them on Farlac call for mention here. The first, which appeared in the Sunday Punch issue of November 22, 1981, and captioned, "FARLAC--the essential cereal for your child's growth," reads thus:

> Farlac is the essential protein-enriched milk cereal that provides ten important vitamins and four vital vitamins for healthy growth. That's why Farlac is recommended not only for infants but for growing children too. Farlac is a formative food that meets your children's nutritional needs. Farlac provides body-building protein, energy producing fat and carbohydrate. For growing children, Farlac makes a nourishing breakfast. Just add freshly boiled and cooled water and serve-- FARLAC.[198]

The second, which appeared in the Sunday Concord issue of September 5, 1982, and captioned, "Give your baby FARLAC for a solid start in life," reads thus:

> At 3 months, your baby needs the extra nourishment of solid foods to ensure healthy growth. This the ideal time to start him on Farlac. Farlac is a specially prepared weaning food that contains protein, carbohydrates and fats for energy, calcium, phosphorous and vitamins for sturdy bones and strong teeth plus iron to keep his blood healthy. Farlac is the ideal solid food for your baby's healthy growth--Just add freshly boiled and cooled water and serve.[199]

What, then, are the costs of breast-milk-substituting baby foods to the developing countries in general, and Nigeria in particular? The first is economic. Undoubtedly, the cost of using such brand-differentiated powdered baby formulas as Lactogen, Ostermilk, Cerelac, Similac, SMA, Cow and Gate, S26, Nan, Farlene, and Farlac (which are virtually the same product)[200] is greater than preexisting substitutes such as breast-milk, cow-milk, and porridges. Second, there is the grave and potential danger posed to the health of millions of newborn children in Nigeria and many Third World countries in the absence of manufacturers' instructions with respect to prepartion or as a result of misapplication, even by literate families, of their difficult-to-observe rules of use.[201] Third, and added to the economic cost to the tight budget of many families, is the pressure on foreign exchange earnings of poor Third World countries through the import of such products as baby formulas, breakfast cereals, toothpastes, and soft drinks, particularly as the cost of their substitutes is considerably less, if not zero.[202]

Just as MNCs have encouraged the consumption of baby formulas through brand names or product differentiation and advertising, multinationals have encouraged the consumption of such food-related products as breakfast cereals and toothpastes. Breakfast cereals (such as Cornflakes, Branflakes, Cocoa Crispies, Wheatabix, Quaker Oats, and Rice Crispies) have virtually replaced the more nutritious porridges (for example, "ogi," made from local grains in Nigeria), while toothpastes (such as Pepsodent, Maclean, Colgate With Gardol, Snow White, Aquafresh, Close-Up with Fluoride, and Aquamint With MFP Fluoride) have replaced, rather unfortunately, chewing sticks ("pako" by the Yorubas), which are much more effective for cleaning and scraping the teeth and gums.

In order to demonstrate that multinationals have not encouraged inappropriate consumption patterns in Nigeria, Biersteker focuses on multinational investments in the cement, saw-milling, textile, and sugar-refining industries.[203] According to him, three elements are common to multinational investments in these industries. The first is that multinational enterprises have often followed the lead of Nigerian enterprises. While the first multinational in the cement industry began production in 1962, four years after the first Nigerian enterprise, the

first multinational textile industry commenced production in 1963, nearly 12 years after the Nigerian
textile company commenced production of textiles in
the country. Second, there were few or no significant product innovations. And third, the products
were nearly identical. With respect to the textile
industry, Biersteker adds:

1. that Nigerian and multinational enterprises, from
   the outset, produced cotton textiles;
2. that both enterprises were engaged in import-
   substitution activities like Nigerian and multinational enterprises in the cement industry;
3. that cotton textiles produced by both enterprises
   were designed to replace imported and local hand-
   woven textiles ("aso oke") that had existed, and
   still exist in Nigeria for centuries.[204]

However, after 1970, most of the new multinational
textile enterprises started producing synthetics
that are not only more expensive than cotton textiles,
as can be seen in Table 3.20, but also inappropriate.

TABLE 3.20

Comparing the Prices of Synthetics
and Cotton Textiles 1969-72

| | Price per Square Yard | | | |
	1969	1970	1971	1972
Synthetics	$2.56	$2.62	$2.56	$2.14
Cotton Textiles	0.42	0.51	0.54	0.67

Source: Thomas J. Biersteker, Distortion or
Development? (Cambridge, Mass.: MIT Press, 1978),
p. 131.

Between 1969 and 1972, synthetics, a new product
line introduced by multinationals, sold for an average of $2.56 per square yard, while cotton textiles
produced by Nigerian textile enterprises sold for an

average of $0.54 per square yard during the same
period. Although the prices for synthetics remained
fairly stable during the four-year period, there is
little doubt that they are much more expensive than
cotton textiles. There is no doubt that synthetics
are of a more questionable substantive value than
cotton textiles. Synthetics are much warmer than
cotton textiles and they are certainly inappropriate
for a tropical country such as Nigeria. Rejecting
the claim that synthetics are inappropriate, Biersteker notes, although quite unconvincingly, that
synthetic textiles "are . . . likely to last longer
in the tropical sun and with repeated handwash-
ings."[205]

     With respect to the sugar industry, Biersteker
observes that all sugar refined in Nigeria is white,
fine-granulated sugar. Although he admits, first,
that white, granulated sugar is more expensive than
the brown, large-crystallized sugar available in
some countries (including Nigeria) and, second, that
white, granulated sugar has a lower substantive
value than brown, large-crystallized sugar, and,
therefore, it may be said that the sugar produced in
Nigeria by multinationals is inappropriate,[206] he
contends that it is difficult to argue that multinationals have introduced or encouraged inappropriate
consumption patterns, because to him "the decision
to process white, granulated sugar was made by a
Nigerian government firm, not by a multinational
corporation intent on altering domestic patterns of
consumption to suit its product."[207] Concluding his
findings, Biersteker contends that multinationals in
the cement, saw-milling, textile, and sugar-refining
industries cannot be held responsible for the creation of tastes for products without prior substitutes. All the four industries, he argues, are import substitution, and they are engaged in the production of substitutes of existing products.[208]

     However, Biersteker joined critics of MNC opera-
tions in arguing that multinationals, in some industries, may well have encouraged inappropriate consumption patterns by way of taste creation. Specifically, he mentioned vitamins, skin lighteners, soft
drinks, cosmetics, and many pharmaceutical and
health-related products that are not only expensive

but also have no prior substitutes and a highly questionable substantive value. More important, through extensive advertising and marketing techniques, multinationals have encouraged the consumption of goods rejected in North America and Western Europe, partly because of their potential danger and partly because they are of lower substantive value. For example, after being banned as potentially dangerous in the markets of Western Europe and North America, as detailed research reveals that they are a potential source of cancer, artificial sweeteners and preservatives containing cyclamates appeared in large quantities on the Nigerian market. Again, color television sets rejected from markets in North America and Western Europe because of their large and potentially harmful emissions of radiation (a potential source of skin cancer) were similarly marketed in Nigeria.[209] To be sure, in the wake of the oil boom (or is it oil doom?), and as a result of salary increases recommended by the Udoji Commission and Udoji salary arrears approved by the Gowon regime, Nigeria became a dumping ground for various brands of electronic goods and household appliances such as transistor radios, stereo sets, tape recorders, videocassette recorders, freezers, refrigerators, cookers, fans, and color television sets (some of which were reconditioned or, simply put, substandard).

Undoubtedly, the economic costs of these products and the drain on Nigeria's foreign exchange earnings on crude oil are enormous. That Nigeria could be a dumping ground of color television sets that have been rejected from markets of North America and Western Europe seems to support the critics of the MNCs that they have engaged in the creation of tastes for inferior goods rejected from the industrialized countries of the North. Perhaps, MNCs doing business with Nigeria could not be blamed for the consumption of large quantities of color television sets;[210] after all, those who received the Udoji salary arrears should have saved or invested them in indigenized enterprises rather than spend them on consumer goods. Lamenting the spending spree of those who received the Udoji salary arrears, a popular columnist, Adetola Adeniyi, has this much to say:

> The whole of the metropolitan city of
> Lagos was thrown into an unprecedented
> fever. This time, the public, the
> private and even what a learned pro-
> fessor tagged "neutral" sectors, were
> all consumed in the ecstacy of reckless
> spending spree. All the electronic
> shops in Lagos . . . look as if burgled.
> TV sets, radios, cookers, fans and
> other types of both electrical and
> electronic appliances had been hurried-
> ly cleared by beneficiaries of Chief
> Jerome Udoji's generous gifts.[211]

To sum up, Third World countries are concerned,
first, about the effects of the marketing practices
of MNC subsidiaries and product differentiation,
namely, shaping or distorting local tastes, and creating a form of cultural dependency. Second, developing countries are concerned that MNCs stimulate
demands for types of products too sophisticated for,
or otherwise inappropriate to, a poor country's
stage of development. Indeed, developing countries
have asserted that MNC subsidiaries produce inappropriate products that are too sophisticated and too
elaborately packaged to meet the needs of the masses
of the people, those who constitute more than 90 percent of the population. For example, critics of the
MNC have often referred to the promotion of baby
formulas for newborn children as a substitute for
breast-feeding; they have also referred to the highly advertised soft drinks based on imported ingredi-
ents or imported technology. Perhaps the undesirable consumption patterns encouraged by MNCs through
their advertising practices and product differentiation (brand names and trademarks) may be more a reflection of an existing uneven distribution of wealth,
income, and privilege in poor Third World countries
than of the effects of MNCs' operations.[212]

MNCs AND TRANSFER OF TECHNOLOGY

It has been said that the MNC is the main vehicle for the transfer of technology to developing

countries. While this view has been challenged by
several critical studies on the political economy of
MNCs, another controversy centers on the appropriateness of the technology so transferred--"technology"
here used in a broad sense to include the nature and
specification of what is produced and the techniques
of production. On the one hand are those who argue
that it is only through DFI or licensing agreements
that developing countries can acquire the technology
and know-how which is a sine qua non for rapid development. On the other hand are those who argue that
MNCs transfer (to developing countries) technology
that is inappropriate, obsolete, overpriced, and inconsistent with the factor endowments of developing
countries. Those who claim that multinationals can
make a meaningful, indeed, significant contribution
to raising the foreign exchange earnings of developing countries through their ability to export, particularly manufactured goods, overlook certain fundamental considerations: (1) Would MNC manufacturing subsidiaries of the same MNC parent compete with
each other through exports? (2) Even where MNC parents have complementary production between subsidiaries so that intrafirm exports and imports are desir-
able, what are the prices on such exports and imports?
(3) Besides the exporting by MNC subsidiaries, what
impact does the licensing of technology by MNC subsidiaries to domestic enterprises have on the latter's ability to export? Let us first examine the
export performance of MNC subsidiaries in developing
countries.

The fact that MNC subsidiaries have the technological and marketing prerequisites does not mean
that they will export from Third World host states.
This is because, and as various studies on transfer
of technology contracts between MNC parents and MNC
subsidiaries and between MNC subsidiaries and domestic firms reveal, MNC subsidiaries are prohibited by
their parents from engaging in exporting. For example, 79 percent of MNC subsidiaries in the member
states of the Andean Common Market were prohibited
by their parents from using the technology so transferred in the production of goods for exports.[213] This
practice is by no means unique to the member states
of the Andean Common Market. To be sure, several

studies have revealed that U.S. manufacturing subsidiaries in Latin America on the average export
less than 10 percent of their total sales; in Europe,
the average stood at about 25 percent.[214]   In fact,
exports by U.S. manufacturing subsidiaries to third
countries remained at 14 percent of total sales in
1967 and 1968, the same percentage as in 1965. Local
sales were 78 percent of the total in 1968, compared
to 82 percent in 1965.[215]   Again, it is true that
U.S. manufacturing subsidiaries in Latin America account for some two-fifths of the region's manufactured exports.   One should not conclude that these
subsidiaries are making a positive impact on the region's balance-of-payments situation.   This is because these exports constitute only 16.6 percent of
the region's total exports, and well over 50 percent
of the exports come from Brazil, Mexico, and Argentina,[216] three of the so-called newly industrializing
countries (NICs), indeed, the same developing countries that are able to attract much DFI (i.e., from
MNCs) and have been able to borrow from the world
capital markets.   What is significant about MNC export performance in these NICs is that compared with
domestic enterprises, "MNC subsidiaries performed
significantly better _only_ in these three countries
and _only_ in terms of export sales to other Latin
American countries."[217]   More important,

> in contrast, for exports to the rest
> of the world, where one would expect
> the technological and marketing su-
> periority of the MNCs to be most cru-
> cial, the export performance was _not_
> _significantly_ different from domestic
> enterprises.   For the remaining coun-
> tries of the region, the MNCs were out-
> performed on exports to the rest of
> the world by firms which had domestic
> participation, while on exports to
> other Latin American countries the
> MNCs performed no differently than
> their domestic counterparts.[218]

When we examined the contributions of MNCs to
the balance-of-payments situations of Third World

host states, references were made to the notions of transfer pricing, overpricing of imports, and underpricing of exports. A study by Ronald Muller and Richard Morgenstern of the export pricing of several manufacturing subsidiaries in Argentina, Brazil, Mexico, and Venezuela has revealed the following: (1) 75 percent of these enterprises sold exports to other subsidiaries of the same parent companies; (2) the average underpricing of exports by these subsidiaries stood at some 40 percent; and (3) the bulk of these exports went to the region. And, in six other Latin American countries where MNCs were exporting to subsidiaries in third countries, the average underpricing of exports stood at 50 percent.[219]

Just how is technology transferred to developing countries between MNCs and domestic enterprises and/or between parent companies (MNCs) and their subsidiaries? First, as noted earlier in this chapter, technology may form part of the initial DFI package by the MNC. Second, technology may be transferred under license or through management/sales contracts to the developing country through permission to use brand names or through joint ventures between MNC subsidiaries and domestic enterprises or between MNC subsidiaries and host governments. Third, technology may be transferred as part of technical assistance programs under bilateral and multilateral agreements.

A close look at transfer of technology contracts between the licensees and licensers in several developing countries has shown that in most cases there are total prohibitions on using the technology so transferred in the production of goods for exports. A study based on 409 "transfer of technology" contracts in the member states of the Andean Common Market[220] showed that 92 percent of domestic-owned enterprises were totally prohibited from using technology transferred for producing goods for exports while 79 percent of MNC subsidiaries were prohibited from exporting by their parent companies although they have the technological and marketing prerequisites.[221] These restrictive business practices are not unique to member states of the Andean Common Market. Indeed, similar results have been revealed by government and United Nations studies in several developing countries including India, Pakistan, Mexico, Iran, and the Philippines.[222]

The restrictive clauses in the transfer of technology contracts, namely, the so-called tie-in clauses, require or oblige the licensee (MNC subsidiaries or domestic enterprises) to purchase materials, components, intermediate parts, and equipment from the licenser (parent companies or MNC subsidiaries) and often at excessive fees.[223] Other contracts include limitation of sales to the domestic market or designated foreign markets and grantback provisions (namely, provisions giving the licenser all rights to improvements). Additionally, the licenser can determine final selling prices and volume of export plus select key personnel in the licensee's business. For example, the Andean Common Market study on transfer of technology contracts revealed that 67 percent of the contracts had tie-in clauses. Similar findings have been reported with respect to other countries, including India and Pakistan. In fact, the practice of entrenching tie-in clauses in transfer of technology contracts seems to be part of the day-to-day operational behavior of MNCs in developing countries.[224] While this practice has been condemned by many critics as well as many international forums, particularly the United Nations Conference on Trade and Development, it could be argued, first, the licensers require licensees to purchase raw materials from them in order to ensure consistent product quality; second, not only is ensuring product quality significant to MNC subsidiaries or parent companies, a tie-in clause entrenched in a licensing agreement "is a matter of keeping one's recipe to oneself." Third, the weak bargaining position of the buyer (either the domestic firm or state-owned company) may enable the seller (MNC parent or MNC subsidiary) to impose all sorts of restrictive conditions on the licensee (domestic firm or state-owned company).

However, in many of the transfer of technology contracts permitting some exports outside host states or to designated countries, namely, where the contracts are liberal (whatever that term means), the effect was really total export prohibition, since

the contracts may limit and have limited the licensee
to a relatively small market in which the MNCs had
little or no interest; alternatively, the contracts
may limit or may have limited exports to distant
countries that the licensees could never hope to
penetrate.

In fact, exports from developing countries had
been greatest in sectors where MNC involvement is
small. This conclusion is derived from several
studies on the role of MNCs in the manufacturing exports of developing countries. For example, it has
been estimated that MNCs account for 15 percent of
the manufacturing exports of developing countries,
and, at that time, ten developing countries accounted
for nearly 80 percent of imports of manufactured
goods by DMEs from developing countries. Five of
these countries, namely, Brazil, Hong Kong, Mexico,
Singapore, and South Korea, along with Greece, Portugal, Spain, Turkey, and Yugoslavia, are among the
NICs whose share in the total imports of manufactured goods to OECD countries increased by more than
300 percent between 1963 and 1977, that is, from 2.5
percent to more than 8 percent. However, of the top
50 exports of manufactured goods in 1976 accounting
for about four-fifths of these countries' exports,
multinationals were only actively involved in about
one-quarter. More significant, these exports included those most competitive to those produced in
OECD countries, notably, textiles, clothing, and
leather goods.[225]

To be sure, another study estimated that MNC
manufacturing subsidiaries account for only about 5
percent of the exports of textiles and clothing while
the percentage of exports for leather goods is even
lower. The one sector dominated by multinationals
is electrical machinery and electronics, the exports
of which rose by 46 percent between 1967 and 1974.
This should not be interpreted to mean that multinationals do not influence the extent and direction of
exports, because they do, particularly those of
Japanese origin. In any event, the figures shown in
Table 3.21 show that in six industries in which NICs
are gaining increased prominence in world trade,
U.S.-related party imports, mainly from U.S. subsidiaries to their parent firms, account for the
major proportion of all imports.[226]

TABLE 3.21

United States-Related Party Imports as a Percentage of Total Imports of Selected
Manufactured Goods from Selected Newly Industrialized Countries 1977

Country	Textiles 65[a]	Nonelectrical Machinery 71[a]	Electrical Machinery 72[a]	Clothing 84[a]	Footwear 85[a]	Scientific Instruments 86[a]	Total Manufacturing
Argentina	0.5	39.1	76.1	2.9	0.8	10.0	9.2
Brazil	9.2	59.9	95.3	18.0	0.5	38.4	38.4
Colombia	1.5	16.8	3.9	15.7	81.2	87.8	14.1
Greece	3.7	52.2	99.1	5.0	0.8	2.2	7.8
Haiti	2.9	33.7	36.5	24.8	77.2	97.9	28.4
Hong Kong	4.9	68.5	43.4	3.4	3.6	30.4	18.1
India	6.1	30.5	58.7	15.8	6.1	16.7	10.1
Ireland	36.3	78.5	77.8	8.3	42.2	91.7	59.0
Israel	18.9	32.8	62.9	14.0	0.0	13.0	18.2
Malaysia	0.2	83.2	97.0	1.9	0.0	91.9	87.9
Mexico	9.6	87.8	95.6	68.0	60.9	93.6	71.0
Philippines	28.9	69.7	31.7	53.4	0.0	27.0	47.5
Portugal	2.8	24.7	78.4	0.4	0.2	32.5	12.5
Singapore	4.3	90.5	97.0	0.5	0.0	85.3	83.3
South Korea	5.5	64.2	67.3	7.1	1.8	12.1	19.7
Spain	1.5	36.3	32.6	3.7	10.1	7.8	24.1
Taiwan	13.1	19.3	58.1	1.2	3.1	67.1	20.5
Yugoslavia	0.1	14.0	2.0	2.3	2.2	3.6	4.9
Total (All Developing Countries)	7.8	63.5	75.2	11.5	4.4	51.2	37.0

[a]SITC category.

Source: Gerald K. Helleiner, "Transnational Corporations and Trade Structure," University of Toronto, Toronto, 1979, Mimeo.

Overall, as importers of private foreign capital and technology, Third World countries can be divided into four fairly distinct groups. The first consists of member states of the Organisation of Petroleum Exporting Countries that, in 1975, accounted for 23 percent of DFI in the Third World and whose technology imports were heavily biased toward petroleum and related activities. The second group, accounting for 13 percent of DFI, consists of the so-called tax-haven countries, having little or no technology transfer. Included in the third group are the larger and NICs whose imports of technology are directed largely to the manufacturing sector; 11 of these countries accounted for 42 percent of DFI in 1975.[227] In the fourth group are countries that attract private foreign capital and technology to specialized resource sectors as well as countries embarking on import-substitution industrialization.

In general, a greater part of DFI by MNCs in developing countries has been directed toward import-substitution and resource-based activities, except in Southern Europe and South East Asia where DFI has been directed to the production of labor-intensive products and/or labor-intensive processes or high/ medium technology products. Until the mid-1970s, most of the growth of manufacturing exports from NICs was in industries in which MNCs did not generally play a dominant role. Additionally, the revealed comparative advantage of developing countries, as Dunning rightly puts it, has improved most significantly in sectors in which MNC involvement is minimal; the exceptions include electrical machinery and photographic supplies.[228]

The interest of the MNC in restricting competition (which is one major reason for placing restrictions on a licensee's exports) is obvious. Equally obvious is the adverse effect on poor developing countries seeking to earn scarce foreign exchange by exporting manufactured goods through a program of import-substitution industrialization. It is interesting to note that while the so-called tie-in clause is a basic violation of the antitrust laws (restraint of trade) of MNCs' home states, particularly the United States, restrictive business practices appear to be the standard routine in several Third World countries. The fact that the legal institutions of developing countries are yet to cope with these problems (among other problems) strongly underlines the differences in the oligopolistic power of MNCs in the industrialized countries of the North versus the agrarian countries of the South. Is it then not strange that when the political leaders of the DMEs are asking and encouraging developing countries to export more manufactured goods, MNCs based in North America and Western Europe are making it not only difficult but also virtually impossible for developing countries to enter into the manufactured export market?

Because Third World countries are, in general, underdeveloped, a subject of the discussion much earlier in this chapter and because the bargaining power of developing countries vis-à-vis MNCs is relatively weak, the technology that MNCs transfer, more often than not, is overpriced and obsolete. The technology often transferred by MNCs to Third World countries is obsolete because some MNCs are motivated to invest in areas where they may still retain a competitive, technological advantage, which is saying that such DFIs are made because of the dynamics of the foreign market for MNCs' products. These motivations are best summarized in the concept of the product life cycle. The theory of the product cycle states that, given a competitive system, no corporation can expect to retain a technological lead for very long. This means that a multinational will expand to new markets to retain its competitive advantage in its existing markets. This expansion into new markets usually entails the introduction or production of products that are no longer competitive in other markets, notably, DMEs. Hans Singer and Javed Ansari have noted:

> Parent firms prefer to issue licences
> for goods with short product cycles
> (e.g. pharmaceuticals). In underde-
> veloped areas, licensing is generally
> easy for the multinational, since the
> technological gap between it and the
> licensee is great and (usually) offers
> no threat to the corporation's techno-
> logical leadership.[229]

Speaking on a similar issue, Jose Epstein notes, and this is very significant, that poor countries are likely to receive "processes which elsewhere are being abandoned or on the verge of being abandoned."[230] This phenomenon, according to many observers of MNCs' operations in developing countries,[231] is more noticeable with respect to consumer goods, notably, refrigerators, transistor radios, washing machines, pharmaceuticals, and, more recently, automobiles. For example, the Colgate-Palmolive Company introduced into African markets Colgate With Gardol, a product that has long been replaced by Colgate With MFP Fluoride in the U.S. market because it was no longer competitive. In essence, Colgate With Gardol has been introduced into African markets where it can retain its competitive advantage.[232] As Barnet and Muller have put it succinctly, "Distributing the last generation's technology to poor countries is a good way to prolong its profitable life."[233]

Just as observers of MNC operations have noted that MNCs transfer obsolete technology to developing countries, detailed studies in Mexico and Colombia, among other Third World countries, have also revealed overpricing of technology by MNCs, and, according to some top executives of MNC subsidiaries as well as investigations conducted in some Latin American and African countries (including Nigeria), overpricing of technology by MNCs is standard practice. From Mexico are reported cases of used or secondhand technology transferred to MNC subsidiaries and being declared as new equipment or valuated at prices much higher than could have been obtained on independent markets.[234] A detailed study by Vaitsos also revealed several cases of excessive overpricing of technology in Colombia. In one case, an MNC (a parent MNC) sold machinery to its own subsidiary at a price 30 percent higher than it was charging a Colombian independent company; and in another case, an MNC subsidiary in the paper industry applied for a permit to import used machinery whose value was put at $1.8 million. Because Colombia is a victim of various sharp business practices by MNCs, a government agency asked for international competitive bids for new models of the same machinery. On investigation, it found that the going price for new models was 50 percent less than what the parent MNC was charging its subsidiary for used models. In essence, the true value of the used machinery stood at $1.2 million.[235]

How does one explain overpricing of technology transferred to poor developing countries by MNCs either as part of a DFI package or under license, through management/sales contracts or as part of technical assistance programs? According to Barnet and Muller, one reason is "to produce politically attractive financial statements. It is an easy way to make one's investment look bigger and one's profits . . . smaller."[236] Second, and more significant, buyers of technology seem to be ignorant of international markets of technology vis-à-vis their contemporaries in the DMEs. Third, technology seems to be much overpriced in developing countries because of inadequate sources of technology. Sanjaya Lall has put the issue succinctly: "the absence of adequate knowledge on the part of the buyer . . . may enable them [MNCs] to charge monopolistic prices."[237] Fourth, because developing countries (DCs) are very much concerned about purchasing technology, whether patented or unpatented, and because parent MNCs tend to regard technology as being sold under monopolistic or oligopolistic conditions, it was small wonder then that technology is often being overpriced. To be sure, "If one regards the technology market as one with very little knowledge on [the] part of the buyer and strict monopolistic control on [the] part of the sellor, it is easy to understand why the price set on the technology may favour the sellor."[238] In any event, whatever reason that can be adduced for overpricing technology, there is no doubt that the practice helps to explain, at least in part, why the gap between the industrialized countries of the North and the agrarian countries of the South is yawning rather than closing.

Two other fundamental issues relating to the technological contribution of MNCs to Third World development lend themselves for examination: (1) appropriateness of technology and extent of technology transfer and (2) cost of technology so transferred to DCs. Let us start with the second issue.

Cost of Technology Transfer

The Advanced Learners' Dictionary defines cost
as the "price (to be) paid for a thing." The Double-
day Roget's Thesaurus in Dictionary Form sees cost
as (1) "price, charge, expense, expenditure, outlay,
rate, figure, amount; damage, tab, sum" and (2) "suf-
fering, detriment, penalty, expense, damage, pain,
sacrifice." Thus, the cost of technology means the
"price (to be) paid for" technology transferred to
DCs (in whatever form) or the "expense" and "penalty"
paid or the "sacrifice" made by DCs for importing
technology from DMEs. Accordingly, an examination
of the cost of technology transfer to DCs should include the following: (1) appropriateness and extent
of technology transfer and (2) impact on the balance
of payments.

Critics of the MNC, for example, have often
questioned the appropriateness of the production
techniques or processes used by MNCs in DCs. The
basic question being asked is: Are production techniques or processes capital intensive or labor intensive? In several case studies, their conclusions,
which seem to be supported by the present study, are
that the production techniques being used by MNC manufacturing subsidiaries are inappropriate, or at best
inconsistent with the factor endowments of DCs.
Simply put, critics of MNC operations contend that
MNC operations in several cases are capital intensive
and that their production processes are appropriate
and best suited to labor-poor rather than labor-rich
economies such as DCs.

Several reasons have been advanced by neoconventional scholars to justify the use of capital-
intensive production techniques by MNC manufacturing
subsidiaries. Reference has already been made to
some of these reasons in this chapter. In addition,
critics of MNCs in DCs--and these include labor/
students' leaders, academics, top officials, and
politicians--contend that the effect of MNC operations in many cases is:

1. to aggravate income inequalities;
2. to exacerbate the unemployment problem;

3. to create or perpetuate a form of sociocultural dependency;
4. to worsen the balance of payments of Third World host states through excessive capital transfers to MNC home states (as a result of overpricing technology, royalties, and fees, to mention but a few; and
5. to create enclave economies.

We have already examined the effects of MNC operations as they relate to 1, 2, 3, and partly 4 (with respect to the incidence of transfer pricing). We will examine item 5 later. Let us, for the moment, examine in detail the cost of technology transfer as it relates to the balance of payments of the host state.

Table 1.2 indicates royalty payments and management/service fees for patents, licenses, brand names, know-how, and trademarks by Argentina, Brazil, Colombia, Mexico, Nigeria, and Sri Lanka (Ceylon) and their relationship to gross domestic product (GDP) and export earnings. Royalty payments and fees by these six DCs represent 7 percent of their combined exports and a little more than half of 1 percent of their combined GDP.[239] According to a United Nations study, royalty payments and fees by 13 DCs representing 65 percent of the total population and 56 percent of the total GDP of DCs stood at approximately $1.5 billion, namely, more than 50 percent of the total flow of DFI to DCs.[240] To be sure, the global total of royalty payments and fees ranges between $3 billion and $5 billion annually; this figure, according to a study, may be higher, because of the possibilities of transfer pricing.[241]

Other studies have revealed huge capital transfers from DCs to MNC home states. According to John Dunning, receipts by some leading OECD countries[242] for technology exports to DCs increased by 15 percent annually during the 1970s.[243] In 1975, about 80 percent of all receipts of royalties and fees by the United States originated from the sale of technology by U.S. foreign subsidiaries.[244] In 1978, royalty payments and fees for technology exports to DCs by seven leading OECD countries stood at $2 billion, namely, 17.9 percent of the total flow of DFI.

Table 3.22 shows that royalties and fees received by U.S.-based MNCs from their subsidiaries have grown rapidly in recent years. In 1964, royalty payments and fees (excluding film rentals) stood at $756 million; they rose to $1.25 billion in 1968 and $1.46 billion in 1969. From Latin American republics and other Western Hemisphere countries, royalty payments and fees stood at $148 million in 1964 and rose to $226 million in 1968 and $239 million in 1969. In areas other than Canada, Western Europe, and Eastern Europe, these payments stood at $140 million in 1964, $248 million in 1968, and $275 million in 1969. Altogether, royalty payments and fees received by U.S.-based MNCs from their subsidiaries in areas other than Canada and Western Europe (increasingly sensitive to domination by U.S.-based MNCs) as well as Eastern Europe stood at $288 million in 1964, $474 million in 1968, and $514 million in 1969.[245]

Obviously, royalty payments and fees to U.S. multinationals by U.S. foreign affiliates cannot but improve U.S. balance of payments.[246] These receipts are used to defray some of the expenses borne by U.S. multinationals for R and D of new products and processes. They also help defray administrative expenses and those incurred by parent companies on behalf of their affiliates.

We have stated in Chapter 1 that royalty payments by Mexico in 1968 for technology imports by MNC subsidiaries (operating in Mexico) as well as Mexican enterprises stood at $200 million, representing 0.76 percent of Mexico's GDP and 15.9 percent of export earnings. Although Mexico has a tradition for regulating DFI, thanks to the Mexican Revolution and the Mexican Constitution of 1917,[247] one major reason that can be advanced for Mexican radical response to the presence of DFI in the manufacturing sector in the 1970s (manifested in The Law to Promote Mexican Investment and Regulate Foreign Investment)[248] was its impact on the balance of payments. The first factor concerns the propensity of foreign-owned enterprises to import capital equipment. Thus, as a percentage of sales, imports by foreign firms were more than twice as great as by Mexican enterprises (majority ownership),[249] although exports of foreign firms were only marginally greater

TABLE 3.22

Receipts of Royalties and Fees[a] by United States Subsidiaries by Areas
($ million)

Areas	1964			1968[b]			1969[c]		
	Royalties, License Fees, and Rentals	Management Fees and Service Charge	Total	Royalties, License Fees, and Rentals	Management Fees and Service Charge	Total	Royalties, License Fees, and Rentals	Management Fees and Service Charge	Total
All Areas	264	492	756	522	724	1,246	641	729	1,369
Europe	147	159	306	294	217	511	381	207	588
European Economic Community	84	66	150	173	96	269	215	84	299
Other Europe Including United Kingdom	13	93	155	121	121	242	165	123	289
Latin American Republics and Other Western Hemisphere Countries	36	112	148	73	153	226	74	165	239
Canada	41	121	162	77	184	261	92	176	268
Other Areas	40	99	139 (140)[d]	78	170	248	94	181	275

aExcludes foreign film rentals.
bRevised.
cPreliminary.
dFigures actually add up to $140 million.

Source: David T. Devlin and George R. Kruer, "The International Investment Position of the United States: Developments in 1969," Survey of Current Business (U.S. Department of Commerce) 50 (1970): 34.

168

than those of Mexican firms. Second, some income of
foreign enterprises is usually remitted abroad, partly as earnings and partly as payments for royalties,
licenses, and technical assistance. As the Report
of the U.S. Senate Subcommittee on Multinational
Corporations shows,[250] such payments are consistently higher for foreign firms than for Mexican or
state-owned enterprises, as shown in Table 3.23.[251]
Next, and particularly with respect to some manufacturing industries, such "foreign payments went more
for trademark licenses and associated management
know-how than for 'hard' technology patents."[252]
What is significant about technology transfer to
Mexico like other DCs such as Bolivia, Colombia,
India, Peru, Philippines, Pakistan, Kuwait, and El
Salvador is that transfer of technology contracts
totally prohibited the use of the technology for
producing goods for exports or restricted exports to
designated markets that the licensees could never
hope to penetrate. Additionally, these restrictions
were more severe with respect to domestic enterprises
than to MNC subsidiaries. This, then, explains the
raison d'être for the Mexican law on investment
and/or divestment of 1973.

Appropriateness and Extent of Technology Transfers

Despite the massive literature on "appropriate"
technology,[253] the precise definition of "appropriate"
technology is not clear; additionally, the "exact
scope for its efficient (and commercially viable)
application in different branches of manufacturing
industry has not been delineated."[254] To some scholars, appropriateness may mean a greater use of labor
and local materials, given the nature of the product;
to others, it may mean the use of the most labor-
intensive technique available with which a given
product may be manufactured; and yet to others, it
may mean a more appropriate product made with a
technique that is unknown but needs to be developed.[255] In essence, the choice of definition
clearly depends on the user's value judgment.

TABLE 3.23

Payments for Importation of Technology in Mexico by Sector and Ownership 1971

Sector	Ownership			
	Foreign	Mexican	State Owned	Total
Food	7.6	2.7	3.0	6.6
Beverage	6.3	3.0	--	5.6
Tobacco	0.4	--	--	0.4
Chemicals, Industrial	12.8	12.3	2.0	12.6
Chemicals, Pharmaceutical	23.9	15.9	--	22.2
Electronic Machinery	11.7	9.7	--	11.3
Transport Equipment	9.9	5.2	1.4	8.9
Total, All Manufacturing	100.0	100.0	100.0	100.0
($ thousand)	(114,760.2)	(28,080.8)		

Source: Van R. Whiting, "International Aspects of National Regulation: Transnationals and the State in Mexico, 1970-1978," paper presented at the 20th Annual Convention of the International Studies Association, Toronto, March 21-23, 1979, p. 31.

In any event, critics of MNCs assert that MNCs tend to introduce production techniques that are inappropriate, indeed inconsistent, with the factor endowments of DCs. Simply put, critics contend that MNCs employ production techniques that are ill-suited to labor-rich DCs but best-suited to labor-poor DMEs. This is because most R and D conducted by parent MNCs is undertaken in MNCs' home states rather than in Third World host states. Critics also contend that MNCs produce inappropriate products that are not only too sophisticated and too highly designed but also too elaborately packaged to meet the consumption demands or needs of the masses.[256] To be sure, much of MNC technology is for the production of high-ticket, sophisticated consumer goods, which is saying that the consumption patterns of the elite groups in the periphery (the DCs) are strongly influenced by tastes created by MNCs, whose head offices are located in the center (the DMEs). In essence, some of the technology supplied by MNCs is undesirable, because it introduces the wrong sets of products (such as baby formulas, soft drinks, artificial sweeteners and preservatives, skin lighteners, cosmetics, and synthetics); some are undesirable, not only because they are overpriced but also because they use an inappropriate combination of factors.[257]

However, while neoconventional scholars do not deny critics' claims that most R and D by MNCs takes place in their home states (the DMEs), they disagree, as Biersteker notes, "with the critical proposition that a complete transfer of production process takes place. Rather, they contend considerable adaptation takes place."[258] To be sure, while they agree with the view that some production techniques employed by MNCs are relatively capital intensive, they (neoconventional scholars) argue that most of these techniques are adapted so that they are not significantly more capital intensive than the production techniques employed by domestic enterprises, which is saying that the MNCs' critics claim that MNCs employ more capital-intensive technologies than their domestic competitors is inconclusive.

In essence, the critical questions are threefold. First, has the adaptation of production

techniques/processes taken place as claimed by neoconventional scholars? If the answer is no, what
reasons can we adduce for nonadaptation? Again, why
do MNCs transfer inappropriate technologies to DCs
or why are appropriate technologies not used by MNCs
in DCs? Second, what reasons can we adduce for the
limited contribution to the local economy of the
technology transferred by MNCs or their subsidiaries?
Third, why are R and D facilities located in MNCs'
home states rather than in host states (DCs)?

Whether MNCs can modify products or production
processes to reflect local circumstances depends, we
believe, on many variables including the type of
product and technology, the socioeconomic environment of the particular state, and the view of the
parent MNC, namely, how its subsidiary can function
most efficiently and profitably over the long term.
In general, fewer MNCs appear willing to adapt their
products than to modify their production processes.
Product adaptation is greatest among manufacturers
of consumer goods. Data on U.S.-based MNCs show
that of their R and D, only 0.5 percent out of 8
percent undertaken outside the United States in 1970
was undertaken in developing countries. According
to an OECD study,[259] most R and D undertaken by U.S.
MNCs in DCs was concentrated in a number of industrial branches having a high level of product differentiation in consumer goods or specific requirements for adaptation to local conditions or production factors. These include World Health Organisation tropical drugs program, some tire development
(in India and the Philippines), as well as product
adaptation in toiletries, food products, and agricultural and industrial machinery. Additionally,
aside from making modifications to reflect variations in tastes, customs, and socioeconomic environment in host states (for example, MNCs may find it
cheaper and more convenient to use local resources
than to import materials or they may be forced by
local-content requirements to use local inputs), MNC
manufacturing subsidiaries, more often than not,
alter their products to take advantage of local resources, the use of which would hardly result in any
reduction of the quality of the goods produced.

By and large, and as many studies have shown,[260] many MNCs make only minor modifications in their products or production processes because of their desire to ensure uniform quality. Although minor changes or modifications in the automotive and heavy machinery industries may be made, and accessories may vary, the basic product is standardized in order to facilitate servicing on a worldwide basis. In general, many pharmaceutical companies have little scope for adaptation, partly because the drugs eventually put on sale are the result of expensive research and partly because these corporations depend on high standards of quality to ensure effectiveness. In fact, the ability of pharmaceutical companies and electronics companies to employ labor in the host state is limited to the final assembly or the final packaging stage. For example, electronics firms believe that final assembly can more readily be adapted to reflect local skill levels and the availability of cheap labor, although it is apparent that their technical processes in the manufacturing of components require uniformity.

The critical proposition that considerable adaptation of production processes by MNCs has not taken place in Third World host states has been confirmed not only by a study sponsored by the Committee for Economic Development[261] but also by Biersteker's study on Nigeria.[262] According to Biersteker,

> Of the multinationals surveyed, about
> 25 percent of those responding suggested that adaptations have been made
> in installed machinery to adjust to
> local conditions. Only five of the
> nineteen firms responding to this
> question[263] had made any adaptations
> to the local climate, employment conditions, raw materials or marketing
> requirements in Nigeria.[264]

Although he observes that slightly more than 40 percent of Nigerian companies responding to the survey (5 out of 12) had made adaptations, meaning that domestic enterprises experience similar economic and technological constraints as MNCs, he concludes that the MNCs "appear to make fewer adjustments and adaptations to installed machinery" than do domestic enterprises. Biersteker's conclusion has been reached by other studies on Nigeria. According to Gerald Helleiner, "Nigerian manufacturing technology, like that of other underdeveloped areas, seems to have been imported from abroad without major modifications,"[265] and with respect to the country's first oil refinery, Terisa Turner found very little adaptation.[266]

The fact that considerable adaptation has not been made by MNCs in their production processes does not mean that MNCs are unwilling to make such adjustments and adaptations. Several MNCs would use local raw materials only if the materials meet stringent quality specifications. In essence, fewer MNCs make adjustments and adaptations because of the need to maintain uniform quality. According to Frank, "the appeal of their products is precisely that they are standardized goods with a reputation for uniform quality."[267] Second, there are market scale and cost considerations. To be sure, MNCs are unlikely to develop a new product or modify an existing one unless the market is sufficiently large enough to permit them to recover operating costs. More fundamental, fewer MNCs make adjustments and adaptations simply because the technologies they employ are developed in the DMEs.

Therefore, although some studies have shown that some MNCs are willing to make adjustments and adaptations in their production processes, in general, fewer MNCs make such adjustments and adaptations, first, because of the need to maintain uniform quality; second, because market-scale and cost considerations militate against such adaptations; and, third, and above all, because the technologies they employ are developed in the DMEs. In essence, the fact that considerable adaptation of production processes by MNCs has not taken place in Third World host states is understandable.

We have already advanced reasons why MNC subsidiaries employ capital-intensive technologies in their operations. At the risk of repetition, let us briefly examine reasons why appropriate technologies

are not used by MNCs in their Third World operations.
First, a range of technologies, combining labor and
capital in different proportions, simply does not
exist. Second, it is much more expensive to develop
labor-intensive technologies, and in any event, factor prices in DCs, more often than not, are distorted, so as to render capital artificially cheap.
Added to this is the fact that it is not feasible to
have labor-intensive technologies capable of performing great feats, such as production of transform-
ers, power generators, heavy chemicals, or machinery
requiring extreme precision.[268] Third, multinationals prefer to employ capital-intensive technologies,
partly to avoid shortage of certain skills and partly to reduce their exposure to labor-union activity.
Fourth, and more important, perhaps MNCs should not
be blamed for transferring inappropriate technologies to DCs, if only because local enterprises demand capital-intensive technologies.

What we have been saying is that the amount of
technology transferred by MNCs or their subsidiaries
to Third World countries is limited; it is limited
because MNCs want to retain monopoly over their
technology and because R and D efforts are concentrated in a few firms in MNC home states. While many
MNCs may have and do have local capabilities for
product testing and adaptation as well as quality
control, which have the potential for evolving into
substantial local R and D capabilities, MNCs generally do not have R and D facilities in DCs:[269]

1. The bulk of R and D is financed by parent MNCs.
2. R and D expenditures are overwhelmingly concentrated in the DMEs, namely, MNC home states. In
   1966 alone, only 6 percent of R and D budgets of
   U.S. manufacturing subsidiaries was spent abroad;
   namely, with a total R and D expenditure of $8.1
   billion, only $526 million was spent abroad. In
   1970, of R and D undertaken by U.S. multinationals, only 8 percent was undertaken outside the
   United States and only 0.5 percent in DCs. To be
   sure, the developing countries account for only 2
   percent of the world R and D compared with 12
   percent of world manufacturing production and 10
   percent of manufacturing exports.

3. While there is little R and D in pharmaceuticals in DCs, no extractive MNC has established R and D facilities in developing countries, although each situation is unique. For example, the three major U.S. aluminum corporations (Alcoa, Kaiser, and Reynolds) have all their R and D operations located in the United States.

4. It is true that manufacturing MNCs have established substantial applied R and D facilities in several DCs where there are large or rapidly growing markets, namely, in Argentina, Brazil, India, Mexico, Nigeria, and Saudi Arabia. These facilities are more geared toward solving MNC subsidiaries' particular problems. As Dunning observed, "where foreign affiliates have established R & D facilities, these have usually been either for purely development programmes or as part of integrated R & D strategy of the MNE."[270]

Although MNCs (for example, two manufacturing subsidiaries in India) may be forced by local partners or host governments to create indigenous R and D institutions and although several manufacturing MNCs agreed that an indigenous R and D may be necessary when the local government "requires substantial product development, testing, and adaptation,"[271] MNCs have a strong tendency to locate R and D facilities in their home states, and for several reasons too. First, because some MNCs are engrossed in ensuring that their products meet uniform specifications, R and D in host states would simply duplicate R and D facilities in their home states. Second, the ability of MNCs to locate R and D facilities abroad is determined not only by the extent of the market, costs, and economics of scale but also by availability of skilled local personnel and adequate infrastructural facilities (for conducting R and D).[272] To be sure, part of the problem of DCs in developing indigenous R and D capability can be attributed to "brain drain" (the tendency of scientists, engineers, and other professionals to migrate from poor DCs to rich DMEs for a variety of reasons that need not detain us here)[273] and high costs of R and D (which are usually borne by MNC home governments). Third, and most important, for some MNCs, the need

for R and D in developing countries simply does not
arise, arguing that R and D facilities would be established in DCs "when it is technically advantageous
and cost-competitive."[274]

While the reasons explaining the tendency of
MNCs to locate R and D facilities in their home
states are valid, as an alternative to establishing
R and D facilities in Third World states, MNCs should
or could contribute financially or technologically
to local R and D facilities through specific training programs and direct financial contributions to
universities and research institutions for applied
research. The contributions of MNCs to local R and D
capability through training programs and skill development have been important, as one study demonstrates,[275] in some industries, namely, rubber tires,
petrochemicals, pharmaceuticals, constructional engineering, and hotels.

We have already noted that in spite of the im-
mense benefits derived by the host state from the
operations of extractive MNCs (in terms of contributions to government revenues, GDP, and foreign exchange earnings as well as local expenditure on
goods and services, to mention but a few), the employment potential of extractive MNCs is very limited, because the extractive industry by its very
nature tends to be capital intensive. By and large,
and this view is shared by critics and neoconventional scholars, the contributions of extractive
MNCs to the local economy are minimal. To be sure,
certain MNC operations have an enclave character,
namely that they have few backward or forward linkages to the local economy. While backward linkages
are the purchase of local inputs, forward linkages
are the domestic use of the company's output in further productive operations. We shall demonstrate
the limited contributions of MNCs to the national
(local) economies by drawing from the experience of
the Nigerian oil industry.

Meanwhile, examples of inadequate backward
linkages are the assembly of automobiles in several
Third World countries from components imported from
MNC home states and the packaging of pharmaceuticals
(and detergents) as well as food-related products
from material imported directly from former parent

companies or associated companies. With respect to
detergents, mention must be made of Lever Brothers
(Nigeria) Limited importing powdered soap directly
from Unilever, its former parent company in the
United Kingdom.[276] Leyland (Nigeria) Limited, Volkswagen of Nigeria Limited, and Peugeot Automobile
Nigeria Limited import practically all the components
for their Nigerian operations from the United Kingdom, the Federal Republic of Germany, and France,
respectively, that is, the home states of the "senior"
partners in the joint ventures, thanks to the Nigerian
Enterprises Promotion Act 1977. Perhaps this explains why "Made-in-Nigeria" automobiles/trucks are
much more expensive than those imported from MNC home
states.[277] Examples of inadequate forward linkages
are the export of ores without further local processing into metals and the export of logs without further local processing into plywood.

We have noted that despite some positive inputs to the host economy (in terms of employment,
government revenue, and foreign exchange), the contributions of extractive MNCs to the host economy
are very limited. For example, a major factor limiting the contributions of the aluminum industry to
host economies (Jamaica, Guyana, Guinea, Surinam,
and Sierra Leone) is that mining operations, as a
rule, are not integrated into the national economy;
if anything, they create enclave economies.[278] According to a study, the aluminum industry "evinces
tight vertical integration."[279] Only a small percentage of the total value of transactions for any
of the six major aluminum companies (Alcan, Alcoa,
Alusuisse, Kaiser, Pechiney Ugine Kuhlmann, and
Reynolds) takes place "outside the corporate networks."[280]

Put simply, few backward linkages to the host
economy exist, first, because production is exported
and, second, because the equipment required for mining is too technologically sophisticated to be manufactured locally. More important, "investment in
infrastructure is usually limited and specific to
the needs of the mining operations; and upgrading of
skills remains company-specific and tends not to be
disseminated throughout the economy."[281] In essence,
although host states may have derived some benefits
from the operations of MNCs,

> mining operations are most integrated
> into the worldwide operations of the
> parent company than into the economic
> system of the host-economy. The impli-
> cations of such a situation are that
> the enclave country not only foregoes
> substantial income but also the benefi-
> cial spin-off effects associated with
> advanced production.[282]

It was small wonder, then, that the Caribbean bauxite-
producing countries (for example, Guyana) wanted the
six major aluminum companies (for example, Alcan in
Guyana) to locate smelting facilities in their terri-
tories through joint ventures between host states
and MNC local subsidiaries.[283]

We have examined in this chapter the contribution of the Nigerian oil industry: creation of employment opportunities and availability of training
opportunities for Nigerians. Other benefits derived
include: (1) local expenditure on goods and services; (2) contributions to revenues, GDP, and foreign exchange earnings; and (3) supply of energy to
industry and commerce. Tables 3.24 and 3.25 show
local expenditure on goods and services and oil expenditure on goods and services. Aside from direct
contributions to government revenues (Table 3.26),
oil industry expenditure in Nigeria takes the form
of payments of wages and salaries, payments to local
(Nigerian and foreign) contractors, scholarships/
staff development program, local rents, and telecommunication charges, to mention but a few. Between
1938 and 1974, oil industry local expenditure on
goods and services stood at ₦ 950 million. During
the 1970-74 Development Plan period, expenditure on
these items totaled ₦ 566.4 million.

Table 3.26 shows that the oil industry accounts
for about 41 percent of GNP (45 percent of GDP). It
is true that the industry's value added helps in
boosting Nigeria's GDP. We tend to overlook the important fact that a substantial proportion of the industry's value added is in the form of factor pay-
ments--profits, dividends, interest, fees, and wages/
salaries of employees paid abroad--since the oil industry is dominated by private foreign capital. In

TABLE 3.24

Local Expenditure on Goods and Services 1967-70

(₦)

Goods and Services	1967-68	1968-69	1969-70
Materials and Supplies	5,481,336	2,865,444	6,951,192
Fuel and Power	2,586,806	2,111,814	4,099,138
Transport (Railway freight etc.)	2,766,224	887,838	1,357,706
Telecommunication Charges	158,800	170,966	221,458
Wages and Salaries	3,728,728	6,259,558	9,696,120
Compensation on Farmland, etc.	819,120	459,860	494,520
Local Rents	608,606	744,844	1,519,870
Scholarships and Training	100,650	118,334	197,998
Donations and Subventions	5,930	81,860	78,686
Harbor and Related Dues	2,780,726	2,524,108	7,164,600
Local Payments to Contractors			
Nigerians	2,733,564	3,169,506	2,459,948
Expatriates	16,128,000	10,918,738	21,775,328
Other Local Expenditure[a]	10,158,228	1,346,646	6,249,128
Total	48,056,718	31,709,516	62,265,692

[a]Excludes direct payments to the government.

Source: S. A. Madujibeya, "Oil and Nigeria's Economic Development" African Affairs 75 (1976): 314.

TABLE 3.25

Oil Industry Expenditure on Goods and Services 1938-74

(₦ million)

Year	Imports of Goods and Services	Local Expenditure on Goods and Services	Total Expenditure on Goods and Services
1938-62	120.2	81.4	201.6
1963	21.2	19.6	40.8
1964	48.0	27.0	75.0
1965	71.4	46.4	117.8
1966	116.0	66.6	182.6
1967	98.0	58.4	156.4
1968	76.2	25.0	101.2
1969	121.6	57.8	179.4
1970	133.6	96.8	230.4
1971	164.2	113.2	277.4
1972	184.3	129.6	313.9
1973	252.1	121.7	373.8
1974	305.5	105.1	410.6
Total	1,712.3	948.6	2,660.9

Source: Central Bank of Nigeria, Annual Reports and Statements of Accounts (Lagos: Central Bank of Nigeria) (Various years).

181

TABLE 3.26

Oil Sector Contribution to the National Income 1974-80
(N million)

Contribution	1974-75	1975-76	1976-77	1977-78	1978-79	1979-80
1. Wages and Salaries Paid Locally	19.3	19.8	22.7	26.0	29.8	33.8
2. Wages and Salaries Paid Abroad	11.4	14.0	14.4	14.8	15.2	15.7
3. Government Revenue	4,346.4	4,804.9	5,328.5	5,894.9	6,528.1	7,231.3
4. Government Investment Income	1,134.9	1,258.8	1,392.9	1,547.7	1,711.5	1,927.2
5. Investment Income Paid Abroad	933.2	1,033.2	1,140.0	1,264.3	1,391.9	1,516.4
6. Value Added to GDP (at Current Factor Cost)	6,445.2	7,130.7	7,898.5	8,747.7	9,676.5	10,724.4
7. Value Added to GNP (Line 6 less Lines 2 and 5)	5,500.6	6,083.5	6,744.1	7,468.6	8,269.4	9,192.3
CONTRIBUTION TO GDP						
8. Total Nigeria GDP	14,410.7	16,288.9	18,608.8	21,512.5	25,131.1	29,664.8
Petroleum Value Added to GDP	6,445.2	7,130.7	7,898.5	8,747.7	9,676.5	10,724.4
as Percentage	44.7	43.8	42.4	40.7	38.5	36.2
CONTRIBUTION TO GNP						
9. Total Nigeria GNP	13,487.3	15,530.1	17,910.7	20,836.1	24,426.1	28,912.7
Petroleum Value Added to GNP	5,500.6	6,083.5	6,744.1	7,468.6	8,269.4	9,192.3
as Percentage	40.8	39.2	37.7	35.8	33.9	31.8

Source: S. A. Madujibeya, "Oil and Nigeria's Economic Development," African Affairs 75 (1976): 284-316.

essence, the Nigerian situation underlines the significant fact that there can be growth--measured by increases in GNP--without development.

Table 3.27 shows the contribution of the oil industry to government revenues in the post-civil war period to 1976-77 financial year, while Table 3.28 shows that the oil sector now accounts for the bulk of foreign exchange earnings--about 86.3 percent in 1974 compared with 15.7 percent in 1966.

TABLE 3.27

Oil Sector Contribution to Government
Revenue 1967-77
(N thousand)

Financial Year	Government Revenue	Oil Revenue	Share of the Oil Sector in Total Revenue
1967-68[a]	300,176	41,884	13.95
1968-69[b]	299,986	29,582	9.86
1969-70[b]	435,908	75,444	17.31
1970-71	755,605	196,390	25.99
1971-72	1,410,911	740,185	52.46
1972-73	1,389,911	576,151	41.45
1973-74	2,171,370	1,549,383	71.36
1974-75	5,177,063	4,183,816	80.81
1975-76[c]	5,252,297	4,568,425	86.98
1976-77[d]	5,756,328	4,833,713	83.97

[a]Excluding the three eastern states created in May 1967.
[b]Excluding the east central state.
[c]Approved estimates.
[d]Estimates.
Sources: Federal Republic of Nigeria, Annual Abstract of Statistics (Lagos: Federal Office of Statistics, 1973), and Federal Republic of Nigeria, Federal Government Budget Estimates (Lagos: Federal Ministry of Information [various years].

TABLE 3.28

Contribution of Oil Companies to the Balance of Payments 1965-77

(₦ million)

| Year | Payments to Governments/ Governmental Institutions | Category | | | Total Contributions to Balance Payments |
		Other Local Payments	Variation in Cash Holdings	Local Receipts	
1965	26.8	46.4	--	2.0	71.2
1966	37.4	66.6	--	17.2	86.8
1967	54.2	58.4	15.6	+0.4	97.4
1968	33.4	25.0	0.8	--	57.6
1969	26.9	28.9	0.4	2.1	53.3
1970	176.4	76.8	4.0	24.0	253.2
1971	542.4	113.2	12.2	38.6	604.8
1972	729.1	129.6	4.3	+46.3	900.7
1973	1,333.1	121.7	4.2	47.3	1,403.3
1974	5,200.6	154.7	+15.1	179.5	5,192.9
1975	4,347.6	+185.6	+8.2	178.4	4,363.0
1976	4,758.3	170.8	+25.0	45.7	4,908.1
1977	5,802.6	+166.0	95.2	58.9	5,814.5

Source: Central Bank of Nigeria, Annual Report and Statements of Accounts (Lagos: Central Bank of Nigeria) [Various years].

It is true that revenues and foreign exchange derived from the oil sector had meant that the government was able to finance the massive public sector programs under the Second National Development 1970-74 without recourse to foreign aid and DFI as had been the case during the 1962-68 Development Plan period. When we examine the nature of its linkage with the Nigerian economy, namely, the extent to which the oil industry contributes to the development of oil-related enterprises (for example, petrochemicals, fertilizers, and liquified petroleum/natural gas), there is little doubt that the oil industry has yet to have any meaningful impact on economic development in Nigeria.

Table 3.25, showing expenditure by the oil industry on goods and services, indicates that expenditure, which is running to about ₦ 411 million annually, stood at about ₦ 2,661 million at the end of 1974 (₦ 1,712.3 million on imports and ₦ 948.6 million on local expenditure), and the figure has been on a steady increase since the late 1970s. What is of significance is:

1. that about 36 percent of the industry's total expenditure was made locally;
2. that many of the contracting firms dealing with the oil industry import most of their supplies, meaning, first, that a large part of the so-called local purchases are in fact disguised imports and, second, that the proportion of the industry's total expenditure spent on locally produced goods and services ranges between 15 and 20 percent;
3. that the locally produced goods and services, as is clear from Table 3.23, consist of local rents, custom duties, compensation for land acquired, grants and subventions, telecommunication charges, and charges for energy supply.

In essence, the oil industry has few backward linkages to the local economy. Locally produced goods and services do not include any of the industry's basic requirements of highly complex equipment, all of which have to be imported. Additionally, the oil industry has few forward linkages to the local economy, meaning that oil-related enterprises (such as fertilizers, petrochemicals, and liquified petro-

leum/natural gas) have been slow to develop. The
situation may, however, change in the 1980s with the
commissioning of the Ajaokuta Steel Complex and
plans to establish oil-related enterprises, namely,
petrochemicals, fertilizers, and liquified petroleum/
natural gas during the 1980-85 Development Plan
period.[285] In any event, the Nigerian oil industry,
like any oil industry in a poor oil-producing country in the Third World, "remains a typical enclave
industry whose contribution to the economy is limited
largely to its contribution to government revenue
and foreign exchange earnings."[286] But why do MNC
operations have few backward and forward linkages to
the economy? The reasons are not hard to find.
First, we must consider the nature of the industry,
and, as already noted, certain MNC operations have
an enclave character. Specifically, mining operations, as a rule, are not integrated into the local
economy; if anything, they create enclave economies.
Second, local content requirements may create problems for MNCs in several DCs. In Mexico, Brazil,
and several Latin American countries, local content
requirements are excessive. More fundamental, government may impose such heavy duties on the finished
products that the plan (for the processing of raw
materials) may become uneconomic. Third, unless the
proposed downstream venture (such as a smelter) is
economically viable, no MNC is willing to get involved in processing raw materials, as processing
entails additional heavy capital outlay. In essence,
MNCs are very much concerned about the profitability
or economic viability of any proposed downstream
venture. Fourth, MNCs may be so concerned about
product quality that they are unwilling to establish
plants for processing raw materials in host states,
given inadequate infrastructural facilities as well
as inadequate and few highly skilled personnel.
Fifth, sometimes MNCs argue that requiring forward
linkages in the natural resource field or forbidding
the export of primary materials in an unprocessed
form is usually not in the best interests of the
host state because such a directive could mean slow-
ing down the rate of capital inflow and, thus, retard
economic development. More fundamental, it could
lead to the development of substitutes, and in any

event, MNC subsidiaries could cease operations in such host states and move their operations to Third World countries that do not enunciate such policies.

With respect to the oil industry, one major reason why multinational oil companies are unwilling to develop oil-related enterprises in DCs is the fear of putting all their "eggs" (investments) in one basket, given the political uncertainty--actual or imaginary--in several oil-producing countries. Peter Odell has noted that the oil companies "have not put their profits in other enterprises, particularly in countries where production has been located, for fear of having too many eggs in the same precarious basket."[287] Another reason why multinational oil companies have generally been slow in developing oil-related enterprises in Third World host states is that the development of the host state is not a priority as long as the essential production facilities (such as flow stations, pipelines, storage tanks, and export terminals) and other infrastructural facilities are provided. Third, we must not overlook the material interests of top public servants who have deliberately delayed implementing the report recommending the establishment of oil-related enterprises. Finally, most oil-related manufacturing enterprises, like extractive enterprises, are highly capital intensive; usually, they have large minimum efficient scales. Therefore, to be viable, such oil-related enterprises need markets that are considerably larger than those existing in oil-producing countries; indeed, they need export markets. In any event, it would be preposterous, from an economic point of view, for multinational oil companies to create in oil-producing countries large export-oriented manufacturing enterprises that would compete effectively with well-established refining and manufacturing plants in DMEs.

Measures have been taken by Third World host states to encourage closer integration of MNC operations with the local economy. They include:

1. prohibitions of the export of materials in their raw form:
2. positive inducements for further local processing of raw materials (such as provision of cheap energy

for MNC subsidiary as in Guyana before Demba,
Alcan's subsidiary, was nationalized in March
1971).[288]
3. greater use of local engineering and consulting
firms;
4. host state's majority (meaningful) participation
in MNC subsidiaries, thus making it possible for
the building of advanced processing facilities;
and
5. progressive increases in the value-added content
of manufacturing products either with MNC subsidiaries or through subcontracting to domestic
firms.

However, some host states have tended not to
depend on multinational oil companies to establish
oil-related enterprises. They have established national oil companies and also invested heavily in
oil-related enterprises. Coming to mind is the decision by the Nigerian government to establish plants
for petrochemicals, fertilizers, and liquified natural and petroleum gas during the 1980-85 Development
Plan period.
Concluding our discussion of the MNC as the
main vehicle for the transfer of technology to DCs,
it is gratifying to note that some DCs, notably,
Mexico, Argentina, Venezuela, Nigeria, and member
states of the Andean Common Market, have taken measures with respect to the transfer of technology by
parent MNCs and/or MNC subsidiaries.[289] First, they
now closely monitor and are becoming more knowledge-
able about licensing arrangements. Indeed, they are
becoming more selective about the kinds of technologies obtained from DMEs. Second, they now obtain
technology through "turnkey" projects and/or "fade-
out" or divestment arrangements. With respect to
turnkey projects, a plant/project (such as TanZam
Railway built by the Chinese) is built by a foreign
enterprise or through a bilateral/multilateral assistance program and handed over, on completion, to the
developing country; and under a fade-out/divestment
arrangement, the foreign investor (natural or juridi-
cal) is allowed to run his business (as under the
Cartagena Agreement establishing the Andean Common
Market) for a specified number of years and then

compelled, by law, to sell to the indigenes, host
state, or interterritorial corporation.[290] Third,
they have imposed limits or restrictions on payments
for technology imported by wholly owned subsidiaries
of MNCs; they have imposed ceilings on royalties and
technical fees, thus making it unattractive for MNCs
or their subsidiaries to transfer technology to DCs.
Fourth, some DCs have excluded foreign firms from
industries producing luxury goods; some DCs have restricted foreign firms to certain areas of economic
activity by insisting that they increasingly use or
employ labor-intensive technologies and produce
goods that are appropriate to the well-being of the
low-income groups. Fifth, some DCs simply include
in licensing arrangements conditions such as export
or local content requirements, namely, "use it or
lose it" regulations, stipulating that patented
technology moves into the public domain if the enterprise or firm holding the patent fails to use or
license the technology.

However, DCs, as a group or in concert with
UNCTAD, may create a system of international review
of patent monopolies; alternatively, they may and
should enact antitrust legislation such as the U.S.
Sherman-Clayton Act.[291] Finally, Third World countries may and can borrow a leaf from Japan and develop alternative technological processes. For example, Japan increased her share of world trade in
manufactured goods from 6.9 percent in 1960 to 16
percent with minimal contribution by MNCs. What she
did was import a very substantial amount of technology and build up an indigenous technology through a
process of adaptation. Between 1950 and 1970, the
Japanese government approved 8,324 contracts involving purchase of Western technology by Japanese enterprises.[292]

Multinational Corporations and Dependent Development

One of the costs of MNC operations in the
Third World is technological dependence. A major
danger posed by the state of technological dependence of most Third World countries is that it im-

pedes, indeed, stifles local development. Not only
does the easy access of Western (foreign) technology
prevent domestic or state-owned enterprises from investing in research. It also makes them, as Sanjaya
Lall put it, "biased against using what innovations
are produced locally. The effect is cumulative,
since R and D generates considerable 'learning by
doing' over time: the less research developing
countries do, the less experience they gather to do
it in the future."[293] More important, the technology transferred by parent MNCs or their subsidiaries
is often inappropriate to the factor endowments of
Third World countries.

In essence, independent national economic development by Third World countries is stunted with
the introduction of DFI, namely, once opportunities
have been appropriated by MNCs rather than by the
national bourgeoisie, indeed, once new consumption
patterns have been created by MNCs, thanks to MNC
product differentiation (or innovation) and adver-
tising/marketing techniques. To be sure, the stunt-
ing of Third World economies has been attributed by
critics of MNC operations to the continuing expansion of the free enterprise economy of the industrialized countries of the North.[294] In his study
of MNCs as "worldwide interest groups," Jonathan
Galloway concludes that MNCs have contributed significantly to the "integration of the Western World's
economy and to the linkage of the Third World to
this more integrated economic growth and is consequently an impediment to stable political and social
development."[295]

To sum up, three general complaints have been
laid at the doors of MNCs. First, critics have generally claimed that MNC operations have had an adverse impact on Third World host states. Second,
MNCs have been accused of engaging in illegal political activity. Third, it has been asserted that MNCs
are beyond national control, and thus they are under-
mining the territorial nation-states. Much of the
discussion in Chapter 1 touched on aspects of the
second and third charges levied against MNCs in the
Third World, and more will be said in Chapter 4.
Let us for the moment deal with the first complaint
by way of summary:

1. It has been argued that MNCs operating in the
   Third World contribute resources that are generally not available or insufficiently available,
   namely, capital, technology, and marketing skills.
2. Again, it has been claimed that MNCs create jobs
   and alleviate balance-of-payments deficits of
   their host states.

These claims have been questioned. Studies carried
out by critical and neoconventional scholars have
produced mixed results:

1. Critical scholars agree that MNCs may well have
   transferred capital to a capital-poor country but
   contend that MNCs, generally, are vehicles through
   which capital is transferred from capital-poor to
   capital-rich countries, thanks to such devices as
   transfer pricing, overinvoicing imports, underinvoicing exports, and overpricing technology.
2. Critical scholars agree that MNCs may well have
   created jobs. While the AFL-CIO accuses U.S.-
   based MNCs of shifting productive facilities
   abroad to avoid demands of powerful labor unions
   for higher wages, on the balance and compared
   with domestic enterprises, MNCs do in fact destroy jobs because they employ capital-intensive
   technologies, namely, technologies that are inconsistent with the factor endowments of Third World
   countries.
3. While it is not denied that MNCs transfer technology to DCs, the technology so transferred is
   inappropriate, obsolete, overpriced, and inconsistent with the factor endowments of Third World
   countries. More fundamental, MNCs often create
   conclave economies; they have few backward and
   forward linkages to the host economy.
4. Critical scholars have claimed that MNCs encourage inappropriate consumption patterns through
   product differentiation (or innovation) and
   marketing/advertising techniques. While neoconventional scholars agree with this claim, they
   contend that the undesirable consumption patterns
   encouraged by MNCs may be more a reflection of an
   existing uneven distribution of wealth, income,
   and privilege in DCs than the effects of MNC operations.

5. Critics have also argued that MNCs contribute to
   the widening elite-mass gap by paying their employees higher salaries and generous fringe benefits than domestic enterprises. While neoconventional scholars agree that MNCs, on the balance,
   pay higher salaries and generous fringe benefits,
   they attribute the higher salaries enjoyed by
   their employees to such factors as the exigency
   of the labor market, public policies, trade union
   pressure, and MNCs' enlightened self-interest (to
   reduce criticisms of their operations).

In essence, while MNCs may confer some benefits on host states, they may do so only at great
costs. Joan Spero was certainly reflecting the position of critics of MNC operations in the Third World
when she noted:

> Multinational corporations often cre-
> ate highly developed enclaves which
> do not contribute to the development
> of the larger economy. These enclaves
> use capital-intensive technology which
> employs few local citizens; acquire
> supplies from abroad, not locally; use
> transfer prices and technology agree-
> ments to avoid taxes; and send earnings
> back home. In welfare terms the bene-
> fits of the enclave accrue to the home
> country and to a small part of the
> host population allied with the cor-
> poration.[296]

NOTES

1. David Colman and Frederick Nixson, Economics of Change in Less-Developed Countries (Oxford,
England: Phillip Allan, 1978), p. 217.

2. Robert Gilpin, "The Political Economy of
the Multinational Corporation: Three Contrasting
Perspectives," American Political Science Review 70
(1976): 187.

3. Colman and Nixson, Economics of Change, p.
217.

4. Gilpin, "The Political Economy," p. 187.

5. Jagdish Bhagwati, ed., Economics and World Order: From the 1970s to the 1990s (New York: (Macmillan, 1972).

6. Stephen Hymer, "The Multinational Corporation and the Law of Uneven Development," in Economics and World Order, p. 113 (emphasis in original).

7. Ibid., p. 114.

8. Similar reasons have been advanced for European penetration of Africa and Asia toward the end of the nineteenth century. See Kwame Nkrumah, Towards Colonial Freedom: Africa in the Struggle Against World Imperialism (London: Heinemann, 1962), pp. 1-23; Parker T. Moon, Imperialism and World Politics (New York: Macmillan, 1936).

9. See Theodore Moran, "Foreign Expansion as an 'Institutional Necessity' for U.S. Corporate Capitalism: The Search for a Radical Model," World Politics 25 (1973): 369-86.

10. See John Hobson, Imperialism: A Study (London: George Allen and Unwin, 1938).

11. Gilpin, "The Political Economy," p. 188.

12. Ibid.

13. Colman and Nixson, Economics of Change, p. 217.

14. Gilpin, "The Political Economy," p. 189.

15. Kari Levitt, Silent Surrender: The American Economic Empire in Canada (New York: Liveright Press, 1970).

16. Gilpin, "The Political Economy," p. 189.

17. See, for example, Herbert Gray, Foreign Direct Investment in Canada, Gray Report (Ottawa, Canada: Queen's Printer, 1972).

18. Gilpin, "The Political Economy," p. 189.

19. Ibid., p. 184.

20. Richard J. Barnet and Ronald E. Muller, The Global Reach: The Power of the Multinational Corporation (New York: Simon and Schuster, 1974), p. 18.

21. Ibid., p. 17.

22. Christopher Tungendhat, The Multinationals (Harmondsworth, England: Penguin, 1971).

23. Harry G. Johnson, Technology and Economic Interdependence (London: Macmillan, 1975), p. 48.

24. Colman and Nixson, Economics of Change, p. 218.

25. Alasdair I. MacBean and V. N. Balasubramanyam, Meeting the Third World Challenge (London: Macmillan, 1978), p. 190.

26. Ibid., p. 191.

27. Ibid.

28. John H. Dunning, Studies in International Investment (London: George Allen and Unwin, 1970), pp. 4-5. For a view that acquisition of majority shares in an enterprise does not necessarily imply control of the enterprise, see Akinsanya, Economic Independence and Indigenization of Private Foreign Investments: The Experiences of Nigeria and Ghana (Columbia: Institute of International Studies, University of South Carolina, 1982).

29. Hymer, "The Multinational Corporation," p. 115.

30. Gilpin, "The Political Economy," pp. 184-85.

31. P. G. Bock and Vincent J. Fuccillo, "Transnational Corporations as International Political Actors," Studies in Comparative International Development 10 (1975): 56-57.

32. MacBean and Balasubramanyam, Meeting the Third World, p. 191.

33. Johnson, Technology and Economic Interdependence, pp. 60-66; Levitt, Silent Surrender.

34. Gilpin, "The Political Economy," pp. 184-85.

35. Colman and Nixson, Economics of Change, p. 219.

36. Fortune (New York), August 10, 1981, p. 205.

37. Raymond Vernon, Sovereignty at Bay--The Multinational Spread of U.S. Enterprises (New York: Basic Books, 1971), p. 4.

38. United Nations, Multinational Corporations in World Development, p. 7.

39. Ibid., pp. 7-8, 127 (Table 1).

40. Ronald E. Muller, "The Multinational Corporation and the Underdevelopment of the Third World," in The Political Economy of Development and Underdevelopment, ed. Charles K. Wilber (New York: Random House, 1973), p. 126.

41. Theodore C. Sorensen, "Improper Payments Abroad: Perspectives and Proposals," Foreign Affairs 54 (1976): 722.

42. See Akinsanya, Economic Independence and Indigenization.

43. Colman and Nixson, Economics of Change, p. 220.

44. See Akinsanya, "Host-Governments' Responses to Foreign Economic Control: The Experiences of Selected African Countries," International and Comparative Law Quarterly 30 (1981): 785-86.

45. See Akinsanya, The Expropriation of Multinational Property in the Third World, pp. 94-106.

46. United Nations, Multinational Corporations in World Development, p. 8.

47. Constantine V. Vaitsos, "Power, Knowledge and Development Policy: Relations between Transnational Enterprises and Developing Countries," in A World Divided: The Less Developed Countries in the International Economy, ed. Gerald K. Helleiner (Cambridge, England: Cambridge University Press, 1976), p. 121.

48. Ibid., p. 122.

49. Colman and Nixson, Economics of Change, p. 220.

50. Ibid.

51. Frank, Foreign Enterprise, p. 9.

52. Ibid.

53. Ibid., pp. 9-10.

54. Lester B. Pearson et al., Partners in Development (London: Pall Mall Press, 1969), p. 155.

55. Frank, Foreign Enterprise, p. 12.

56. Akinsanya, Economic Independence and Indigenization; Id., "Indigenisation or Nationalisation of Private Foreign Investments: Alternative Strategies for Dealing with Transnational Corporations in Member-States of ECOWAS," in Development Planning Priorities and Strategies for the 1980s in the ECOWAS, ed. R. E. Ubogu et al. (Ibadan, Nigeria: Heinemann Educational, 1983), pp. 365-409; Id., "Host-Governments' Responses," pp. 776-80.

57. Sampson, The Seven Sisters, pp. 243-61.

58. United Nations, Multinational Corporations and World Development, p. 177.

59. Ibid., p. 19.

60. Grant L. Reuber et al., Private Foreign Investment in Development (Oxford, England: Oxford University Press, 1973), Appendix A.

61. Colman and Nixson, Economics of Change, p. 189.

62. See Akinsanya, "The United Nations Charter of Economic Rights and Duties of States: International Protection of Economic Independence of Third World Countries," The Annual of the Nigerian Society of International Law [forthcoming].

63. See Akinsanya, "Permanent Sovereignty Over Natural Resources and the Future of Foreign Investment," Nigerian Journal of International Affairs 5 (1979): 70-92; Id., The Expropriation of Multinational Property in the Third World, pp. 48-68.

64. Ian Brownlie, Principles of Public International Law (Oxford, England: Clarendon Press, 1973), p. 4.

65. Akinsanya, "Indigenisation or Nationalisation of Private Foreign Investments."

66. Barnet and Muller, The Global Reach, pp. 123-46; Akinsanya, "United States Multinationals in South Africa and Policy Options for the United States," Third Press Review of Third World Diplomacy 1 (1982): 98-102.

67. Colman and Nixson, Economics of Change, p. 205.

68. Ibid.

69. See Raymond F. Mikesell, "Effects of Direct Investment on Development," Economic Impact 35 (Washington, D.C.: United States International Communication Agency, 1981), pp. 36-41; Muller, "The Multinational Corporation and the Exercise of Power: Latin America," in The New Sovereigns, ed. Abdul A. Said and Luiz R. Simmons (Englewood Cliffs, N.J.: Prentice-Hall, 1975), p. 60; Johnson, Technology and Economic Interdependence, pp. 48-60, 70-86; MacBean and Balasubramanyam, Meeting the Third World Challenge, pp. 200-22.

70. Muller, "The Multinational Corporation and the Exercise of Power: Latin America," pp. 56-59; Id., "The Multinational Corporation and the Underdevelopment of the Third World," in The Political Economy of Development and Underdevelopment, pp. 125-30.

71. Muller, "The Multinational Corporation and the Exercise of Power: Latin America," p. 57.

72. Gustav Ranis, "The Multinational Corporation as an Instrument of Development," in The Multinational Corporation and Social Change, ed. David E. Apter and Louis W. Goodman (New York: Praeger, 1976), p. 105.

73. Ibid., pp. 107-11.

74. Muller, "The MNC and the Exercise of Power," p. 58.

75. Akinsanya, "United States Multinationals in South Africa and Policy Options for the United States," pp. 108-9.

76. Ibid., pp. 107-11.

77. Muller, "The MNC and the Exercise of Power," p. 58.

78. Pinelo, The Multinational Corporation as Force in Latin American Politics: A Case Study of the International Petroleum Company in Peru, p. x. Orlando Letelier was killed along with his friend Ronni Macfitt in a car-bombing on September 21, 1976. The Washington Post Book World 12 (1982): 4.

79. Barnet and Muller, Global Reach, p. 150.

80. Robert Gilpin, Power and the Multinational Corporation (New York: Council on Foreign Relations, 1975).

81. Richard E. Caves and Grant L. Reuber, Capital Transfers and Economic Policy: Canada (Cambridge, Mass.: Harvard University Press, 1971).

82. Barnet and Muller, Global Reach, pp. 152-53.

83. Ibid., p. 154.

84. Daniel S. Blanchard, "The Threat to U.S. Investment in Latin America," Journal of International Law and Economics 5 (1971): 224; James Fred Rippy, Latin America in World Politics (New York: Crofts, 1958), pp. 47-52.

85. Vaitsos, "Power," p. 125.

86. Ibid.

87. Ibid.

88. Barnet and Muller, Global Reach, p. 408.

89. Ibid., p. 409. See also United Nations, The Flow of Financial Resources: Private and Foreign Investment: Main Findings of a Study of Private Foreign Investment in Selected Developing Countries, Publication No. TD/B/C.3/III, 1973.

90. Barnet and Muller, Global Reach, p. 409.

91. Frank, Foreign Enterprise, pp. 61-62.

92. Ibid., pp. 61-64.

93. Ibid., p. 70.

94. Colman and Nixson, Economics of Change, p. 227.

95. Barnet and Muller, Global Reach, p. 278.

96. Sanjaya Lall, "Transfer-Pricing by Multinational Firms," Oxford Bulletin of Economics and Statistics 35 (1973): 175-78.

97. Barnet and Muller, Global Reach, p. 279.

98. See James S. Hanson, "Transfer Pricing in the Multinational Corporation: A Critical Appraisal, World Development 3 (1975): 861.

99. Vaitsos, "Power," p. 122.

100. Hanson, "Transfer Pricing," p. 861.

101. Lall, "Transfer Pricing," pp. 183-85.

102. Barnet and Muller, Global Reach, p. 159.

103. Colman and Nixson, Economics of Change, p. 229.

104. Lall, "Transfer Pricing," p. 186.

105. Barnet and Muller, Global Reach, pp. 159-60.

106. Johnson, Technology and Economic Interdependence, p. 59 (emphasis added).

107. Ibid.

108. MacBean and Balasubramanyam, Meeting the Third World Challenge, p. 218.

109. Ibid.

110. Vaitsos, "Interaffiliate Charges by Transnational Corporations and Inter-Country Income Distribution," pp. 69-73.

111. See Claes Brundenius, "The Anatomy of Imperialism: The Case of the Multinational Mining Corporation in Peru," Journal of Peace Research 9 (1972): 189-207.

112. Ibid., pp. 199-201.

113. Vaitsos, "Bargaining and the Distribution of Returns in the Purchase of Technology by Developing Countries," in Underdevelopment and Development: The Third World: Selected Readings, ed. Henry Bernstein (Harmondsworth, England: Penguin, 1973), p. 319.

114. United Nations, Multinational Corporations in World Development, p. 190.

115. Ibid.

116. Thomas N. Gladwin and Ingo Walter, Multinationals Under Fire: Lessons in the Management of Conflict (New York: Wiley, 1980), p. 534.

117. United Nations, Multinational Corporations in World Development, p. 50.
118. Barnet and Muller, Global Reach, p. 161.
119. International Labour Office, Employment,
Incomes and Inequality: A Strategy for Increasing
Productive Employment in Kenya (Geneva: International
Labour Office, 1972), pp. 456-57.
120. Barnet and Muller, Global Reach, p. 161.
121. Akinsanya, Economic Independence and Indigenization.
122. MacBean and Balasubramanyam, Meeting the
Third World, p. 217.
123. Streeten, "New Approaches to Direct Private Overseas Investment in Less Developed Countries,"
in The Frontiers of Development Studies, ed. Paul
Streeten (London: Macmillan, 1972), p. 213.
124. See Thomas J. Biersteker, Distortion or
Development? Contending Perspectives on the Multinational Corporation (Cambridge, Mass.: MIT Press,
1978), pp. 119-62.
125. See Olukunlc Iyanda and Joseph A. Bello,
"Employment Effects of Multinational Enterprises in
Nigeria," Faculty of Business Administration, University of Lagos, Lagos, Nigeria, Mimeo, n.d., p. 12.
126. Federal Republic of Nigeria, Second National Development Plan 1970-74 (Lagos: Federal
Ministry of Information, 1970), p. 34.
127. Muller, "The Multinational Corporation
and the Underdevelopment of the Third World," pp.
132-33.
128. Akinsanya, "Host-Governments' Responses
to Foreign Economic Control," pp. 769-73.
129. Vaitsos, "Employment Effects of Foreign
Direct Investments in Developing Countries," in Employment in Developing Countries, ed. Edgar Edwards
(New York: Columbia University Press, 1974), pp.
336-37.
130. Sanjaya Lall and Paul Streeten, Foreign
Investment, Transnationals and Developing Countries
(Boulder, Colo.: Westview Press, 1977), p. 84.
131. Richard Jolly, "International Dimensions,"
in Redistribution with Growth, ed. Hollis B. Chenery
(London, England: Oxford University Press, 1974),
p. 171.

132. See Brian F. Wallace, "Multinational Corporations and Governments in Developing Nations: Effects on the Distribution of Wealth and Power in Colombia," paper presented at the 22nd Annual Convention of the International Studies Association, Philadelphia, Pa., March 18-21, 1981, p. 16.

133. Colman and Nixson, Economics of Change, p. 246.

134. Wallace, "Multinational Corporations," p. 16.

135. Ibid., p. 17.

136. These include Bogotá, Medellin, Cali, Barranquilla, Cartagena, Manizales, Pereira, and Bucaramanga.

137. Albert R. Berry, "Open Unemployment as a Social Problem in Urban Colombia: Myth and Reality, Economic Development and Cultural Change 23 (1975): 278.

138. Albert R. Berry and Francisco Thoumi, "Import Substitution and Beyond: Colombia," World Development 5 (1977): 90.

139. International Labour Office, Towards Full Employment: A Programme for Colombia (Geneva: International Labour Office, 1970), p. 107.

140. Barnet and Muller, Global Reach, p. 166.

141. Ibid.

142. Wallace, "Multinational Corporations," p. 17.

143. Jaime Silva, "Direct Foreign Investment in the Manufacturing Sector of Colombia" (Ph.D. dissertation, Northwestern University, 1976), p. 234.

144. Wallace, "Multinational Corporations," p. 16.

145. Livio W. R. De Carvalho, "Comparative Performance of Domestic and Foreign Firms in Latin America" (Ph.D. dissertation, Cornell University, 1977).

146. Wallace, "Multinational Corporations," p. 19.

147. Ibid.

148. Iyanda and Bello, "Employment Effects," p. 15.

149. Ibid.

150. See Hal. R. Mason, "Some Observations on the Choice of Technology by Multinational Firms in

Developing Countries," <u>Review of Economics and Statistics</u> 55 (1973): 351; Louis Wells, Jr., "Economic Man and Engineering Man: Choice of Technology in a Low Wage Country," <u>Public Policy</u> 21 (1973): 323; Somsak Tambunlertchai, "Foreign Direct Investment in Thailand's Manufacturing Industries" (Ph.D. dissertation, Duke University, 1976), p. 238; Jamuna P. Agarwal, "Factor Proportions in Foreign and Domestic Firms in Indian Manufacturing," <u>Economic Journal</u> 86 (1976).

151. Barnet and Muller, <u>Global Reach</u>, p. 168.
152. Ibid.
153. Colin Leys, <u>Underdevelopment in Kenya: The Political Economy of Neo-Colonialism</u> (Berkeley: University of California Press, 1975), pp. 138-40.
154. International Labour Office, <u>Employment, Incomes and Equality: A Strategy for Increasing Productive Employment in Kenya</u>, p. 451.
155. Wallace, "Multinational Corporations," p. 19.
156. Biersteker, <u>Distortion</u>, p. 127.
157. Ibid.
158. See generally, S. A. Madujibeya, "Oil and Nigeria's Economic Development," <u>African Affairs</u> 75 (1976): 284-316; S. B. Falegan and G. O. Okah, "The Contribution of Petroleum to Nigeria's Economy," in <u>Oil and the New International Economic Order</u>, ed. Femi Kayode and Ibidayo Ajayi (Ibadan: Nigerian Economic Society, 1976).
159. Falegan and Okah, p. 174.
160. Organisation for Economic Cooperation and Development, <u>Development Assistance: 1970 Review</u> (Paris: OECD, 1970), p. 17.
161. MacBean and Balasubramanyam, <u>Meeting the Third World</u>, p. 210 (emphasis added).
162. See Akinsanya, "Host-Governments' Responses to Foreign Economic Control," pp. 769-70; Id., "State Strategies Towards Nigerian and Foreign Business," in <u>The Political Economy of Nigeria</u>, ed. I. W. Zartman (New York: Praeger, 1983), pp. 145-84; Id., "Indigenisation or Nationalisation of Private Foreign Investments."
163. United Nations, <u>Multinational Corporations in World Development</u>, p. 50.

164. Colman and Nixson, Economics of Change, pp. 261-62.
165. Ibid., pp. 261-68; Gerald K. Helleiner, "The Role of Multinational Corporations in the Less Developed Countries' Trade in Technology," World Development 3 (1975): 169.
166. Streeten, "Costs and Benefits of Multinational Enterprises in Less Developed Countries," in The Multinational Enterprise, ed. John H. Dunning (London: George Allen and Unwin, 1971), p. 252.
167. Robert B. Sutcliffe, Industry and Underdevelopment (London: Addison-Wesley, 1971), p. 186.
168. Biersteker, Distortion, p. 137.
169. See John H. Dunning, International Production and the Multinational Enterprise (London: George Allen and Unwin, 1981), pp. 273-74.
170. See International Labour Office, International Comparison of Real Wages: A Study of Methods, Studies and Reports (Geneva: International Labour Office, 1956).
171. International Labour Office, Wages and Working Conditions in Multinational Enterprises (Geneva: International Labour Office, 1976).
172. Mason, "Some Observations," p. 352; Wells, "Economic Man," p. 323; Sung-Hwan Jo, The Impact of Multinational Firms on Employment and Incomes: The Case Study of South Korea (Geneva: International Labour Office, 1976); Y. Sabolo and R. Trajtenberg, The Impact of Transnational Enterprises in the Developing Countries (Geneva: International Labour Office, 1976); M. L. Possas, Employment Effects of Multinational Enterprises in Brazil (Geneva: International Labour Office, 1979); J. V. Sourrouille, The Impact of Transnational Enterprises on Employment and Incomes: The Case of Argentina (Geneva: International Labour Office, 1976); Steve Langdon, "Multinational Corporation in the Political Economy of Kenya" (Ph.D. dissertation, University of Sussex, 1975); and V. A. Papandreou, "Multinational Enterprises, Market Industrial Structure and Trade Balance in Host Less-Developed Countries: The Case of Greece" (Ph.D. dissertation, University of Reading, 1980).
173. Dunning, International Production, pp. 274, 278-82.

174. Mason, "Some Observations," p. 352.

175. Iyanda and Bello, "Employment Effects," pp. 22-29.

176. Biersteker, Distortion, pp. 137-42.

177. See Tambunlertchai, "Foreign Direct Investment," pp. 232-33.

178. Benjamin I. Cohen, Multinational Firms and Asian Exports (New Haven, Conn.: Yale University Press, 1975).

179. Wallace, "Multinational Corporations," pp. 4-10.

180. Barnet and Muller, Global Reach, p. 169.

181. Biersteker, Distortion, p. 151.

182. Ibid.

183. Ibid., pp. 151-52; Akinsanya, "The Nigerianization of the Western Nigeria Higher Public Service" (Ph.D. dissertation, University of Chicago, 1973), pp. 233-73; Federal Republic of Nigeria, Public Service Review Commission: Main Report (Lagos: Federal Ministry of Information, 1974); Id., The Public Service of Nigeria: Government Views on The Report of the Public Service Review Commission (Lagos: Federal Ministry of Information, 1974); Id., The Public Service Review Panel: Main Report (Lagos: Federal Ministry of Information, 1975); Id., The Public Service of Nigeria: Government Views on the Report of the Public Service Review Panel (Lagos: Federal Ministry of Information, 1975); Id., Report of the Presidential Commission on Parastatals (Lagos: Federal Government Press, 1981); Id., Views of the Government of the Federation on the Report of the Presidential Commission on Parastatals (Lagos: National Assembly Press, 1982).

184. Akinsanya, "State Strategies Towards Nigerian and Foreign Business."

185. Akinsanya, "The Nigerianization of the Western Nigeria Higher Public Service," pp. 268-69.

186. Ibid., p. 270.

187. Biersteker, Distortion, p. 152.

188. Akinsanya, "The Nigerianization of the Western Nigeria Higher Public Service," p. 270.

189. Federal Republic of Nigeria, Second National Development Plan 1970-74.

190. Barnet and Muller, Global Reach, p. 173.

191. Ibid., p. 176.

192. Peter Drucker, The Age of Discontinuity
New York: Harper & Row, 1969), p. 119.
193. Albert Stridsberg, "New Marketing, Ad
Message May Save Underdeveloped Nations," Advertising
Age (New York), September 22, 1969, p. 64.
194. Barnet and Muller, Global Reach, p. 176.
195. Ibid., p. 184.
196. Ibid., p. 183.
197. Biersteker, Distortion, p. 131. The advertisements appearing on Farlac in the Sunday Punch
and Sunday Concord indicated below have pictures not
only of a professional mother feeding her baby while
the father of the newborn child, holding a feeding
bottle, watches with admiration, but also of a naked
healthy baby as well as passport-size photograph of
a baby and his mother mounted on the 350-gram can of
Farlac. See Sunday Punch (Lagos), November 22, 1981;
Sunday Concord (Lagos), September 5, 1982.
198. Sunday Punch (Lagos), November 22, 1981.
199. Sunday Concord (Lagos), September 5, 1982.
200. Sunday Sketch Private Eye, "Nestle, Glaxo
Defy Nigeria," Sunday Sketch (Ibadan), November 22,
1981.
201. In order to demonstrate its concern about
the dangers posed to several millions of newborn
children in the Third World following the introduction of baby formulas, the World Health Organisation
in May 1980 adopted a code imposing a ban on direct
advertising and other forms of promotion to the general public, sales incentives to marketing personnel,
as well as wide-ranging controls. While there had
been a dramatic decline in the promotional tactics
of many food companies in Nigeria, ostensibly in
compliance with the code, Glaxo (Nigeria) and Nestle
of Switzerland, at time of writing, continue to ad-
vertise (in defiance of the Code of Conduct) their
products on television and radio and in print. In
November 1981, the Federal Ministry of Health banned
two brands of baby custard powder from circulation
because they contained only cornflour, starch, artificial flavoring and coloring in violation of the
Food and Drugs Act of 1974. See Sunday Punch (Lagos),
November 22, 1981; Sunday Sketch (Ibadan), November
22, 1981; Sunday Concord (Lagos), September 5, 1982;
Daily Times (Lagos), September 7, 1982; Sunday Punch

(Lagos), October 17, 1982, pp. 12, 17; Nigerian Tribune (Ibadan), October 18, 1982, p. 8. We might note that Nigeria is perhaps the only Third World country where the circulation of expired drugs and the sale of drugs by unauthorized persons appear to be routine. We might also note here that the Kenyan government instituted criminal proceedings against some food-related companies, claiming compensation for the deaths of thousands of newborn children.

202. Biersteker, Distortion, p. 133.
203. Ibid., p. 130.
204. Ibid.
205. Ibid., p. 131.
206. Ibid.
207. Ibid.
208. Ibid., p. 132.
209. For example, Colgate With Gardol, a toothpaste which is no longer competitive in the U.S. market and has been replaced by Colgate With MFP Fluoride, has been introduced into African markets where it can retain its competitive advantage. See Biersteker, U.S. Multinational Investments in Africa: The Dynamics of a Changing Relationship, prepared for the Council on Foreign Relations Survey Discussion Group on U.S. Policy Toward Africa, February 1977, p. 12.

210. For a view that multinationals should not be blamed for encouraging the consumption of color television sets in Nigeria, see Biersteker, Distortion or Development?, p. 133.

211. 'Tola Adeniyi, "A Week after Udoji Bonanza," Sunday Times (Lagos), January 25, 1975, p. 5.

212. Akinsanya, "The Nigerianization of the Western Nigeria Higher Public Service," pp. 234-38; Frank, Foreign Enterprise, pp. 73-74.

213. Muller, "The Multinational Corporation and the Underdevelopment of the Third World," p. 140.

214. Ibid., p. 141; Vaitsos, "The Process of Commercialization of Technology in the Andean Pact: A Synthesis," Andean Group Document, Lima, October 1971, pp. 20-26; David R. Belli, "Sales of Foreign Affiliates of U.S. Firms," Survey of Current Business 50 (1970): 20. The Survey of Current Business is a U.S. Department of Commerce publication.

215. Belli, "Sales," p. 20.

216. Muller, "The Multinational Corporation and the Underdevelopment of the Third World," p. 141.

217. Ibid. (emphasis added).

218. Ibid. (emphasis added).

219. Ronald Muller and Richard Morgenstern, "The Impact of Multinational Corporations on the Balance of Payments of LDCs: An Econometric Analysis of Pricing in Export Sales," presented at the American Economics Association Annual Meeting, Toronto, December 27, 1972. See also Muller, "The Multinational Corporation and the Underdevelopment of the Third World," p. 142.

220. These include Bolivia, Colombia, Ecuador, and Peru.

221. See Vaitsos, "The Process of Commercialization," pp. 20-26.

222. See United Nations Conference on Trade and Development, Restrictive Business Practices, TD/122/Supp. 1, Santiago, Chile, January 7, 1972, pp. 9-11; Id., Transfer of Technology Policies Relating to Technology of the Countries of the Andean Pact: Their Foundations: A Study by the Junta del Acuerdo de Cartagena, TD/107, December 29, 1971, pp. 44-45; P. Patnaik, "Imperialism and the Growth of Indian Capitalism," in Studies in Imperialism, eds. Robert Owen and Robert B. Sutcliffe (London: Longman, 1972).

223. See Frank, Foreign Enterprise, pp. 78-82.

224. United Nations Conference on Trade and Development, Restrictive Business Practices, pp. 44-45.

225. Dunning, International Production, pp. 337-38.

226. See ibid., p. 338; Gerald K. Helleiner, "Transnational Corporations and Trade Structure," University of Toronto, 1979, Mimeo; D. B. Keesing, World Trade and Output of Manufactures: Structural Trends and Developing Countries' Exports (Washington, D.C.: World Bank, 1978); N. B. Kawaguchi, "The Role of Japanese Firms in the Manufactured Exports of Developing Countries," November 1978, Washington, D.C.: World Bank, Mimeo; P. A. Plesch, "'Developing Countries' Exports of Electronics and Electrical Engineering Products," February 1978, Washington, D.C.: World Bank, Mimeo. The newly industrialized coun-

tries, according to OECD, UNCTAD, and other sources, include Argentina, Brazil, Greece, Hong Kong, Hungary, India, Israel, Malaysia, Malta, Mexico, Pakistan, Philippines, Portugal, Poland, Rumania, Singapore, South Korea, Spain, Taiwan, Turkey, and Yugoslavia.

227. These included Argentina, Brazil, Hong Kong, India, Malaysia, Mexico, Philippines, Singapore, South Korea, Taiwan, and Thailand.

228. Dunning, International Production, p. 339.

229. Hans Singer and Javed Ansari, Rich and Poor Countries (London: George Allen and Unwin, 1977), pp. 205-6.

230. Barnet and Muller, Global Reach, p. 164.

231. Biersteker, U.S. Multinational Investments in Africa, p. 12; Barnet and Muller, Global Reach, p. 164; Barbara Rogers, White Wealth and Black Poverty: American Investments in Southern Africa (Westport, Conn.: Greenwood Press, 1976), pp. 124-27; John Suckling, Ruth Weiss, and Duncan Innes, Foreign Investment in South Africa: The Economic Factor (Uppsala, Sweden: Africa Publications Trust, 1975), pp. 27-28.

232. Biersteker, Distortion, p. 12. On the theory of product life cycle, see Louis Wells, The Product Life Cycle and International Trade (Cambridge, Mass.: Harvard University Press, 1972); Vernon, Sovereignty at Bay (New York: Basic Books, 1971); Id., "The Product Cycle Hypothesis in a New International Environment," Oxford Bulletin of Economics and Statistics 41 (1979).

233. Barnet and Muller, Global Reach, p. 164.

234. See Leopaldo Solis, "Mexican Economic Policy in the Post-War Period: The Views of Mexican Economists," American Economic Review 16 (1971).

235. Vaitsos, "Inter-Affiliate Charges by Transnational Corporations and Inter-Country Income Distribution," pp. 55-56.

236. Barnet and Muller, Global Reach, p. 165.

237. Lall, Developing Countries and Multinational Corporations: Effects on Host Countries' Welfare and the Role of Government Policy (London: Commonwealth Secretariat, 1976), p. 28.

238. Ibid.

239. United Nations, Multinational Corporations in World Development, p. 50.

240. Ibid.

241. Colman and Nixson, Economics of Change, p. 229.

242. These include France, the Federal Republic of Germany, Italy, Japan, Holland, the United Kingdom, and the United States.

243. Dunning, International Production and the Multinational Enterprise, p. 329.

244. United Nations, Transnational Corporations in World Development, Publication No. E.78.II, A.5, 1978.

245. David T. Devlin and George R. Kruer, "The International Investment Position of the United States: Developments in 1969," Survey of Current Business 50 (1970); 34.

246. Ibid.

247. Akinsanya, The Expropriation of Multinational Property in the Third World, pp. 115-21.

248. The Law to Promote Mexican Investment and Regulate Foreign Investment was published on March 9, 1973, and came into force on May 9, 1973. See Akinsanya, pp. 333-40.

249. Majority ownership does not necessarily imply effective control by the majority shareholders. In fact, it is possible for a minority shareholder to exercise effective control in many cases. See Akinsanya, Economic Independence and Indigenization.

250. See Richard S. Newfarmer and Willard F. Mueller, Multinational Corporations in Brazil and Mexico: Structural Sources of Economic and Noneconomic Power. Report to the Subcommittee on Multinational Corporations of the Committee on Foreign Relations, United States Senate (Washington, D.C.: Government Printing Office, 1975).

251. See Van R. Whiting, "International Aspects of National Regulation: Transnationals and the State in Mexico, 1970-1978," paper presented at the 20th Annual Convention of the International Studies Association, Toronto, March 21-23, 1979, p. 31.

252. Ibid., p. 14.

253. F. Stewart, Technology and Underdevelopment (London: Macmillan, 1977); H. Pack, The Capital Goods Sector in LDCs: A Survey (Washington, D.C.: World Bank, 1978); G. Jenkins, Non-Agricul-

tural Choice of Technique: An Annotated Bibliography
(Oxford, England: Institute of Commonwealth Studies,
1975); C. Cooper and R. Kaplinsky, Second-Hand Equipment in a Developing Country (Geneva: International
Labour Office, 1974); A. S. Shalla, ed., Technology
and Employment in Industry (Geneva: International
Labour Office, 1975).
    254. Lall, Developing Countries in the Inter-
national Economy: Selected Papers (London: Macmillan,
1981), p. 139.
    255. Ibid.
    256. Frank, Foreign Enterprise, p. 73.
    257. Lall, Developing Countries and Multina-
tional Corporations, p. 27.
    258. Biersteker, Distortion, p. 122.
    259. Organisation for Economic Cooperation
and Development, North/South Technology Transfer:
The Adjustments Ahead (Paris: OECD, 1981).
    260. Frank, Foreign Enterprise, pp. 73-78;
Helleiner, Peasant Agriculture, Government, and Economic Growth in Nigeria (Homewood, Ill.: Richard D.
Irwin, 1966), p. 330; Babatunde D. Thomas, Capital
Accumulation and Technology Transfer (New York:
Praeger, 1975), p. 111; Terisa Turner, "Two Refineries: A Comparative Study of Technology Transfer to
the Nigerian Refining Industry," World Development 5
(1977): 238-39.
    261. Frank, Foreign Enterprise, pp. 73-78.
    262. Biersteker, Distortion, pp. 122-29.
    263. The question posed by Biersteker to top
executives of MNC subsidiaries reads thus: "Have
any adaptations been made in installed machinery to
suit local conditions, raw materials, or local marketing requirements?" See Biersteker, Distortion,
p. 122.
    264. Ibid.
    265. Helleiner, Peasant Agriculture, p. 330.
    266. Turner, "Two Refineries," pp. 238-39.
    267. Frank, Foreign Enterprise, p. 74.
    268. Lall, Developing Countries and Multina-
tional Corporations, p. 27.
    269. Biersteker, Distortion, p. 120; United
Nations, Multinational Corporations in World Development, pp. 59, 189; Frank, Foreign Enterprise, pp.
82-84; Michael Morris, Farid G. Lavipour, and Karl P.

Sauvant, "The Politics of Nationalization: Guyana vs. Alcan," in Controlling Multinational Enterprises, ed. Karl P. Sauvant and Farid G. Lavipour (Boulder, Colo.: Westview Press, 1976), p. 138, n. 10; Dunning, International Production, pp. 333, 335, 367-68; Colman and Nixson, Economics of Change, pp. 261-62.

270. Dunning, International Production, p. 368.

271. Frank, Foreign Enterprise, p. 84.

272. Dunning, International Production, pp. 367-68; Frank, Foreign Enterprise, pp. 83-84.

273. Barnet and Muller, Global Reach, pp. 162-63; Frank, Foreign Enterprise, p. 83; Kochi Hamada, "Taxing the Brain Drain: A Global Point of View," in The New International Economic Order: The North-South Debate, ed. Jagdish N. Bhagwati (Cambridge, Mass.: MIT Press, 1977), pp. 125-58.

274. Frank, Foreign Enterprise, p. 83.

275. Organisation for Economic Cooperation and Development, North/South Technology Transfer.

276. An insider, during a conversation with the author, revealed, first, that Lever Brothers (Nigeria) Limited does not do more than packaging of various brands of detergents (Omo and Surf, to mention only two) for sale on the Nigerian market; second, that Lever Brothers imports large quantities of powdered soap from its former parent company, Unilever, as a result of overproduction and low demand in the United Kingdom (for a variety of reasons); and third, that much of the imported powdered soap is destroyed en route to Nigeria. Needless to mention is the fact that the transaction is fully paid for in scarce, hard (foreign) currency. This information seems to be supported by claims made by Nigerians holding top positions in Cadbury (Nigeria) Limited and Food Specialities (Nigeria) Ltd., namely, that the companies do no more than package beverages, Bournvita (by Cadbury) and Milo (by Food Specialities).

277. Leyland (Nigeria) Limited and Volkswagen of Nigeria Limited, at the time of writing, face very serious problems arising from overproduction and lack of demand, attributed largely to the high costs of "Made-in-Nigeria" cars and importation of various automobiles/trucks which are relatively cheaper than "Made-in-Nigeria" automobiles. This

situation has led to mass retrenchment of workers.
For example, the Nigeria Police, for reasons which
are inexplicable, buys Land Rovers from abroad
rather than from Leyland (Nigeria), the makers of
Land Rovers and Range Rovers, while the Nigerian
Armed Forces (Army/Navy/Air Force), hitherto consumers of Land Rovers, now consume new brands of trucks,
obviously imported from Western Europe.

278. On the characteristics of the aluminum
industry, see Morris, Lavipour, and Sauvant, "Poli-
tics of Nationalization," pp. 112-19; Vaitsos,
"Power, Knowledge and Development Policy: Relations
Between Transnational Enterprises and Developing
Countries," in A World Divided: The Less-Developed
Countries in the International Economy, ed. Gerald
K. Helleiner (Cambridge, England: Cambridge Univer-
sity Press, 1976), pp. 132-33.

279. Morris, Lavipour, and Sauvant, "Politics
of Nationalization," p. 112.

280. Ibid.

281. Ibid., p. 119.

282. Ibid., p. 120.

283. Guyana, in the late 1960s, initiated efforts to gain greater control over Demba, a subsidiary of Alcan, in order to force Demba to locate
smelting facilities. When participation negotiations yielded no results, Demba was nationalized in
March under the Bauxite Nationalisation Bill. See
Morris, Lavipour, and Sauvant, "Politics of Nationalization," pp. 120-33.

284. See Madujibeya, "Oil and Nigeria's Economic Development," African Affairs 85 (1976): 284-
316; Falegan and Okah, "The Contribution of Petroleum
to Nigeria's Economy," pp. 163-98.

285. On why the oil industry has few backward
and forward linkages to the Nigerian economy, see
Madujibeya, "Oil and Nigeria's Economic Development,"
pp. 293-99.

286. The World Bank, Nigeria--Options for
Long Term Development (Baltimore, Md.: Johns Hopkins
University Press, 1974), p. 70.

287. Peter R. Odell, An Economic Geography of
Oil (London: Bell, 1963), p. 185.

288. Morris, Lavipour, and Sauvant, "Politics
of Nationalization," pp. 120-23.

289. Akinsanya, The Expropriation of Multinational Property in the Third World, pp. 336-42; Whiting, "Transnationals and the State in Mexico, 1970-1978," pp. 23-30.

290. See Dale B. Furnish, "The Andean Common Market's Common Regime for Foreign Investments," in Controlling Multinational Enterprises, pp. 181-93.

291. See Emmettee S. Redford et al., Politics and Government in the United States (New York: Harcourt, Brace and World, 1965), pp. 663-69.

292. Dunning, International Production, p. 345.

293. Lall, Developing Countries and Multinational Corporations, p. 28.

294. A. G. Frank, Capitalism and Underdevelopment in Latin America (New York: Monthly Review Press, 1969); Harry Magdoff, The Age of Imperialism (New York: Monthly Review Press, 1969); and Paul A. Baran, The Political Economy of Growth (New York: Prometheus, 1960).

295. See Jonathan F. Galloway, "Multinational Enterprises as World-wide Interest Groups," Politics and Society 1 (1971): 1-20. On dependency generally see Lall, Developing Countries in the International Economy, pp. 3-23; Id., "Is 'Dependence' a Useful Concept in Analysing Underdevelopment?," World Development 3 (1975): 799-810; Theotonio Dos Santos, "The Structure of Dependence," in The Political Economy of Development and Underdevelopment, pp. 109-17.

296. Joan E. Spero, The Politics of International Economic Relations (London: George Allen and Unwin, 1977), p. 199. See also Dunning, International Production, pp. 369-70; and Raymond F. Mikesell, "Effects of Direct Foreign Investment on Development," Economic Impact 35 (1981): 36-41.

4.

Third World Responses to the Multinational Challenge

Many of the arguments advanced today by proponents of the MNC are reminiscent of the classic liberal rationale, such as those that see the MNC as an agent of economic development and world peace. To be sure, advocates and apologists claim that MNCs contribute to DCs by providing access to foreign markets required by DCs and providing the much-needed capital resources, diffusing scarce technology and allocating management skills, thus increasing world production and employment. Multinationals, they say, "deploy resources so as to rationalize worldwide production in accordance with economic efficiency, thereby, helping the world function as a unit."[1] With particular reference to the developing Third World, proponents claim that MNCs help to integrate the DCs into the world (albeit, capitalist) economy and overcome the gap between rich and poor countries, thereby contributing to a more equitable distribution of world's resources and wealth. Therefore, the consequence of MNC activity "is a contribution to world integration, peace, order and justice."[2] What we have been able to demonstrate in Chapter 3 is:

1. While MNCs may well have transferred capital resources from capital-rich countries to capital-poor countries, MNCs, generally, are vehicles through which capital resources are transferred from capital-

poor to capital-rich countries, thanks to such
devices as transfer pricing, overinvoicing imports,
and overpricing technology.

    2. While MNCs may well have exported jobs to
DCs (as claimed by the AFL-CIO) or created jobs, on
balance, and when compared with domestic enterprises,
multinational enterprises do in fact destroy jobs
because they employ technologies that are inconsistent with the factor endowments of Third World host
countries.

    3. While it is not denied that MNCs transfer
or diffuse "scarce" technology to DCs, the technology so diffused or transferred, more often than not,
is inappropriate, obsolete, and overpriced. More
fundamental, this study has supported the claim by
critics of MNC operations that MNCs often create
enclave economies, namely, that MNC operations have
few backward or forward linkages to the local
economy.

    Other conclusions of this study of the role of
MNCs in the development (or underdevelopment) of
Third World countries can be briefly stated.
The first is that MNCs, on the balance, encourage
inappropriate consumption patterns through product
differentiation (or innovation) and massive mar-
keting/advertising techniques. Second, multinationals contribute to the widening elite-mass gap
in the host states by paying their employees higher
salaries and more generous fringe benefits than do
domestic enterprises. Third, through a variety of
sharp business practices by MNCs, the gap between
the industrialized countries of the North and the
agrarian countries of the South is in fact yawning
rather than closing. Fourth, independent national
economic development by Third World countries is
stunted with the introduction of DFI by MNCs.

    Essentially, critics not only view with skep-
ticism claims by proponents that MNCs are engines
of development in DCs, they are also alarmed about
MNC activities, particularly in the Third World.
Some of their arguments recall the theories developed by Karl Marx, Frederich Engels, and John Hobson.
The state, to Marx, is merely an instrument of exploitation of the masses by the dominant bourgeois

class, while Lenin has argued that the fundamental motivation for colonialism and imperialism is economic determinism.[3] More recent Marxist exposition by Paul Sweezy and Harry Magdoff contends not only that all capital is nationally based but also that the spread of the multinational is a mere facade for the growth of Western (and U.S.) capital that perpetuates the colonial structure of the world economy.[4] In The Age of Imperialism,[5] Magdoff sees MNCs as the vehicle of the "new imperialism" of the wealthy and powerful classes in the rich (capitalist) countries pursuing policies to the detriment of the majority of the world's population in the DCs.

In general, Marxists and neo-Marxists have tended to see multinationals as fronts or agents for capitalist states or having a symbiotic relationship and working in concert with those states rather than being independent actors. A cause of concern by critics of U.S.-based MNCs,

> lies in the identification of American multinationals with the foreign policies of the United States. The foreign connections of large American firms leads them to seek "friends" in Washington. Such friendships may be cultivated for mutual advantage, firms expecting U.S. Government support in their foreign operations in return for information or assistance in foreign countries penetrated by the firms. Not only is this inimical to the detachment with which foreign policy should ideally be conducted, but it implants in foreigners an image of the United States in which private firms are identified with official policy.[6]

There are, however, instances in which MNCs pursue their own foreign policies. For example, they may attempt not only to prevent the expansion of socialism but also to destroy or destabilize political institutions or structures inimical to their continued profitable operation.[7] Addressing

the General Assembly of the United Nations on
December 4, 1972, when he denounced the U.S. "financial and economic blockade applied against"
Chile as well as acts of aggression by the Kennecott
Copper Corporation and the International Telephone
and Telegraph Company, President Salvador Allende
said:

> We are witnessing a pitched battle be-
> tween the great transnational corpora-
> tions and sovereign States, for the
> latter's fundamental political, eco-
> nomic and military decisions are being
> interfered with by world-wide organiza-
> tions which are not dependent on any
> single State and which as regards the
> sum total of their activities, are not
> accountable to or regulated by any par-
> liament or institution representing the
> collective interest.[8]

Specifically,

> The trouble with multinational corpo-
> rations . . . is accountability. . . .
> Business is worldwide; government or
> law is not. Consequently, world-corps
> are free of effective control. And
> lacking accountability, they lack
> legitimacy, for a government or a
> world-corp to have legitimacy, it must
> be responsible to people and institutions
> outside itself and must be supported by
> an informed labour and consumer con-
> stituency which is so intimately af-
> fected. Multinational firms are free
> of such restraints. To whom are they
> responsible? To those who govern them?
> Who are they? A self perpetuating oli-
> garchy. Who selected them? . . . They
> selected themselves. The question at
> issue, therefore, is whether a set of
> institutions and devices can be worked
> out which will guide the MNC's exercise
> of powers and introduce some form of
> accountability into their activities.[9]

Unfortunately, the international community has not been able to reach agreement on these and many other issues.

Giving a liberal interpretation of colonialism and imperialism, Hobson argued that international finance was the motivating force in imperialist foreign policies as various capitalist interest groups tried to "use their governments in order to secure for their use some distant undeveloped country by annexation and protection."[10] It is true that Hobson later said that he had distorted the situation by oversimplification. Neo-Hobson arguments have made the point that the competitive struggles for overseas markets and raw materials inevitably lead to international tensions and conflicts and, ultimately, to war. Hobson, a non-Marxist, and other non-Marxists have been critical of MNCs and capitalism. First, they reject the claim that MNCs allocate global resources efficiently and contribute to the growth of DCs, if only because the gap between the rich and poor countries is yawning rather than closing. Second, they also reject MNCs' claims to economic rationality and efficiency, again because multinationals create artificial demands and produce unnecessary goods and services, namely, that MNCs create or distort tastes and encourage inappropriate consumption, and because "'rationalization of production' often is really the transfer of capital across national boundaries in search of low tax havens."[11] Third, and more fundamental, a number of practices by MNCs "detract from rather than add to economic development: profits often are exorbitant with too small a proportion reinvested; the shifting of production from one market to another adds to unemployment, erosion of the tax base and concomitant social dislocations; and MNCs, obsessed with production and profits, give no consideration to undesirable environmental and ecological consequences."[12] Fourth, the sheer economic power of MNCs as shown in Table 3.2, which intersperses billion-dollar or more MNCs (in terms of sales) with 100 nation-states ranked by the size of their GNPs, makes a prima facie case for considering them significant political actors. Not only do they constitute imperium in imperio (a state within a state), more often than not MNC operations are at variance with the goals and aspirations of several Third World host states. To sum up, the trend toward increasing MNC control of the global economy has meant undesirable economic, social, and political consequences. Simply put, instead of reducing barriers between peoples, MNC activity aggravates international tensions and stimulates economic nationalism in the Third World.

As a consequence of economic nationalism that has characterized the politics of DCs since the late 1960s--indeed, as a consequence of the changing relations between MNCs and host countries on the one hand and between DCs and DMEs on the other hand-- several governments in the Third World have reacted differently to the multinational challenge. In general, all countries, explicitly or implicitly, adopt some stance on DFI. This may range from no policy or a laissez-faire approach to DFI to the other extreme of outlawing DFI. To be sure, responses to the multinational challenge differ from one to another; in fact, it is possible to identify attitudes of countries toward DFI by such variables as size, stage of development, culture, and political ideology. For example, changes in form of governments (through military/palace/parliamentary coups d'état, revolution, or civil war) have induced far more dramatic policy changes toward DFI than any action on the part of MNCs.

In any event, the response to the multinational challenge is manifested by such policy measures as:[13]

1. nationalization or expropriation of all foreign-owned enterprises;
2. indigenization of foreign-owned enterprises to reduce or completely outlaw foreign equity participation in such enterprises;
3. renegotiation, restructuring, or termination of concession agreements or state contracts (with aliens);
4. negotiated sales or purchases of foreign-owned enterprises; and
5. "intervention" or effectively taking over control or management of foreign-owned enterprises,

thereby effectively impairing operations of such enterprises and forcing the enterprises to cease operations.

DIRECT FOREIGN INVESTMENTS IN THE
DEVELOPING COUNTRIES

Let us recall Table 3.5 showing that of a total estimated stock of DFI of some $165 billion by the end of 1971, most of which is owned by MNCs, the U.S. share stands at 52 percent. The United States is trailed by the United Kingdom (14.5 percent), France (5.8 percent), and the Federal Republic of Germany (4.4 percent). Let us again recall Table 3.13 showing regional and sectoral distribution of DFI in the Third World by the end of 1970. Of a book value of $40 billion, representing about 25 percent of the world's total DFI, just over 30 percent is in manufacturing, followed by petroleum 33.3 percent, mining 10.3 percent, while others account for 24.9 percent. By the early 1970s, investment in manufacturing accounts for approximately 50 percent of total DFI, given the growing assertiveness of many Third World countries to exercise greater control over the exploitation of their vital and irreplaceable natural resources. For example, Table 4.1 shows that 41.3 percent of U.S. DFI by the end of 1970 was manufacturing, followed by petroleum (27.9 percent), while others (including agriculture, shipping, trade, banking, and tourism) and mining represent 23 and 7.9 percent, respectively. In fact, investment in the extractive sector stood at 35.8 percent.

However, as stated in Chapter 3, most MNC activities are concentrated in the DMEs rather than in the DCs. Table 4.2, showing the distribution of DFI of DMEs, indicates that 41 percent of this investment, at the end of 1975, was located in Canada, the United States, the United Kingdom, and the Federal Republic of Germany.

While the share of total stock of DFI located in the DMEs increased from 69 percent in 1967 to 72 percent in 1971 and again to 74 percent in 1975, the share located in DCs fell from 31 percent in

1967 to 28 percent in 1971 and 26 percent in 1975. To be sure, only 17 percent of total stock of DFI was actually located in the Third World when we consider the fact that 3 and 6 percent of total stock of DFI going to the DCs went to tax-haven and OPEC countries, respectively. In essence, less than 20 percent of total stock of DFI was exposed at the end of 1971 to politics of economic nationalism in the Third World.

TABLE 4.1

Stock of United States Direct Foreign Investment
by Industrial Sector Year-End 1970

Sector	$ million	%
Mining	6,137	7.9
Petroleum	21,790	27.9
Manufacturing	32,231	41.3
Others	17,932	23.0
All Sectors	78,090	100.0[a]

Source: United Nations, Multinational Corporations in World Development. Publication no. E.73.II.4.11, pp. 151-52.
[a]Percentages do not add up to 100 because in a number of cases the form of ownership is unknown.

TABLE 4.2

Stock of Direct Foreign Investment of Developed
Market Economies by Host Country/Area:
Selected Years

	1967	1971	1975
Host Country and Country Group			
Total Value ($ billion)	105	156	259
Distribution of Stock (%)a			
Developed Market Economies	69	72	74
Canada	18	17	15
United States of America	9	9	11
United Kingdom	8	9	9
Federal Republic of Germany	3	5	6
Others	30	32	33
Developing Countries	31	28	26
OPEC Countries	9	7	6
Tax Havens	2	3	3
Others	20	17	17
Total	100	100	100

Source: United Nations, Transnational Corporation in World Development: A Re-Examination,
Publication no. E/C. 10/38, March 20, 1978, p. 237.
aPercentages do not add up to 100 because of
rounding.
bAlgeria, Ecuador, Gabon, Indonesia, Iran,
Iraq, Kuwait, Libya, Nigeria, Qatar, Saudi Arabia,
United Arab Emirates, and Venezuela.
cBahamas, Barbados, Bermuda, Cayman Islands,
Netherlands Antilles, and Panama.

RESPONSES TO ECONOMIC NATIONALISM IN
THE THIRD WORLD

When we examine the politics of economic
nationalism in the Third World, it seems apparent
that the United States has been hardest hit by expropriatory measures taken by several DCs, followed
by the United Kingdom and France. Although Japan's
share of some $165 billion of DFI at the end of
1971 stood at 2.7 percent, available evidence and
data suggest that Japanese investors have fared better than investors from the United States, Switzerland, the United Kingdom, France, Canada, Federal
Republic of Germany, and the Netherlands. Because
the United States dominated the investment picture
in Latin America and Asia (as shown in Table 4.3),
we should naturally expect the U.S.-owned enterprises to be more vulnerable to expropriation than
their counterparts from the United Kingdom, France,
and the Netherlands (see also Table 4.4).

When we consider investor nationality and vulnerability to expropriation in Latin America, certain facts stand clear. The first is that U.S.-
owned enterprises were more vulnerable than their
U.K., Dutch, French, or Canadian counterparts.
Second, U.S. enterprises' vulnerability was exceeded
only by that of the Swiss: Swiss-owned enterprises
were expropriated in Argentina (1974, communications), Peru (1972, public utilities; 1974, cement),
and Venezuela (1974, dairy production). Surpris-
ingly, the Swiss, with relatively small amounts of
DFI in Latin America compared with the United
States, which had $16.6 billion (66 percent) out
of $25.2 billion DFI in the Third World located in
Latin America, were caught in the net of widespread
expropriatory actions while U.S. enterprises were
expropriated in virtually all the Latin American
countries during the period 1968-76 except Brazil,
Colombia (which expropriated U.K., Dutch, and
Canadian enterprises), Nicaragua, Paraguay, and
Uruguay. Third, Canada took the third position as
Canadian investments were expropriated in Guyana
and Jamaica (bauxite); Colombia and Trinidad and
Tobago (banks) Panama and Peru (agriculture); and
Trinidad and Tobago (manufacturing). Fourth, although
it is difficult to separate Canadian enterprises from

TABLE 4.3

Distribution of Foreign Direct Investment in Latin America and Asia
by Sector and Investor Country 1967
($ million)

Investing Country	Petroleum	Production	Refining	Marketing	Transport	Mining	Agriculture	Manufacturing	Trade	Utilities	Transport	Banking	Tourism	Other	Total
United States	3,329	2,055	732	258	285	1,720	382	3,627	1,286	489	231	134	152	425	11,777
United Kingdom	492	252	129	71	40	10	203	487	176	41	81	51	67	85	1,693
Switzerland								200	19	10		9		90	427
Sweden						2		74	4					1	81
Portugal								2	2			2			6
Norway								5	1						6
Netherlands	638	315	178	84	60	24	1	218	21	22		13	1	3	940
Japan						32	5	292	73			5			405
Italy							1	367	8	2		15			392
Germany						5	2	731	29	1	13			9	788
France						21	14	377	28	1	1	6		2	468
Denmark								3	2						5
Canada	26	6		5	15	202	1	159	18	706	53	24	34	120	1,343
Belgium								108	1			4			113
Austria								4	1						5
Australia															
Total	4,486	2,628	1,039	418	401	2,016	608	6,653	1,668	1,371	368	287	260	678	18,449

Source: Organisation for Economic Cooperation and Development, Stock of Private Direct Investments by Development Assistance Committee Countries in Developing Countries, End 1967 (Paris: OECD, 1972).

U.S. ownership and control, if only because we know
that about 49 percent of the equity interest in
Alcan is owned by U.S. nationals, the vulnerability
of U.S.- and Canadian-owned enterprises to expropriation is partly due to their images as colonial
powers who have exercised a hegemonial relationship
over Latin America and the Caribbean; it is also a
function of the concentration of their investments
in sensitive, therefore vulnerable sectors (natural
resources and public utilities) that, in turn, reflects the timing of their penetration into the
economies of the countries concerned. This situation, certainly, can be compared with the Dutch,
Italians, French, and Germans who penetrated the
region at a much later date and to a lesser degree
than did the North Americans, and their investments
were located, in general, in less sensitive sectors
of the host economies.

Let us now examine the extent and distribution
of U.S. and U.K. direct foreign investment since
both countries followed by France and Japan were the
major capital-exports to the developing countries.
In 1960, the year of independence for many African
countries, 38 percent of the book value of U.S. DFI
was in DCs; seven years later, the figure had dropped
to 26, and by 1973, a year after the U.S. government
made clear its intention, through the Gonzalez Amendment on multilateral assistance, to assist U.S. investors by voting against loan applications in multilateral development institutions submitted by countries expropriating U.S. investments "without adequate, effective and prompt compensation," the figure
was only 24 percent.

The pattern with respect to U.K. DFI was similar, and, as Table 4.5 reveals, 28 percent of U.K.
DFI in 1962 was sited in the former British colonies
in Africa, Asia, the Middle East, and the Western
Hemisphere. Eight years later the figure stood at
20 percent, and it dropped by 5 percent four years
after that.

Because all available evidence points to the
fact that U.S. investors had been hardest hit by expropriatory measures taken by a number of DCs, particularly in Latin America and the Middle East, our
illustrations on expropriatory measures as well as

TABLE 4.4

United States Direct Foreign Investments by Country/Area and Year-End

$ million

Country/Area	1950	1957	1960	1962	1965	1967	1968	1969	1970	1973	1978
All Countries	11,788 (100%)	25,262 (100%)	32,778 (100%)	39,226 (100%)	49,474 (100%)	56,583 (100%)	64,983 (100%)	70,763 (100%)	78,090 (100%)	100,675 (100%)	165,100 (100%)
Developed Countries	5,312 (45%)	13,905 (55%)	17,879 (55%)	22,618 (61%)	29,393 (59%)	37,708 (69%)	43,500 (67%)	47,701 (67%)	47,572 (61%)	72,214 (70%)	120,700 (72%)
Developing Countries	5,864 (50%)	10,316 (41%)	12,478 (38%)	12,960 (35%)	16,373 (33%)	14,928 (26%)	18,753 (29%)	20,000 (28%)	23,772 (30%)	25,266 (24%)	40,500 (24%)
Others	612 (5%)	1,041 (4%)	2,412 (7%)	1,647 (4%)	3,798 (8%)	2,947 (5%)	2,731 (4%)	3,061 (5%)	7,048 (9%)	6,195 (6%)	6,900 (4%)

Sources: Devlin and Kruer, "The International Investment Position of the United States: Developments in 1969," Survey of Current Business 50 (1970): 28; U.S. Department of Commerce, Business Investment in Foreign Countries (Washington, D.C.: Government Printing Office, 1960); Id., Survey of Current Business, August 1964 and August 1979; Id., Revised Data Series on U.S. Direct Investment, 1966-1974 (Washington, D.C.: Government Printing Office, 1974).

the consequences of such measures for government-business relations will be drawn from the U.S. experience, particularly in Latin America.

TABLE 4.5

United Kingdom Direct Foreign Investments*
by Country/Area and Year-End

Country/Area	1962		1970		1974	
	£m	%	£m	%	£m	%
All Areas	3,405	100	6,404	100	10,623	100
Developed Common- wealth (inc. Canada)	1,470	43	2,759	43	3,961	37
Developing Common- wealth	936	28	1,300	20	1,633	15
United States	301	9	769	13	1,678	16
European Economic Community (The Six)	272	8	808	13	2,095	20
European Free Trade Area (The Seven)	82	2	182	3	373	4
Other	344	10	593	9	883	8

*Excludes oil, banking, and insurance.
Source: John M. Stopford, "Changing Perspectives on Investment by British Manufacturing Multinationals," Journal of International Business Studies (1976): 15.

EXPROPRIATIONS AND GOVERNMENT-
BUSINESS RELATIONS

Diplomatic Interventions in
Investment Disputes

Let us recall and amplify four assumptions underlining this study as stated in Chapter 2. First, expropriatory actions taken by several DCs can be

defended or justified on grounds of "public interest."
In any event, expropriations of foreign-owned assets
have generally not been questioned by investors
and/or investor states (including the United States)
unless the measures were patently discriminatory
(namely, directed against particular national/racial
groups) or the measures were inconsistent with the
treaty obligations of the taking states. Usually,
the investor state stays in the background while its
national, whose assets are affected, is encouraged
to pursue his claims with the taking state, availing
himself of appropriate available local remedies. The
second assumption is that private investors engage
in business not for philanthropic reasons but to
make profits. Thus, barring "superior" needs of the
state, they naturally expect to carry on with their
operations.

Third, when foreign-owned assets are expropriated, a conflict of interest arises between the taking state and the alien investor; the conflict, more
often than not, centers on the quantum of compensation. Thus, while the taking state favors the "book
value" (since the investor uses "book value" for tax
purposes), the investor naturally favors the "market
value" or "going-concern value" since this guarantees him greater, and to him "adequate," compensation.
While compensation received by the investor, in most
instances, is less than adequate, the bargaining
power of the investor is enhanced if there is a convergence of interest between the investor and his
home state and/or a major investor state, as demonstrated by the compensation negotiations between the
Aluminium Company of Canada and the government of
Guyana following the nationalization of Demba,
Alcan's subsidiary. Sometimes, the investor, other
things considered, is prepared to settle for less
than adequate compensation.

Fourth, when the assets of an alien investor
are expropriated, he will, among other things, seek
the support or intervention of his home state. If
he is a U.S. investor, he may suggest cutting off
bilateral/multilateral assistance under the Hicken-
looper/Gonzalez Amendment to the Foreign Assistance
Acts, the Fisheries Act, the Sugar Act, and Food Aid
Program or a denial of trade preferential treatment

under the Trade Act of 1974.[14] There is nothing bizarre in making such suggestions. But the United States, or better still the Department of State, may well have a series of other matters either with the taking state or with a regional group (of which the taking state is a part).

For example, it would be very difficult to maintain an Alliance for Progress in Latin America if every investment dispute,[15] large or small, threatened to terminate or suspend U.S. bilateral assistance to such a taking state. Therefore, the Department of State and the aggrieved U.S. investor may differ about the tactics to follow. The former may attempt to seek answers to the following questions:

1. Is the investor a model or a good corporate citizen deserving U.S. diplomatic support?
2. Would it be better to press hard now or to wait in order to allow feelings or tempers to cool down?
3. Is the problem really his investment in the taking state or his world-wide investment position?
4. Would exhaustion of local remedies produce a fair result?
5. What about the issues on the merits?
6. Is the investor threatened with expropriation or is the host state engaged in legitimate regulatory activity?
7. Does the investor's call for the suspension of bilateral/multilateral assistance or the denial of trade preferential treatment have the support of the entire foreign business community?
8. Is there something to the host state's claim that the investor has not made the maximum production effort required by the contract or that he has fallen behind on his program for training indigenes?

In essence, the Department of State cannot simply agree with the contention that what is good for the U.S. investor abroad is also good for the United States.

Put differently, much depends on timing, the volume of investments expropriated, the influence and power that can be wielded by the investor in the politics of his home state, and the way that the investor state perceives the taking in terms of its overall foreign policy interests. For example, when the Bolivian subsidiary of the Standard Oil Company of New Jersey was expropriated on March 13, 1937, and Standard Oil put pressure on the Department of State to take up its case in demanding compensation from the Bolivian government, the U.S. government refused to play the game. This was certainly a historic precedent in that for the first time the "United States did not act harshly against a country that had mistreated U.S. business interests."[16] And, as explained by Bryce Wood:

> The . . . policy which does not appear to have been stated explicitly by the Department of State, may, it is suggested, be regarded as being based on the principle that the interests of United States business enterprises in Latin America were not identical with the interests of the government of the United States but were of substantially less importance. The interests of business enterprises would be protected so far as protection did not interfere with what the Department regarded as the essential requirements for the maintenance of good political relations with Latin American countries.[17]

And, again, when the International Petroleum Company, the Peruvian subsidiary of Standard Oil, was expropriated by the Velasco regime and Standard Oil asked the Department of State to apply the Hickenlooper Amendment, arguing that only a tough policy could deter future expropriations or ensure "prompt, adequate, and effective compensation," officials in the State Department took the position that aid sanctions (as required by the Hickenlooper Amendment) "would only strengthen nationalist hostility to foreign investment throughout Latin America."[18] In any case, almost all other U.S. investors, led by Marcona Corporation (which was expropriated in 1973),[19] opposed

the application of the Hickenlooper Amendment. Therefore, we venture to hypothesize that:

> Whereas expropriations of the service
> sector (banking, insurance, hotels,
> etc.) do not generate much diplomatic
> controversies between the taking and
> investor states because the assets are
> usually valued only in hundreds of
> thousands of collars, expropriations
> of the mining (extractive), power, com-
> munications, and agricultural sectors
> usually and generally generate much
> diplomatic controversies between the
> taking and investor states and could
> lead to government-to-government con-
> frontation, particularly if such in-
> vestments carry government insurance
> coverage.

We hold this view for a number of reasons. The
first relates to the size of the investments expropriated, and as it is demonstrated in Table 4.7, extractive (petroleum or mining) enterprises are highly capital intensive. They entail a heavier financial (capital) outlay than investments in the service industries (for example, banking and insurance).
Second, several developed countries including the
United States have regulations excluding alien capital investments from the banking industry, if only
because banking and fiduciary activities are considered a sensitive sector of the economy.[20] Thus, the
nationalization of the service sector (which includes
the banking industry) does not generate much controversy between the taking and investor states.
Third, the investments, so expropriated, are
regarded as the patrimony of the investor states.
Fourth, and more fundamental, one has to consider
the benefits derived by the investor states in terms
of easing the problems of balance of payments, providing jobs for nationals of investor states, and
revenues accruing to the investor states. For example, Table 4.6 shows the tax revenues accruing to
the United States from the foreign operations of
U.S. oil companies (U.S. "Sisters"). Fifth, many
investor states invoke Palmerstonian imagery, con-

ceptualizing corporations as citizens entitled to
the full protection of their governments with respect to their properties. Sixth, extractive (natural resources), power/communication, and agricultural sectors are considered (by the taking states) as
basic to future industrialization. Since these sectors are controlled by alien investors who, naturally, owe their loyalties to their home states and cannot be trusted during periods of international crises
and grave national emergencies, alien control of
these sectors raises fundamental and sensitive issues
of national sovereignty.

We must emphasize here that expropriatory measures need not automatically lead to government-to-
government confrontation, first, if such measures
are accompanied by compensation, which may be far
from being adequate; second, if prospects for DFIs
continue to exist in the taking states; and third,
because a state expropriating private-owned assets
is in fact exercising its power of eminent domain.
In essence, whether an investor state intervenes on
behalf of its nationals depends on the influence
that those nationals have over domestic and foreign
policies.

Table 4.7 shows the size of expropriated assets
in selected DCs in the Third World. In several
cases, diplomatic representations on behalf of the
affected aliens have been made by their home states
with varying results. In many other cases, the investor states have been content to ask their nationals to avail themselves of local remedies; they have
come into the investment dispute only when there is
manifest denial of justice or when they are convinced that their nationals are unlikely to get
proper justice--and in which case, the investor
states, through exchange of diplomatic notes with
the taking states, suggest the resolution of the
dispute through international arbitration or meet-
ings of officials of investor and taking states.
Expropriation proceedings carried out in Mexico,
Guatemala, and Nicaragua were settled by arbitra-
tions while the Peruvian expropriations carried out
between 1968 and 1969 were settled following extensive discussions carried out between President Richard
Nixon's Special Envoy, James R. Green, and top Peruvian officials representing the Velasco regime.

TABLE 4.6

Size of Expropriated Assets in Selected Developing Countries

Year	Country	Enterprise or Type of Investment	Book Value or Compensation Claim	Nationality	Insurance Coverage	Compensation Settlement and Year
1975	Afghanistan	Industrial Dev. Bank of Afghanistan	$3,428,000	U.S.A.	None	n.a.
1967	Algeria	Detersav-Algerie	$2,100,000	U.S.A.	None	n.a.
1967	Algeria	Mobil, Exxon, Newmont Mining	n.a.	U.S.A.	n.a.	n.a.; 1970
1971	Algeria	Compania Francaise des Petroles (CFP) and Enterprises de Recherches d'Applications Petrolieres (ERAP)	n.a.	France	n.a.	CFP got $54 million plus other concessions
1971	Algeria	Mobil, ARCO, Sinclair, Exxon, Phillips, Getty, Atlas, (Dresser), Magcobar (Dresser), Drilling Specialities (Phillips sub.)	$4,500,000	U.S.A.	n.a.	n.a.
1976	Algeria	Compagnie Algerienne de Methane Liquide	n.a.	France	n.a.	n.a.; 1976
1958	Argentina	American and Foreign Power Co.	$60,000,000	U.S.A.		$56,300,000 arbitral award; 1961
1963	Argentina	Argentine Cities Service Development Co., Continental Oil Co. of Argentina, Marathon Petrol Argentina, Esso Argentina Inc., Pan American International Oil, Tennessee Argentina, S.A., Trans World Drilling Co., Union Oil of California, etc.	$300,000,000–$395,000,000	U.S.A.	n.a.	$51,700,000 for five companies; 1965
1963	Argentina	Shell Production Co. (U.K.)	n.a.	U.K.	n.a.	$21,500,000

232

Year	Country	Enterprise	Book Value	Owners	Compensation	Settlement
1973	Argentina	Cabot Corporation	n.a.	U.S.A.	Yes	$1,000,000; 1973
1973	Argentina	Banking industry	n.a.	Local/Foreign	n.a.	Four U.S. banks received $16,500,000; 1974
1974	Argentina	Exxon, Cities Service Development Co.	n.a.	U.S.A.	n.a.	Denationalized with compensation; 1976
1974	Argentina	Public utilities	n.a.	Switzerland	n.a.	n.a.
1974	Argentina	Standard Electric of Argentina (ITT)	$64,000,000	U.S.A.	n.a.	n.a.; compensation settlement
n.d.a.	Burma	Value of expropriated assets	$100,000,000	1. British: $70,000,000 2. Indian: $25,000,000 3. Pakistan/Swedish/Chinese/Others: $5,000,000	n.a.	n.a.
1967–73	Chile	Enterprises Chileanized/nationalized under Frei and Allende	$1 billion	Mostly U.S.A.	$389,000,000–$400,000,000	Negotiated
1967	Chile	Kennecott Copper Corp. (51 percent); Cerro Corp. (30 percent); Anaconda (25 percent)	n.a.	U.S.A.	Yes	$115,250,000
1969	Chile	Anaconda (51 percent)	n.a.	U.S.A.	Yes	$203,000,000
1970–73	Chile	Enterprises nationalized under Allende[a]	$700,000,000	U.S.A.	Yes	
		1. Anaconda, Kennecott, and Cerro Corporations	$616,500,000	U.S.A.	Yes	$362,800,000; 1974
		2. Guías Telefonicas de Chile and Chile Telephone Co.	$153,000,000	U.S.A.	Yes	$125,000,000; 1974 plus $35,000,000 from OPIC[a]
		3. South American Power Co.	$81,300,000	U.S.A.	n.a.	$31,000,000; 1971
		4. Bethlehem Steel Co.	$22,000,000	U.S.A.	Yes	
		5. Bank of America/Citibank	$3,800,000 (Bank of America)	U.S.A.	None	$5,000,000 for Bank of America and Citibank
		6. Anglo-Lautara	$6,700,000	U.S.A.	Yes	n.a.; 1971

(continued)

233

Table 4.6, continued

Year	Country	Enterprise or Type of Investment	Book Value or Compensation Claim	Nationality	Insurance Coverage	Compensation Settlement and Year
		7. Industrias Nacional de Neumaticos, S.A.	$25,000,000	U.S.A.	None	n.a.
		8. Industrias NIBCO SGM Sudamericana	$300,000	U.S.A.	Yes	n.a.
		9. Ford Motor Co.	n.a.	U.S.A.	Yes	$910,885 from OPIC
		10. Sociedad Quimica y Minera de Chile, S.A.	$8,000,000	U.S.A.	None	n.a.
		11. Petroquimica Dow, S.A.	$2,000,000	U.S.A.	None	n.a.
		12. Shell, COPEC, Exxon	$40,000,000	U.S.A.	n.a.	n.a.
		13. Purina de Chile, S.A.	$448,000	U.S.A.	Yes	$448,000
		14. Quimicas Dupont S.A.	$1,000,000	U.S.A.	None	n.a.
1919	Cuba	Condemned property	$595,999	U.S.A.	n.a.	$190,000; n.d.a.
1959-60	Cuba	Cattle ranches; sugar lands and mills; oil refineries; banks, nickel plant; manu-facturing plants; public utilities; hotels; etc.	over 5,800 claims valued at $3,346,000,000	Mostly U.S.A.	n.a.	Compensation settlement pending. Cuban assets of $30,000,000 frozen by U.S. (1963)
1970	Ecuador	All American Cables and Radio	$4,500,000- $8,900,000	U.S.A.	None	$600,000; 1971
1970	Ecuador	Forestal Equatoriana S.A.	n.a.	U.S.A.	Yes	£100,000
1971	Ecuador	Minas y Petroles	n.a.	U.S.A.	None	n.a.
1972	Ecuador	Ada Concession	n.a.	U.S.A.	None	No compensation
1972	Ecuador	All American Cables and Radio (estates/agrarian assets)	$1,500,000	U.S.A.	None	n.a.
1974	Ecuador	Texaco/Gulf Consortium	n.a.	U.S.A.	n.a.	$148,000,000

1977	Ecuador	Gulf Oil Co.	$122,000,000	n.a.	U.S.A.	$82,000,000
1928	Guatemala	Chicle	$561,000	n.a.	U.S.A.	$225,000; 1930
1953-54	Guatemala	United Fruit Co. (uncultivated lands)	$15,854,849	n.a.	U.S.A.	denationalized after overthrow of Colonel Arbenz
1968	Guatemala	International Railways of Central America	n.a.	None	U.S.A.	n.a.
1971	Guatemala	Empressa Electrica	n.a.	None	U.S.A.	Book value; n.d.a.
1958	Indonesia	Dutch-owned enterprises following Indonesian Independence and dispute over Irian Barat	n.a.	n.a.	Netherlands	Dfl. 683,000,000; 1966
1960-65	Indonesia	Estates; plantations producing agricultural crops; banks; merchant houses; agency firms; factories; insurance companies[b]; extractive and manufacturing firms (Shell, Unilever, British American Tobacco Co.)	£150,000,000	n.a.	U.K.	n.a.
	Indonesia	P. T. Baud	$6,000,000	None	U.S.A.	Indonesia offered $450,000
1966	Indonesia	Manhattan Securities Co.	$750,000	n.a.	U.S.A.	n.a.
	Indonesia	Shell Indonesia	$110,000,000	n.a.	U.S.A./U.K.	n.a.
1951	Iran	Anglo-Iranian Oil Co.	n.a.	n.a.	U.K.	Firm to receive from Iran £25,000,000 and £214,000,000 from other members of the consortium
1973	Iran	International Oil Consortium	n.a.	n.a.	International Consortium	n.a.
1961	Iraq	Iraqi Petroleum Co.	n.a.	n.a.	Consortium[c]	n.a.
1963	Iraq	American Eastern Tankers	n.a.	n.a.	U.S.A.	n.a.

(continued)

235

Table 4.6, continued

Year	Country	Enterprise or Type of Investment	Book Value or Compensation Claim	Nationality	Insurance Coverage	Compensation Settlement and Year
1963	Iraq	Bisra Shipping Co.	n.a.	U.S.A.	n.a.	n.a.
1963	Iraq	Everett Shipping Co.	n.a.	U.S.A.	n.a.	n.a.
1964	Iraq	Insurance industry	n.a.	Local/foreign	n.a.	n.a.
1964	Iraq	Banking industry	n.a.	U.K./ Lebanon	n.a.	n.a.
1967	Iraq	Iraqi Petroleum Co.	$350,000,000	Consortium[c]	n.a.	n.a.
1973	Iraq	Mobil/Exxon	n.a.	U.S.A.	n.a.	n.a.
1973	Iraq	Basrah Petroleum Co.	n.a.	Consortium[d]	n.a.	n.a.
1975	Iraq	Dutch/Portuguese enterprises	n.a.	Netherlands/Portugal	n.a.	n.a.
1975	Jamaica	Jamaica Telephone Co.	$31,075,000	U.S.A.	n.a.	$31,075,000
1976	Jamaica	Aluminum firms	n.a.	Canada	n.a.	n.a.
1976	Jamaica	Alcoa (51 percent)	$10,500,000	U.S.A.	Yes	n.a.
1977	Jamaica	Kaiser Aluminum (51 percent)	$20,110,000	U.S.A.	Yes	n.a.
1977	Jamaica	Reynolds Aluminum	$22,000,000	U.S.A.	Yes	n.a.
n.d.a.	Kenya	Industrial and commercial enterprises; public utilities (electric power); banking industry; petroleum refining (Exxon, Mobil, Caltex)	n.a.	U.S.A./U.K.	n.a.	n.a.
		Value of U.S. assets affected	$80,000,000	U.S.A.	n.a.	n.a.
1974	Kenya	Saul/Miller Ruby Mine (Kenya)	n.a.	U.S.A.	n.a.	n.a.
1969-73	Libya	1. 50-100 percent equity interests in oil industry	n.a.	U.S.A./U.K.	n.a.	n.a.

Year	Country	Item	Amount	Ownership		Status
		2. 50 percent equity interests in some oil companies and outright takeover of some oil companies		U.S.A./U.K.	n.a.	n.a.
		3. Oasis Petroleum Co.	n.a.	U.S.A.	n.a.	$17,000,000; 1974
		4. Standard Oil Co. (Exxon)	n.a.	U.S.A.	n.a.	$350,000
		5. Gulf Oil Co.	n.a.	U.S.A.	n.a.	n.a.
		6. Chappaqua Oil Co.	n.a.	U.S.A.	n.a.	Negotiated; 1974
		7. Mobil Oil (Libya) Limited	n.a.	U.S.A.	n.a.	Negotiated; n.d.a.
		8. Texaco Overseas Petroleum Co.	n.a.	U.S.A.	n.a.	Negotiated; n.d.a.
		9. Grace Overseas Petroleum Co.	n.a.	U.S.A.	n.a.	Negotiated; n.d.a.
		10. California Asiatic Oil Co. (SOCAL)	n.a.	U.S.A.	n.a.	Negotiated; n.d.a.
		11. Occidental Petroleum Co.	n.a.	U.S.A.	n.a.	Negotiated; 1973
		12. Hunt International Petroleum Co.	n.a.	U.S.A.	n.a.	Negotiated; 1975
		13. British Petroleum	£250,000,000	U.K.	n.a.	Libya offered £75,000,000-100,000,000
		14. Insurance/Banking Industries	n.a.	Local/foreign	n.a.	n.a.
		15. Libyan Engineering and Construction Co.	n.a.	Libya/U.S.A.	None	n.a.
1917-41	Mexico	Landholdings, 1917-41	$37,000,000	U.S.A.	None	n.a.
1937	Mexico	National Railways	$75,000,000	U.S.A.	None	$41,000,000; 1941
1938	Mexico	Petroleum industry	$262,000,000-$450,000,000	U.S.A./U.K./Netherlands	None	$13,000,000; 1940 $24,000,000; 1942
1960	Mexico	American and Foreign Power Co.	$69,500,000	U.S.A.	n.a.	$70,000,000; 1960
1965	Mexico	Asarco Mexicana	n.a.	U.S.A.	n.a.	n.a.
1965	Mexico	Industrias Petroles	n.a.	U.S.A.	n.a.	n.a.
1967	Mexico	Compania Azufrera Mexicana Companie Explotadora del Istimo	$49,500,000	U.S.A.	n.a.	n.a.
1969	Mexico	Compania de Azufre Veracruz S.A.	$24,000,000	U.S.A.	n.a.	n.a.
1969	Mexico	Other claims	$3,000,000	U.S.A.	n.a.	n.a.

(continued)

Table 4.6, continued

Year	Country	Enterprise or Type of Investment	Book Value or Compensation Claim	Nationality	Insurance Coverage	Compensation Settlement and Year
1970–76	Nigeria	1. Two phases of indigenization under 1973 and 1977 Nigerian Enterprises Promotion Acts				
		2. 60 percent equity interests in foreign-owned banks and insurance and oil companies	n.a.	U.S.A./U.K./France Italy/Netherlands	n.a.	n.a.
		3. Bank of America, First National Bank of Chicago, and Chase Manhattan	n.a.	U.S.A.	n.a.	Negotiated settlement
		4. Esso Standard Limited	n.a.	U.S.A.	n.a.	$3,175,000
		5. American International Insurance Co.	n.a.	U.S.A.	n.a.	Received $353,058 with reservations
		6. Shell, Mobil, Agip, Phillips Gulf, Texaco/Chevron, Elf, and British Petroleum	n.a.	U.S.A./U.K./Netherlands France/Italy	None	Participation and Sharing Agreements with Nigeria
1979		7. British Petroleum	£1 billion	U.K.	n.a.	Compensation settlements reached. Possibility of denationalization
1972	Pakistan	Insurance industry	n.a.	Local/foreign	None	American Life Insurance Co. received compensation but rupee devalued by 130 percent
1976	Pakistan	Esso Standard	n.a.	U.S.A.	n.a.	$5,800,000
1976	Pakistan	Modern Cotton Ginning and Seed Oil Factory	n.a.	U.S.A.	n.a.	$66,000
1976	Pakistan	Gul Flour and General Mills	n.a.	U.S.A.	n.a.	Compensation claim filed with Pakistan
1968–69	Peru	International Petroleum Co. and several enterprises	n.a.	U.S.A.	None	Lump sum compensation of $76,000,000 to be distributed by U.S.A.

Year	Country	Enterprise	Book value	Owner	Compensation	Remarks
1970	Peru	Peruvian Telephone Co.	$18,500,000	U.S.A.	n.a.	$17,900,000; 1970
1970	Peru	Chase Manhattan Bank	n.a.	U.S.A.	n.a.	$6,300,000; n.d.a.
1970	Peru	American Smelting and Refining Co.	n.a.	U.S.A.	n.a.	n.a.
n.d.a.	Peru	Uncultivated lands	n.a.	Canada	n.a.	n.a.
1970	Peru	Andes del Peru (Anaconda)	n.a.	U.S.A.	n.a.	n.a.
1970	Peru	Cerro de Pasco Corp. (iron ore, estates, animals)	n.a.	U.S.A.	n.a.	n.a.
1972	Peru	Public utilities	n.a.	Switzerland	n.a.	n.a.
1973	Peru	Four fishmeal subsidiaries; three road construction companies; Standard Oil Co.	n.a.	U.S.A.	n.a.	Negotiated as part of lump-sum settlement. $7,000,000 in unremitted profits to fishmeal companies plus $3,500,000
1974	Peru	Manufacturing firms (cement)	n.a.	Switzerland	n.a.	n.a.
1975	Peru	Marcona Mining Co.	$174,000,000	U.S.A.	None	$61,440,000; 1976
1974	Peru	Gulf Oil Co.	$2,000,000	U.S.A.	n.a.	$1,540,000; 1977
1970	Sierra Leone	Sierra Leone Selection Trust	£2,550,000	U.K.	None	Joint-venture (National Diamond Mining Co.) and £2,550,000 to trust from Sierra Leone
1962	Sri Lanka	Caltex Ceylon Limited (California Texas Oil Co.)	$8,000,000	U.S.A.	n.a.	Suspension of bilateral assistance under Hickenlooper Amendment. Negotiated settlement after change in power
1970	Sri Lanka	Esso Standard Eastern (Exxon)	n.a.	U.S.A.	n.a.	$146,000
1967-73	Tanzania	1. Banking/insurance industries	n.a.	Local/foreign	n.a.	Seven insurance companies (German/U.K./India/Kenya) received $170,000. Negotiated settlements for banks nationalized. But currency devaluation.

(continued)

Table 4.6, continued

Year	Country	Enterprise or Type of Investment	Book Value or Compensation Claim	Nationality	Insurance Coverage	Compensation Settlement and Year
		2. Export and import firms/ millers	n.a.	U.K.	n.a.	Negotiated
		3. Landholdings				
		a. sisal estates				
		b. coffee plantations		Foreign		
		c. other landholdings				
		(1) Missouri plantation (6,700 acres)	n.a.	U.S.A.	n.a.	$628,850; n.d.a.
		(2) British properties	£4,000,000	U.K.	n.a.	Negotiated
		(3) Rental properties				
		(a) Captain J. May	n.a.	U.S.A.	n.a.	$5,000; n.d.a.
		(b) Stadler/Forbes	n.a.	U.S.A.	n.a.	$8,810; n.d.a.
		4. Bata Shoe Company	n.a.	Canada	n.a.	Full/fair compensation
		5. Singer Sewing Machine of Kenya	n.a.	U.S.A./Kenya	n.a.	n.a.
		6. Caltex (marketing facilities)	n.a.	U.S.A.	n.a.	n.a.
1972	Trinidad and Tobago	Trinidad and Tobago Telephone Co.	$7,200,000	U.S./Trinidad and Tobago	None	$7,200,000
1972	Trinidad and Tobago	Trinidad Flour Mills Limited	n.a.	U.S.A.	None	n.a.
1976	Trinidad and Tobago	Texaco (marketing facilities)	$8,500,000	U.S.A.	n.a.	n.a.
1952–70	United Arab Republic	Landholdings	n.a.	Local/foreign	n.a.	n.a.
		Investments affected				
		1. U.S.A.	$3,750,000	U.S.A.	n.a.	Compensation through bilateral agreements
		2. Greece	$20,000,000	Greece	n.a.	ibid.
		3. Switzerland	$10,000,000	Switzerland	n.a.	ibid.

Date	Country	Enterprise nationalized	Value	Nationality		Terms/settlement	Source
		4. Italy/Netherlands	$5,000,000	Italy/Netherlands	n.a.		ibid.
		5. Belgium	n.a.	Belgium	n.a.		ibid.
		6. Anglo-Egyptian Oil Fields	$3,500,000	U.K./Netherlands	n.a.		ibid.
		7. Shell Oil	n.a.	U.K./U.S.A.	n.a.		ibid.
1961	United Arab Republic	1. Financial, industrial, and commercial enterprises 2. Banking and insurance industries 3. Land reclamation companies	n.a.	Egypt/U.S.A./ Switzerland/ Netherlands/Greece	n.a.		ibid.
1971–76	Venezuela	21 oil companies	$5–10 billion	U.S.A.	n.a.	$1,010,000,000 (minus $134,000,000 for equipment after deficiencies; plus technology services and sales control	
1971	Venezuela	Banking industry	n.a.	U.S.A.	n.a.	n.a.	
1975	Venezuela	Bethlehem Steel and U.S. Steel subsidiaries	$200,000,000	U.S.A.	n.a.	$101,400,000; 1975 plus management/ technical contracts and five-year supply of iron ore	
1976	Venezuela	Owens–Illinois Glass subsidiary	n.a.	U.S.A.	n.a.	Nationalization proceedings discontinued; 1979	
1969–74	Zambia	1. Standard Bank Commercial Bank of Zambia Barclays Merchant Bank of Zambia National and Grindlays	n.a.	U.K./U.S.A. U.S.A./South Africa/Neth. U.K./U.S.A. Switzerland U.K./U.S.A.	n.a.	Nationalization proceedings discontinued; n.d.a.	
		2. Insurance industry	n.a.	U.K.	n.a.	n.a.	

(continued)

241

Table 4.6, continued

Year	Country	Enterprise or Type of Investment	Book Value or Compensation Claim	Nationality	Insurance Coverage	Compensation Settlement and Year
		3. 51 percent equity interests in Lever Brothers; Refined Oil Products; National Milling Co. Ltd.; Supra Bakeries Ltd.; Central Cigarette (BAT/Rothman)	n.a.	U.K.	n.a.	n.a.
		4. Roan Selection Trust	n.a.	U.K./U.S.A.	n.a.	$117,800,000
		5. Zambian Anglo-American	n.a.	South Africa/U.K.	n.a.	$175,000,000
		6. Roan Selection Trust (cancellation of management contracts)	n.a.	U.K./U.S.A.	n.a.	$34,200,000
		7. TAW International	Zambia claiming £125,000,000 TAW claiming $21,200,000	U.K./U.S.A.	n.a.	n.a.; Arbitration not available

n.a.   Not available.

n.d.a. No date available.

aOPIC is the Overseas Private Investment Corporation.

bDenationalized under Pinochet (Chile) and Suharto (Indonesia).

cConsists of British Petroleum (23.75 percent) Shell (23.75 percent); Mobil and Exxon (11.875 percent each); CFP (23.75 percent); Other (5 percent).

dBasrah Petroleum is registered in the United Kingdom but managed by an international consortium.

Sources: Ellen C. Collier, "Expropriation of American-Owned Property by Foreign Governments in the Twentieth Century," International Legal Materials 2 (1963): 1075–91; United States, Department of State, Bureau of Intelligence and Research, Disputes Involving U.S. Foreign Direct Investment: July 1, 1971 Through July 31, 1973, February 28, 1974; Id., Disputes Involving U.S. Foreign Direct Investment: August 1, 1973–January 31, 1975, March 20, 1975; Id., Disputes Involving U.S. Foreign Direct Investment: February 1, 1975– February 28, 1977, September 19, 1977; Paul E. Sigmund, Multinationals in Latin America (Madison: University of Wisconsin Press, 1980), pp. 35–39; E. Lauterpacht, British Practice in International Law (1964): 194–201; Id., British Practice in International Law (1967): 118–22; Monroe Leigh, Expropriation of Foreign-Owned Investment—Recent Trends (New York: Matthew Bender and Company, 1973), pp. 197–223.

TABLE 4.7

United States Taxes Paid by United
States Oil Companies 1962–71, 1972

Company	1962–71		1972	
	Net Income before Taxes ($ billion)	% Paid in U.S. Taxes	Net Income before Taxes ($ billion)	% Paid in U.S. Taxes
Exxon	19.653	7.3	3.700	6.5
Texaco	8.702	2.6	1.376	1.7
Mobil	6.388	6.1	1.344	1.3
Gulf	7.856	4.7	1.009	1.2
Socal	5.186	2.7	0.941	2.05

Source: United States, Congress, Senate, Multinational Corporations and United States Foreign Policy. Hearings Before the Sub-Committee on Multinational Corporations of the Committee on Foreign Relations, Part 4 (Washington, D.C.: Government Printing Office, 1974), p. 104.

At the height of diplomatic controversy between the United States and Mexico following Mexican land expropriations affecting several U.S. nationals, Mr. Saenz, the Mexican Minister for Foreign Affairs, in his Note to the U.S. Secretary of State Kellog dated October 7, 1926, observed:

The right of States to protect their citizens or subjects abroad is recognized. . . . But the foreign private persons are also given the right to apply to their governments for protection; the exercise of this right is

subject to the will of the parties in
interest and therefore, they may forgo
its exercise without thereby affecting
the right of the State concerned. The
Mexican Government . . . does not deny
that the American Government is at lib-
erty to intervene for its nationals;
but that does not stand in the way of
carrying out an agreement under which
the alien agrees not to be the party
asking for the diplomatic protection
of his Government. In case of infringe-
ment of any international duty, such as
a denial of justice would be, the right
of the American Government to take with
the Mexican Government appropriate action to seek atonement for injustice or
injury which may have been done to its
nationals would stand unimpaired.[21]

In essence, Mr. Saenz was denying the right of
the United States to intervene on behalf of its national who has bargained away his right to diplomatic
protection although he agreed that the United States
may take "appropriate action" to "seek atonement for
injustice or injury which may have been done to its
nationals."

Again, the Mexican Presidential Decree of March
18, 1938, expropriating the properties of 17 oil companies "representing chiefly the Royal Dutch Shell,
the Standard Oil and the Sinclair groups,"[22] not only
generated a sharp exchange of diplomatic notes between Mexico and the United Kingdom that the United
Kingdom had to recall its Ambassador from Mexico
City in May 1938 after a final British note of May
20, 1938; the oil expropriations also brought into
the open pressures by the United Kingdom and the
Netherlands on the United States to establish a
"'united front' against Mexico, and not to seek any
settlement, by direct negotiations or by resort to
arbitration, which would in any way prejudice the
other claimants' demands for the return of the seized
oil companies to their original management."[23] In
essence, while the United Kingdom and the Netherlands
questioned the validity of the oil expropriations on

legal grounds and demanded retribution, the United
States was only content for monetary compensation to
the dispossessed owners.

On March 21, 1938, the day when four U.S. oil
companies petitioned the Department of State that
they had suffered a "denial of justice," the United
Kingdom informed Mexico that it reserved all its
rights with regard to the expropriation of British
interests in the Aguila (Mexican Eagle) Oil Company,
a subsidiary of the Royal Dutch Shell, and on April
8, the United Kingdom, in a firmly worded diplomatic
note to the Mexican government, demanded the restitution of the expropriated assets to the company because the oil expropriation was essentially arbitrary:

> H.M. Government of the United Kingdom
> do not question the general right of a
> government to expropriate in the pub-
> lic interest and on payment of ade-
> quate compensation; but this principle
> does not serve to justify expropria-
> tions essentially arbitrary in charac-
> ter.

Replying, the Mexican government denied that the U.K.
government had any right to intervene on behalf of
the Aguila (Mexican Eagle) Oil Company, which, according to Article 27 of the Mexican Constitution of
1917, is a Mexican company although several British
nationals may have equity interests in the company.
As in the case of the Mexican land expropriations,
the Mexican government contended that the U.K. government cannot intervene on behalf of an alien who
agrees, within the meaning of Article 27 of the Mexican Constitution, not to ask for the diplomatic protection of his home government. In a diplomatic
note dated April 21, 1938, the U.K. government, as
the U.S. government,[24] maintained that foreign nationals cannot bargain away the right of diplomatic
protection of their home governments (without the
consent of their home governments) because of the
so-called Calvo clauses entrenched in states' contracts with aliens:

> If the doctrine were admitted that a
> Government can first make the operation
> of foreign interests in its territories
> depend upon their incorporation under
> local law, and then plead such incor-
> poration as the justification for re-
> jecting foreign diplomatic interven-
> tion, it is clear that the means would
> never be wanting whereby foreign Gov-
> ernments could be prevented from exer-
> cising their undoubted right under in-
> ternational law to protect the commer-
> cial interests of their nationals
> abroad. His Majesty's Government can-
> not admit such a doctrine as debarring
> them from intervention any more than
> they have ever regarded themselves as
> precluded from intervening on behalf of
> their nationals by the existence of the
> so-called Calvo clause.

As both the U.K. and Mexican governments were unwilling to compromise their position on the right of diplomatic intervention, the U.K. government, after a
final diplomatic note of May 20, 1938, recalled its
Ambassador from Mexico City.

Meanwhile, President Lizaro Cardenas on October
23, 1938, asked the oil companies to negotiate directly with him for compensation, saying:

> Mexico is willing to settle "in justice
> and equity" under Mexican law. The
> Government consider that the only fair
> basis of settlement is for us to pay
> every penny of the investments of Brit-
> ish and American companies from the day
> they first began the exploitation of
> operation of the oil fields in Mexico.
> We shall pay every dollar or pound that
> has been put into the properties we
> have taken over. We do not, however,
> regard the oil expropriation as a mat-
> ter for diplomatic intervention or dis-
> cussion.[25]

Following evaluations of the oil interests taken
over, the Mexican government agreed to pay between
$262 million and $450 million compensation while the
oil companies, in turn, renounced all rights and
claims with respect to properties, rights, and interests which belonged to them and were affected by
the expropriation decree of March 18, 1938.

Expropriatory actions in many other instances
have been preceded or followed by satisfactory compensation settlements or negotiations leading to
compensation settlements. In other cases, there
were frictions between the investor and taking states,
particularly over subrogated assets (assets that
carry government-guaranteed insurance schemes) as
had been the case with Bolivia (when the government
of Bolivia expropriated the assets of Gulf Oil Company, International Metals Processing Company, and
Mina Matilde Corporation), Jamaica (when the government of Jamaica introduced the controversial "Bauxite
Levy" and eventually acquired majority equity interests in Kaiser Aluminum and Reynolds Aluminum), and
Chile (when the government of Chile under President
Salvador Allende Gossens expropriated several U.S.-
owned enterprises carrying political risk insurance
provided by the Overseas Private Investment Corporation). In several other cases, there were frictions
between the taking and investor states in the absence
of diplomatic relations (for example, Iraq v United
States; Indonesia v United Kingdom; Algeria v United
States; Tanzania v United Kingdom; Yemen v United
States; Libya v United States; and the People's Republic of the Congo v United States), although such
investment disputes were eventually resolved to the
satisfaction of the parties concerned. With respect
to Indonesian expropriation measures carried out during President Sukarno's last years, all the expropriated enterprises, except National Cash Register
which sold out, were denationalized by President
Suharto, a U.S. protégé who enunciated a new policy
encouraging DFI. Threats of application of the sanctions provided under the Hickenlooper Amendment
and/or the Trade Act of 1974 forced the governments
of Sri Lanka and the People's Republic of the Congo
to reach compensation settlements with U.S. oil companies whose assets were expropriated in these coun-

tries while the fact that Somalia was denied the
status of a beneficiary developing country under
Sections 502 and 504 of the 1974 Trade Act forced
the Somali government to commence compensation negotiations with Caltex. And, with respect to Tanzanian
nationalization measures, the government of Tanzania
reached compensation settlements but subsequently de-
valued the country's currency.

   The position of the Canadian government with
respect to Guyana's decision to acquire 51 percent
equity interest in Demba, Alcan's subsidiary, and
subsequent decision to nationalize Demba was rather
interesting when compared with U.S. position of the
treatment of U.S. DFI. First, the Canadian government made it clear that the right of Guyana to control her natural resources remained unimpaired. Second, it only expressed the hope that Alcan would be
given "fair and nondiscriminatory" treatment, unlike
the U.S. practice of threatening economic sanctions
as a lever in support of its corporate investors.
Third, when Prime Minister Linden Forbes Burnham announced on February 23, 1971, the decision to nationalize Demba after participation negotiations col-
lapsed, the Canadian Minister of Trade and Industry
explained the Canadian position:

> We regret that negotiations between the
> company and the government of Guyana
> have not been successful . . . it is
> not the right of the government of
> Canada to dictate the conduct of the
> government of Guyana in these matters.
> We put the case that we expect Canadian
> companies not to be discriminated
> against in these matters. . . . I
> would not like to leave the impression
> that the Canadian government has not
> made proper representations to the gov-
> ernment of Guyana. Conversations were
> held to that effect. The point . . .
> that we expect the Canadian companies
> to be properly treated was made in
> these bilateral negotiations.[26]

To be sure, unlike the U.S. government, which
insists that its nationals receive "prompt, adequate,

and effective compensation" from the taking state,
the Canadian government was "without a clearly formu-
lated policy in that regard. It hoped to see Alcan
compensated fairly for its investments in Demba, but
it left the company to work out for itself a satisfactory compensation agreement with the Guyanese government."[27] It was then small wonder that it was the
U.S. "intervention" in the Demba takeover,[28] largely
because of roughly $25 million investments in the
bauxite industry by Reynolds Guyana Mines Limited
carrying a $16 million Overseas Private Investment
Corporation expropriation insurance, that forced the
government of Guyana to reach a $54 million compen-
sation agreement with Alcan on July 14, 1971, the
day before the vesting of Demba was to take place.

In other cases, compensation negotiations have
proved to be tedious. For example, compensation
agreement on U.S.-owned enterprises expropriated by
the Peruvian military junta led by Major-General
Juan Velasco Alvardo between 1968 and 1973 was not
reached until February 19, 1974. This agreement
represented more than a milestone in U.S. relations
with Peru in particular and Latin America in general;
for the first time since the U.S.-Mexican oil compensation settlement of 1942, the United States and
a Latin American government agreed on a comprehensive
settlement of all outstanding claims between U.S.
nationals and a foreign government. Under the agreement, the Peruvian government paid $76 million to the
U.S. government for subsequent distribution to the
claimants covered by the agreement.[29] What is significant about the Peruvian expropriations is that
while the question of compensation for expropriated
assets remained unresolved, the United States quietly
suspended bilateral assistance to Peru without a formal application of the Hickenlooper Amendment. Again,
the government of Chile reached compensation agreements with several U.S.-owned enterprises; but compensation agreement for Kennecott, Anaconda, and ITT
proved very tedious and difficult, and in the end,
Kennecott and Anaconda reached compensation settlements with the military junta which overthrew the
government of President Allende in September 1973.
In essence, in some cases, compensation settlements
were reached or the enterprises were simply denationalized following a change of regime. For example,

compensation settlements were reached or expropriated enterprises were denationalized in Chile (1973), Bolivia (1971), Brazil (1962), Indonesia (1967), Sri Lanka (1963), and Peru (1976) after a change of government (more often than not through the barrel of the gun), when the new regime, for a number of reasons which need not detain us, decides to be accommodating to DFI.

Table 4.8 shows the proportion of U.S. DFI expropriated by sector between 1960 and 1977. Of 70 reported investment disputes between 1960 and mid-1971, and involving nationalization or negotiated/coerced sales in 34 countries, 27 (38.6 percent) are associated with the natural resource industries (15 in petroleum alone). The most conspicuous expropriatory actions involved large extractive enterprises in Latin America and Africa, particularly in Bolivia, Algeria, Peru, Libya, Zaire, Somalia, People's Republic of the Congo (Congo-Brazzaville), United Arab Republic, Guyana, and Chile. The value of assets expropriated ranges between $1.2 billion and $1.3 billion, representing 6 to 7 percent of the estimated book value of U.S. DFI in DCs. Of this, 95 percent is located in Latin America, half of which in Chile's large copper mining and smelting companies--which perhaps explains the "invisible blockage" of Chile, for which more will be said later.

By July 1973, when there were 143 reported investment disputes, 79 (over 55 percent) were resource related. The balance was distributed as follows: eight (5.6 percent) in public utilities; 21 (14.7 percent) in banking and insurance; and 35 (24.5 percent) in other industries. There were 39 countries, distributed geographically, involved: Latin America with 84 cases (and 38 in Chile alone) while Africa and Middle East/Asia had 33 and 26, respectively. These countries represent 25 percent of the independent countries of the world and 35 percent of some 110 DCs. The preponderance of the investment disputes in Latin America can be attributed primarily to the fact that Latin America received $16.6 billion out of $25.2 billion U.S. DFI in the Third World and also perhaps to the socialist programs of President Salvador Allende of Chile.

TABLE 4.8

Proportion of United States Direct Foreign
Investment Expropriated by Sector 1960-77

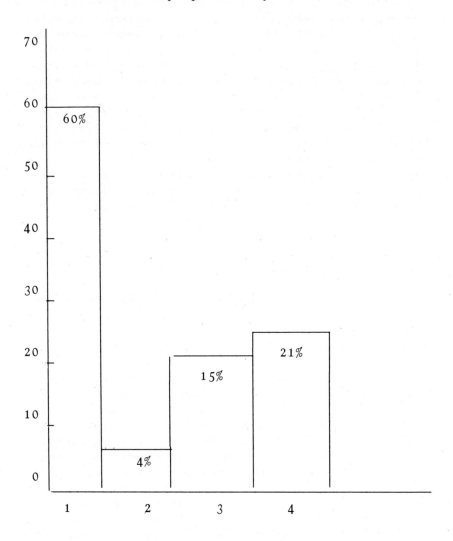

Sources: Same as for Table 4.7.
1.   Resource or resource related.
2.   Public utilities.
3.   Banking and insurance.
4.   Others including agriculture and manufacturing.

The period between August 1973 and January
1975 witnessed 42 investment disputes, and of these,
36 (86 percent) were resource related; two (4.8 percent) in public utilities: one (2.4 percent) in banking and insurance; and three (7.1 percent) in other
industries. While the number of disputes dropped
markedly during this period as opposed to 79 between
1971 and 1973, a higher percentage of the disputes
were still resource related, and this is much as expected, given the increasing militancy and economic
nationalism in several DCs that are primary producers.
And, between February 1975 and February 1977, some 78
investment disputes were reported compared with 42 in
the previous period. Once again, resource and re-
source-related industries accounted for 63 percent
of the disputes, followed by banking, indicating the
importance attached to the financial sector by the
host government.

Domestic Disorder and Expropriation

It has been argued, and quite rightly, that
the foreign investment decision-making process of
MNCs is influenced primarily by the management's
perception of the stability of the polity (country)
in which they want to invest.[30] Ceteris paribus,
there will be a lower propensity to invest in presumably unstable polities because of the increasing
risks to the operating autonomy and financial returns of the corporation. While this argument is
useful, most scholars fail to specify the crucial
intervening factor between domestic political violence (or disorder) and investment risk, namely,
public policy change. Essentially, risk to foreign-
owned enterprises results largely from changes of
government (public) policy which may or may not be
related to or caused by domestic political disorder.
We have stated in Chapter 3 that of a total
estimated stock of DFI of some $165 billion by the
end of 1971, the U.S. share stands at 52 percent,
followed by the United Kingdom (14.5 percent), France
(5.8 percent), and the Federal Republic of Germany
(4.4 percent). In 1973, as shown in Table 4.4, U.S.
DFI stood at $165 billion; of this amount, $120 bil-

lion (72.7 percent) is located in the DMEs and $40
billion (24.2 percent) is located in the Third World.
One striking feature of the data in Table 4.4 is the
much greater expansion of U.S. DFI in the DMEs than
in the DCs. For example, investment in DMEs grew
from $5.3 billion in 1950 to $47.6 billion in 1970,
or by a factor of approximately nine. Conversely,
investment in DCs grew from $5.8 billion in 1950 (the
same amount as in DMEs) to $23.8 billion in 1970, or
by a factor of only four.

      Therefore, from a cursory look one could argue
that even if U.S. DFI is a major determinant of U.S.
foreign policy,[31] U.S. DFI in DCs is certainly not a
major determinant of the country's foreign policy.
From a closer examination, however, one could in fact
make the point that U.S. DFI in DCs is a major determinant of the country's foreign policy in that
part of the world.

      First, as Thomas Weisskopf noted, "although the
value of U.S. direct private investment is now much
higher in the developed than in the underdeveloped
countries, there is much less of a difference in the
level of income from that investment."[32] Thus, of
total earnings of $10.2 billion from U.S. DFI at the
end of 1971,[33] earnings from the DMEs stood at $5.3
billion (52 percent) while earnings from DCs stood
at $4.3 billion (42 percent). Additionally, of $7.3
billion repatriated to the United States by U.S. MNC
subsidiaries and other U.S. firms in the form of
"interest, dividends, and branch earnings" (see also
Tables 1.2 and 1.3), some $3.7 billion (51 percent)
and $3.1 billion (43 percent) came from developing
and developed countries, respectively. Put differently, a much higher proportion of earnings from U.S.
investments in DCs, compared with earnings from similar investments in DMEs, is repatriated to the United
States rather than reinvested in the host country.

      Second, and perhaps more important, much of
U.S. investment in the developed countries is dependent on the petroleum sector (which became one of
the targets of nationalization measures in several
DCs in the late 1960s and early 1970s),[34] either
directly, namely, that $13 billion (22 percent) of
$58.3 billion invested in DMEs at the end of 1971
was in the petroleum sector or indirectly, namely,

that much of U.S. manufacturing in Western Europe runs on Middle Eastern oil.[35] What is significant is that the oil corporations have not only been supporters of the North Atlantic Treaty Organization but also the largest of the oil corporations, and five of the world's 20 largest industrial companies in terms of sales and net income at the end of 1980 (Exxon, Mobil, Texaco, Standard Oil of California, and Gulf Oil),[36] have had major investments in the Middle East for some time, such as in Venezuela before the Venezuelan oil expropriations.[37] For example, the total sales of the four "Sisters" and Standard Oil of California stood at $281 billion while their net income totaled $15.4 billion (Table 3.1).

In essence, given these aggregate data on U.S. DFI, particularly in the DCs, it was small wonder then that scholars have argued that U.S. DFIs in the Third World are a primary determinant of U.S. foreign policies toward Third World countries. The results, it has been argued, "are foreign policies that are protective both of these investments and of opportunities for their future expansion, which therefore are profoundly counterrevolutionary in their intent, and which undertake foreign interventions and military alliances in pursuit of these ends."[38] Talking on the same issue, James Petras and others have noted:

> Since World War II, the U.S. position as a dominant imperial power in a competitive world capitalist system has been largely rooted in the continually growing opportunities for capital expansion and accumulation through the exploitation of social classes throughout the different areas of the world economy.[39]

Commenting on similar issues, Henry Kissinger has observed:

> The international economic system has been built on these central elements: Open and expanding trade; Free movements of investment capital and tech-

nology; Readily available supplies of
raw materials; and Institutions and
practices of international cooperation.[40]

Therefore, any fundamental challenge to the arrangements comprising this "present economic system" is
regarded by U.S. policy makers as inimical to basic
U.S. interests. According to Kissinger, U.S. pros-
perity "requires international economic stability"
and, by extension, international political stability.
     From these observations, we can derive our
second hypothesis:

> Whereas it is in the interest of DMEs
> (core societies) and their MNCs (here-
> after referred to as core actors) not
> to support political violence in LDCs
> (periphery societies) when the domestic
> conditions in these countries continue
> to protect and promote their (core so-
> cieties') interests, when LDCs (periph-
> ery societies) attempt to "opt out of
> the world system" or attempt to re-
> structure the economic relations favor-
> able to the core societies, then eco-
> nomic actors (MNCs) in core societies
> work with their home governments to
> cause economic and political disrup-
> tions in the periphery societies (LDCs)--
> disruptions which could be used as a pre-
> text for foreign military intervention
> (ostensibly, to protect political and
> strategic interests) or used as an ex-
> cuse by the military establishment to
> stage a coup d'état and restore the
> old political order.

What we are saying in effect is that there is a positive correlation between government change and expropriation of DFI. Just as one set of political elites
may, as a last resort, expropriate foreign enterprise
as a demonstration of state power vis-à-vis internal
(MNC subsidiaries, pressure groups, and comprador
class-particular socioeconomic classes associated

with MNCs) and external (other states, MNCs, and multilateral lending institutions such as the Inter-American Development Bank and the World Bank) actors, one set of political elites, backed by internal and external actors, may overthrow the existing government and restore the status quo ante.

But does it necessarily mean that every taking of foreign-owned assets (particularly, U.S.-owned investments) in a DC, regardless of the size of the assets/investments, must be followed, sooner or later, by a change of regime and a restoration of the old political order? If our answer is in the affirmative, how does one explain why the Venezuelan expropriations under President Carlos Andres Perez do not generate "a hostile and conflictive response on the part of U.S. policy makers"[41] and, therefore, a change of the Perez administration whereas the Chilean expropriations under President Salvador Allende Gossens did generate "a hostile and conflictive response on the part of U.S. policy makers," eventually leading to the overthrow of President Allende in the bloody military coup d'état of September 11, 1973?

Since the Chilean and Venezuelan expropriations provoked different responses on the part of U.S. policy makers, we must then examine the behavior of investor states, particularly the United States, toward economic nationalism in several Third World countries. It has been suggested that U.S. policy makers "anchor nationalist policies within the context of the class structure and political process."[42] Specifically, U.S. policy makers may ask these questions:

1. Do the nationalist policies manifested in nationalization measures represent an effort on the part of the ruling regime to restructure or constrain capitalism?
2. What is the impact of the new policies (on nationalization) on the distribution of power and nature of the class struggle?
3. Is the new regime operating within the confines of the existing class

(social) structure or attempting
to change it?[43]

To provide answers to these rather intriguing questions, it is necessary to consider the primary in-
terests of MNCs and those of their home states, par-
ticularly as various accounts seemed to have laid
the "destabilization" of "nationalist" regimes in
Iran (Mossadegh), Guatemala (Arbenz), Zaire (Lumumba),
British Guiana (Jagan), Brazil (Goulart), Argentina
(Illia), Bolivia (Estenssoro and Torres), Indonesia
(Sukarno), and Chile (Allende), the abortive Bay of
Pigs operation (Castro), as well as the crushing of
the popular "constructionalist" rebellion in the
Dominican Republic (1965) at the doors of the United
States.[44] In essence, is there any convergence of
interests between U.S.-based MNCs and agencies of
the U.S. government, especially the Departments of
State and Treasury?

What, then, are the primary interests of MNCs
and those of their home states? On the one hand,
the main concerns of the MNC are profits and economic
hegemony. To be sure, the MNC is primarily concerned
with whether the host country offers or provides a
climate which ensures a high rate of return on investments. For example, Table 1.1 shows that the
average rate of return on U.S. DFI in DCs was 17.5
percent. More significant is Africa, where the rate
of return on investment stood at 22.3 percent. It
is therefore understandable why MNCs and the governments that they influence and/or control are hostile
or opposed to nationalist (socialist) revolutions or
the spread of socialism, particularly in Latin America
since socialism or nationalist (socialist) revolution
"reduces their opportunities to profit from doing
business with and in the newly socialized area."[45]

The history of the Standard Oil Company of New
Jersey (Exxon), currently the world's largest industrial company in terms of sales and net income, gives
us a textbook example of why MNCs and their home
states, particularly the United States, are profoundly hostile and/or opposed to nationalist (socialist)
revolutions or the spread of socialism. At the end
of 1958, while 67 percent of Standard Oil's assets
was located in North America, only 34 percent of its

profits came from the region; more significant, while
20 percent of Standard Oil's assets was located in
Latin America, 39 percent (about two-fifths) of its
profits came from that region, and while 13 percent
of Exxon's assets was located in the Eastern Hemisphere, 27 percent of its profits came from that region. Put differently, while Standard Oil's foreign
investments were half as large as its domestic investments, interestingly enough its foreign profits
were twice as large as its domestic profits.[46] In
essence, Exxon, far from being a "large and consistent exporter of capital," has, in fact, been a
"large and consistent importer of capital."[47]

It was small wonder, therefore, that while U.S.
DFI stood at $13.7 billion in the period 1950-61, re-
turned earnings stood at $23.2 billion, namely, a
profit of $9.5 billion; and between 1961 and 1965,
profit remittances and royalties/fees to the United
States from the Latin American operations of U.S.
MNCs increased by some $260 million annually.[48] In
1958 alone, Exxon's total profits stood at $841 mil-
lion. Of this sum, $538 million were paid out as
dividends to shareholders, the majority of whom are
U.S. residents, while $303 million were retained
earnings.[49]

On the other hand, the home state of the MNC,
especially the United States, is very much concerned
with the "nature and context of change (structural
versus sectoral issues) and to such associated issues
as the impact of change on trade relations and access
to strategic raw materials."[50] In several cases,
there is a convergence of interests between the MNC
and its home state. For example, the U.S. government, through the Investment Guarantee Program of
the Agency for International Development and its
successor, the Overseas Private Investment Corporation, has committed itself in many Third World countries to creating a favorable climate for DFI. Thus,
the linkage of Washington and U.S. investors vis-à-
vis several Third World countries is "explicit and
concrete. Any attempt by these governments to exercise their sovereignty by expropriating private U.S.
investors, immediately confronts the U.S. government."[51] To be sure,

> U.S. business interests are strongly
> represented in important policy-making
> positions and are in a position to
> direct national resources and legisla-
> tion to increasing their sales, profits
> and control over Latin America [and
> the rest of the colonial so-called
> "third world"].[52]

Consequently, in the event of a conflict between the
MNC and the host government, the investor state becomes directly involved on the side of the MNC. In
some cases, some investor states have adopted a more
flexible approach in defending their nationals abroad.
In the wake of expropriations of U.S. investments in
Cuba (1959-60) and Brazil (1959 and 1962), Secretary
of State Dean Rusk advised:

> I don't believe the United States can
> afford to stake its interests in other
> countries on a particular private in-
> vestment in a particular situation. . . .
> I would hope we would not use legisla-
> tive mandates which in effect would
> cause us to break relations with impor-
> tant countries over particular points
> of policy, because in the longer run,
> it seems to me, that leads us into many
> blind alleys.[53]

The investor state becomes directly involved
on the side of the MNC: (1) when the host government, in exercise of its power of dominium eminens
(eminent domain), expropriates the assets of local
MNS subsidiary and (2) when and if major DFIs are
threatened by a "nationalist" regime in a developing/
dependent country and the local allies (comprador
class) are not in a strong position to give them
(foreign economic elite) much support or offer any
resistance to the regime. This is because compensation for expropriated assets raises fundamental questions about the "nature and content of overall change"
for DFI in the Third World including the taking
state. One official of the U.S. Department of State
has noted:

> If [a country] is doing something
> grossly in violation of its laws, or
> international laws, then we are pre-
> pared to go in. . . . If there is a
> serious problem that a particular com-
> pany can't handle then we will come in.
> Where we get involved is where local
> remedies seem to be exhausted and a
> company comes in and asks for our
> help.[54]

To be sure, because the United States has always
taken the position that the legality of any expropriatory measure is contingent on the payment of
"prompt, adequate, and effective compensation,"[55] it
is small wonder the payment of "prompt, adequate,
and effective compensation" continues to be an important determinant of U.S. response to economic
nationalism in several Third World countries:

> Satisfactory compensation is a critical
> index of the nature and content of
> overall changes. A regime that compen-
> sates satisfactorily does so because it
> is prepared to pursue further economic
> relations with the United States.[56]

By extension, uncompensated nationalization and/or
unsatisfactory compensation can only be regarded as
a challenge to the United States and economic hegemony of U.S. MNCs, particularly oil corporations
which are an important faction of the U.S. ruling
class. For those Third World countries pursuing
politics of economic nationalism, the position of
the policy makers in Washington is explicit and concrete:

> We should continue to seek full national
> treatment for U.S. investment abroad,
> and we must insist on prompt, adequate
> and effective compensation in the few
> cases of nationalization. Where needed
> and appropriate, we will bring to bear
> available political and economic influ-

ence to get a satisfactory resolution,
recognizing that the basic sanction is
the damage the host country does to
his future investment prospect.[57]

Enunciating the Nixon Doctrine, which has become protective of U.S. investments abroad, former President
Richard Nixon was very forceful and blunt:

> Under international law, the United
> States has a right to expect:
>   --that any taking of American private
>   property will be non-discriminatory;
>   --that it will be for a public pur-
>   pose; and
>   --that its citizens will receive
>   prompt, adequate, and effective
>   compensation from the expropriating
>   country.
> Thus, when a country expropriates a
> significant U.S. interest without mak-
> ing reasonable provision for such com-
> pensation to U.S. citizens, we will
> presume that the U.S. will not extend
> new bilateral economic benefits to the
> expropriating country. . . . In the
> face of the expropriatory circumstances
> . . . described, we will presume that
> the United States Government will with-
> hold its support from loans under con-
> sideration in multilateral development
> banks.[58]

In essence, uncompensated nationalization and/or unsatisfactory compensation will incur the wrath of
the United States in terms of foreign-aid sanctions
under the Hickenlooper and Gonzalez Amendments to
the United States Foreign Assistance Acts.[59]
    It would appear, then, that the critical de-
terminant in U.S. response to development strategy
of any Third World country is the larger political-
economic context within which decisions have been
made. Specifically, can we say that the investor
state's response to acts of nationalization depends
on the "political context of nationalization--the

social nature of the regime pursuing policies of
state ownership, the area(s) of the economy subject
to nationalization, and the extent of nationalization"?[60] Can we attribute "hostile and conflictive"
reactions on the part of the investor state to the
fact that key policy makers in such a state have had
links with or have financial interest/stakes in corporations whose assets have been expropriated or
threatened by the host government? Again, can we
conclude that "hostile and conflictive" reaction on
the part of an investor state to acts of nationalization was motivated by strategic interests and/or
opposition to communism? Finally, do MNCs influence
their home states to undertake covert (proxy) or
overt (military) intervention in pursuit of corporate
interests threatened by acts of nationalization?

Unfortunately, these questions are easy to
formulate but difficult to answer. However, we
shall make an attempt, particularly as a great deal
about U.S. cold war conflicts (employment of subversive tactics and the use of direct military intervention) came to be known through congressional committee hearings and books written by former CIA
agents and observers of post-World War II conflictual
relations between the United States and Latin America.
In May 1951, the Iranian Parliament (Majlis) under
the leadership of Mohammed Mossadegh ("a shrewd poli-
tician from a rich landowning family who perceived
the nationalist mood")[61] nationalized the oil industry and, by implication, the Anglo-Iranian Oil Company, a company whose majority assets are held by
the U.K. government.

At the time of the takeover, the Atlee (Labour
Party) government (which had recently nationalized
major industries) was in power; consequently, the
takeover proved an embarrassment, namely, should the
United Kingdom use force to protect British interests? It was apparent that U.K. and not U.S. economic interests were involved in the Iranian oil
nationalization. However, since oil interests were
affected, and U.S. oil corporations are an important
faction of the U.S. ruling class, it is small wonder
that the "American Sisters" joined Anglo-Iranian
(later, British Petroleum) in their boycott of Iranian
oil, a boycott which "brought on a near-impossible

economic situation"[62] in Iran and induced a statement by the Department of State on May 18, 1951,
namely, that "no American company would step into
the place of the Anglo-Iranian Oil Company if it was
evicted."[63] Overall, the Truman administration was
sympathetic to Mossadegh, much to the chagrin of the
Churchill (Conservative Party) government, because
the nationalization had "almost universal Iranian
support" and Mossadegh was pictured as being "strongly anti-Communist."[64]

However, General Dwight D. Eisenhower, elected
President in November 1952, and John Foster Dulles
(who was to become Secretary of State under Eisenhower), decided in March 1953 that Mossadegh would
have to go. According to Nathan and Oliver,[65] Eisenhower, Dulles, and Under-Secretary Walter B. Smith,
former CIA Director, agreed with British Foreign
Secretary Anthony Eden to seek "alternatives to
Mossadegh," particularly after Mossadegh had rejected the U.S. suggestion that the crisis with the
United Kingdom be resolved in return for U.S. economic assistance. It must be stated here that plans
to remove Mossadegh through CIA covert operation
were kept secret by Allen Dulles, then-CIA Deputy
Director and brother of John Foster Dulles, from
President Harry Truman and Secretary of State Dean
Acheson. But why would Mossadegh have to go? Certainly not because the United States was interested
in retrieving the sagging British interests and influence in Iran. Then must Mossadegh be ousted from
power simply because the United States was concerned
that the Soviet Union would occupy a politico-stra-
tegic vacuum created by the collapse of British power
in Iran? This may well be true. During the two
years that he was in power, Mossadegh had consoli-
dated his hold on the Majlis; reduced the power of
the Shah, a Western protégé; expelled the U.K. Embassy from Iran in 1952; and was feared would become
a Soviet puppet. More important, however, were the
realities of oil:

> Eisenhower's election had been heavily
> financed by the American oil industry;
> and of the men Eisenhower counted as
> his closest friends numerous oil men,

investment bankers, and other titans of
the corporate world constituted a clear
majority. He was, therefore, intuitively responsive to their interests
and concerns, and his entire conception
of the national economy and America's
role in the global economy was pervaded
with their views concerning free enter-
prising, access to raw materials, and
world markets.[66]

Additionally, there was concern about the domino effect, namely, that a success of economic nationalism
in Iran would encourage economic nationalism in the
Middle East, and that would adversely affect U.S.
oil interests in the region.

In essence, U.S. "intervention" in the Iranian
oil crisis was influenced by four major considerations. First, it would provide an opportunity to
replace not only sagging British political power but
also British economic presence. Second, by ousting
Mossadegh and restoring the status quo ante, Eisenhower was "intuitively" responding to U.S. corporate
"interests and concerns." Third, a defeat of Mossadegh meant a defeat of forces of economic nationalism
in the Middle East. Fourth, the overthrow of the
nationalist regime in Iran would put at bay Soviet
intentions in Iran.

Operating from a basement apartment (used as a
command post), Kermit Roosevelt, former CIA bureau
chief in the Middle East and a grandson of President
Theodore Roosevelt, directed and funded pro-Shah
street mobs backed by pro-Shah army officers (led by
General Fazollah Zahedi) who were "given refuge in
the CIA compound adjoining the U.S. Embassy."[67] After
the street demonstrations and the overthrow of Mossadegh (who was arrested and imprisoned for three
years) in a military coup d'état, the Shah, who had
fled Tehran in August, returned to Tehran "in qualified triumph--conscious that it was more of the CIA's
victory than his, though he did not care to admit
it."[68] The cost of the CIA operation, according to
Roosevelt, stood at about $75,000.[69] The point to
emphasize here is, first, that in the Iranian Oil
Consortium concluded after the overthrow of Mossadegh,

the share of U.S. oil companies (Exxon, Mobil, Gulf, Texaco, Socal, and others) stood at 40 percent. Second, Roosevelt later became the Vice-President of Gulf Oil Company in 1960 and served as the communication channel between Gulf and the Shah.[70]

While the U.S. proxy intervention in Iran can be explained by U.S. oil interests in addition to what the United States (the intervening state) would gain in the future, particularly since U.S. investments and markets at the time of intervention were small, how does one explain U.S. proxy intervention in Guatemala (1954), Cuba (1961), British Guiana (1963), and Chile (1973), alleged proxy intervention in Brazil (1964), and direct military intervention in the Dominican Republic (1965) not to mention proxy intervention in Greece (1967) and Indonesia (1967)? This question is significant given President Dwight Eisenhower's foreign policy statement: "Any nation's right to form a government and an economic system of its own choosing is inalienable. . . . Any nation's attempt to dictate to other nations their own form of government is indefensible."[71] As demonstrated below, business interests are strongly represented in important policy-making positions and are able to influence policy decisions leading to intervention in "underdeveloped, dependent [and] colonial economies."

Prior to the 1954 coup d'état in Guatemala, a series of dictators had served as a front for powerful U.S. business interests, primarily the United Fruit Company (later United Brands) which virtually owned the country. These dictators included Manuel Estrada Cabrera and General Jorge Ubico, who was overthrown by a military junta which included Colonel Jacobo Arbenz Guzman in 1944. The United Fruit Company, since the nineteenth century, had bought hundreds of square miles of banana-producing and non-producing acreage; employed forced labor; coerced small farmers, through threats of physical violence, to sell exclusively to the company and at company prices; and controlled the only railroad in the country. The company, in addition, had private armies; bribed public officials; and sponsored coups, earning the United Fruit the popular name of el pulpo (the octopus).[72]

Juan Jose Arevalo, elected civilian President in 1945, promoted fundamental social reforms. His successor, Jacobo Arbenz Guzman (1951-54), initiated far-reaching, indeed, radical socioeconomic and political changes which, not unnaturally, evoked strong U.S. opposition, since "the status quo . . . provides valuable sources of profits and resource payoffs to U.S. capitalism."[73] Among other things, Arbenz Guzman:

1. co-opted Guatemalan communists/leftists (including Argentine Ernesto Che Guevara) in his regime;
2. attempted to integrate the Indian majority into the mainstream of Guatemalan national life through labor organization and agrarian reform; and
3. broadened Guatemala's diplomatic contacts with Soviet-bloc nations. For example, Arbenz Guzman ordered arms from the Soviet bloc; the arms, from Czechoslovakia, arrived aboard <u>Alfhem</u> (Swedish freighter) in Guatemala on May 15, 1954, through Poland. (The United States had refused arms sales to Guatemala since 1948.)

Additionally, in June 1952 an agrarian legislation empowering the Arbenz Guzman regime to expropriate uncultivated land and, presumably, to redistribute same to the Guatemalan peasants was introduced. In March 1953, Arbenz Guzman expropriated about 400,000 acres of uncultivated land belonging to United Fruit and offered United Fruit 3 percent agrarian bonds maturing in 25 years and compensation at book value as of May 5, 1952.

By embarking on agrarian reforms and expropriating the assets of United Fruit valued at $16 million, Arbenz Guzman alienated powerful alien business interests. More important, by offering United Fruit $627,000 in long-term interest-bearing bonds which the Department of State did not consider "prompt, adequate, and effective compensation" since the "bonds were of uncertain market value and many of the holders would realize very little of the bonds during their life time,"[74] Arbenz Guzman further strained U.S.-Guatemalan relations. Petras and others have observed, and quite rightly: "The issue of 'swift, adequate, and effective' compensation for expropriated U.S. investors continues to be an important determinant of the U.S. response to economically nationalist regimes in the Third World."[75] This means that a decision to adopt a "policy of accommodation or conflict" with a taking state depends on the payment of "prompt, adequate, and effective compensation," namely, satisfactory compensation. Arbenz Guzman also seized the Guatemalan Electric Company and the railroad owned by United Fruit.

Reacting to the seizure of the railroad, the president of the company had this much to say: "From here on out it's not a matter of the people of Guatemala against the United Fruit Company: the question is going to be communism against the right of property, the life and security of the Western Hemisphere."[76] Also branding Colonel Arbenz Guzman as a "Communist" was Ambassador John E. Peurifoy, who was assigned to Guatemala specifically to coordinate CIA activities directed at the overthrow of the Arbenz Guzman regime. Peurifoy also personally participated in the coup d'état:[77]

> It seemed to me that the man thought
> like a Communist, and if not actually
> one, would do until one came along. I
> so reported to Secretary Dulles, who
> informed the President; and I expressed
> to them the view that unless the Communist influences were counteracted,
> Guatemala would within six months fall
> completely under Communist control.[78]

In essence, the overthrow of the Arbenz Guzman regime was simply a question of time.

In early 1953, the CIA began training Guatemalan exiles in Honduras and Nicaragua, preparatory to a planned invasion to be led by Colonel Carlos Castillo Armas, a graduate of the U.S. Army Command and General Staff School at Fort Leavenworth, Kansas. As a way of weakening Guatemala's position in the Western Hemisphere, and perhaps justifying U.S. intervention in Guatemala, Secretary of State Dulles secured the adoption of an anticommunist resolution at the Tenth Inter-American Conference at Caracas in 1954. Specifically, the resolution declared that intervention against a state whose political institutions were dominated and/or controlled by "the international Communist movement" would not constitute an abrogation of hemisphere principles of political and territorial integrity.[79] Additionally, the arrival of an arms consignment from Czechoslovakia in May 1954 prompted an additional shipment of arms to the Guatemalan exiles by the United States. At a press conference on May 25, 1954, Dulles stated that the arms shipment to Guatemala where "communist influence is very strong" had brought Guatemala "into a position to dominate militarily the Central American area."[80] More significant, he added the arms might be used to close the Panama Canal. To be sure, a communist-dominated Guatemala was seen as potentially dangerous to the United States, not only because of Guatemala's proximity to the Panama Canal but also because Guatemala would provide a sanctuary for Soviet "one-way" bombers.[81]

Faced with a CIA-financed rebel force led by Colonel Castillo Armas, indeed, a rebel force given air cover by a CIA air force of four P-47s and a handful of B-26s (some say C-46s); harassed by the Voice of Liberation, a rebel radio station manned by CIA propaganda expert David Phillips; and faced with a possible rebellion within the Guatemalan army, Arbenz Guzman resigned the presidency on June 27, 1954. He handed power over to Colonel Diaz, who only proscribed the Communist party and later turned over power to Colonel Castillo Armas, who arrived in the Guatemalan capital in Peurifoy's private plane.[82] Arbenz Guzman went into permanent exile, lived for many years in Cuba, and died in Mexico in 1971.[83] Following the invasion Che Guevara took refuge in the Mexican Embassy and managed to flee the country; he was hunted down and murdered in 1967 by CIA agents in Bolivia. All the CIA officers (except two) who were involved in the Guatemalan affair were promoted to a CS grade.[84] Colonel Castillo Armas denationalized United Fruit, returning all land belonging to United Fruit; his regime received $90 million of U.S. bilateral assistance over the next two years compared with less than $1 million received by any regime between 1944 and 1954. However, he was assassinated in 1957 along with two Guatemalans who had worked closely with David Phillips.

Undoubtedly, the destabilization of the Arbenz Guzman regime was an exercise in economic imperialism. This is also the position taken by the North American Congress on Latin America, which linked the Dulles brothers, other top U.S. officials, and Sullivan and Cromwell (John Foster Dulles's law firm) with powerful U.S. economic interests, especially United Fruit. What we are saying in essence is that the United States intervened in Iran and Guatemala primarily to protect particular interests of political benefactors and/or past business associates of U.S. policy makers/President and protect present U.S. investments and/or future investment opportunities. We have already noted the influence of the U.S. oil industry in the overthrow of Mossadegh. With respect to Guatemala, mention must be made of the links between United Fruit and top U.S. policy makers. First, Sullivan and Cromwell drew up the 1930 and 1936 contracts between United Fruit and the government of Guatemala, by which large tracts of land were sold to United Fruit. Second, John Moors Cabot, Assistant Secretary of State for Inter-American Affairs, was a major stockholder in United Fruit. Third, Allen Dulles, CIA Director, had been President of United Fruit. Fourth, Under-Secretary of State Walter Bedell Smith would join the Board of Directors of United Fruit on leaving the State Department in 1955. Fifth, Ambassador to the United Nations Henry Cabot Lodge was a major stockholder in United Fruit.

By way of summary, the Iranian and Guatemalan coups must be placed in a broader context of policy development during the early Eisenhower administration, when anti-Western nationalism and/or radical socioeconomic and political change was perceived by Washington as "externally derived," indeed, the product of international communism. At the height of McCarthyism men such as Eisenhower and Dulles could neither believe nor accept the fact that "revolutionary change in the non-Western world could result solely or even primarily from indigenous conditions."[85]

Again, from documented sources,[86] U.S. proxy intervention in British Guiana (1963) can be explained by U.S. investments in bauxite, while alleged proxy intervention in Brazil (1964) can be explained by U.S. oil and mining interests whose assets were threatened and/or nationalized by President Joao "Jango" Goulart. In British Guiana the United States penetrated the trade union movement and employed other covert instruments to thwart Cheddi Jagan's nationalist movement.

The events which culminated in the overthrow of President Goulart began in 1959 when Governor Brizola of the state of Rio Grande do Sul expropriated the American and Foreign Power Company. In 1960, the Brazilian government rejected ITT's offer to invest in manufacturing facilities in return for new telephone rate increases and established a state-owned telephone company, inviting ITT to participate. At that stage, the Brazilian government, like any Latin American government, was very much concerned about alien domination of such a sensitive sector as a public utility. Thereupon, ITT agreed to divest. The sum ($7.3 million) tentatively agreed to by ITT and government officials as representing the valuation of ITT assets was ultimately rejected by the government of Brazil as too high and by the ITT as too low. As a result, Governor Brizola decreed the expropriation of ITT local subsidiary on February 16, 1962, and paid $400,000 into the company's account as compensation. The ITT put its expropriated assets as between $7 million and $8 million.

In any event, the expropriation of ITT raises fundamental issues not only in terms of the immediate reaction of the U.S. Congress to the security of U.S. DFI but also because grave concern was expressed that seizures of U.S. investments abroad anywhere would encourage economic nationalists everywhere and, therefore, expropriations must be deterred by threatening U.S. aid sanctions against any expropriating country.[87] More fundamentally, Brazil, occupying about half the land area of South America, containing about half its population, and liberally endowed with natural resources, is a key country in Latin America. From the standpoint of policy makers in Washington, Brazil, by expropriating the American and Foreign Power Company and ITT, has joined the ranks of countries dedicated to changing the status quo which "provides valuable sources of profits and resource payoffs to U.S. capitalism."[88]

An analysis of 1,800 Brazilian corporations at
about the time of these takeovers indicated that 28
percent were foreign owned.[89] Of 650 leading corporations with a capital of at least $1 million, 35
percent were controlled by Brazilian private capital,
30 percent by private foreign capital, while 35 percent fell within the public sector. We can then assert that private foreign capital pervaded the Brazilian industry. In terms of distribution, of the
total DFI of approximately $3.5 billion at the end
of 1966, the U.S. share stood at over 37 percent or
at best 45 percent, given substantial U.S. equity
interests in Canadian and Brazilian corporations.
These investments can be found in automobile and
chemical industries as well as heavy-duty machinery.
        While foreign domination of significant sectors
of the economy has caused grave concern in many countries including the United States, France, Canada,
Mexico, Japan, and Nigeria,[90] the one sector that
has created much anxiety among Brazilian nationalists, because of its foreign ownership, is public
utility. It was small wonder then that the issue of
telephone utility rates generated so much tension
between ITT and Rio Grande do Sul, tension which not
only led to the expropriation of ITT holdings but
also created alarm among policy makers in Washington
that a successful takeover of U.S. investments in
Brazil would encourage similar takeovers in other
Latin American countries.
        Incidentally, the ITT takeover occurred at a
time when President Goulart had arranged a trip to
the United States in April 1962 to secure additional
financial assistance. Plus Brazil promised ITT that
it would assist in securing fair compensation for
its expropriated assets. And, during Goulart's visit,
President John F. Kennedy and President Goulart agreed
that the transfer of public utility enterprises to
state ownership, principle of fair compensation, and
investment in other sectors of the Brazilian economy
should be maintained.[91] Meanwhile, Senator Bourke
Hickenlooper (R-Iowa) secured the passage of an
amendment to the U.S. Foreign Assistance Act of 1962.
Known as the Hickenlooper Amendment, the language of
the amendment was very clear: it required the U.S.
President to suspend bilateral assistance to any country which expropriates U.S. investments and does not:

> within a reasonable time (not more than
> six months . . .) take appropriate
> steps, which may include arbitration,
> to discharge its obligations under in-
> ternational law . . . including equit-
> able and speedy compensation for such
> property in convertible foreign ex-
> change.[92]

In the meantime, while the lawmakers and corporate
executives were demanding foreign-aid sanctions
against countries threatening and/or expropriating
U.S. investments, the Department of State adopted a
more flexible approach which worked, because the ITT
reported in early 1963 an interim agreement providing for "advances to ITT of the cruzeiro equivalent
of $7,300,000 . . . of which $3,650,000 has been reinvested in Standard Electrica, S.A., a Brazilian
manufacturing subsidiary."[93] This agreement was
followed by yet another between American and Foreign
Power Company and Brazil on the sale to Brazil of
all of the power company's electric utility subsidiaries for $135 million, three-quarters of which were
to be reinvested "in enterprises of primary importance to the economic development of the country."[94]
At this stage, a plan to oust the Goulart administration was in the offing. The final push for
the ouster of President Goulart stemmed from the determined effort of the U.S. oil industry and the U.S.
government to "open up" the Brazilian oil industry,
having broken the resistance to the granting of oil
concessions in Argentina (with the ouster of President Arturo Illia) and in Bolivia with promises of
U.S. bilateral assistance. Put simply, the petroleum
oil industry was opposed to the establishment of
state-owned oil companies including Pemex (Mexico),
Yacimientos Petroliferas Fiscales (Argentina), and
Petrobas in Brazil. In a posthumous message to the
nation, President Vargas (who had committed suicide)
declared that his administration had been ruined by
the pressure of oil companies and their allies:

> Once more, anti-national forces and in-
> terests, coordinated have become in-
> furiated with me. I wanted to create

> national freedom in realizing our na-
> tional wealth through Petrobas; hardly
> had it begun to function when the wave
> of agitation grew. They don't want
> the people to be free.[95]

Although Vargas was dead, the man who was to carry
on the mantle of "national freedom in realizing
[Brazilian] national wealth through Petrobas" was no
less than Joao Goulart, who was ousted as Labour
Minister under President Vargas in 1954.

Meanwhile, continued U.S. pressure on Brazil
to accept terms on petroleum concessions neither
broke Brazil nor slowed the growth of gross national
product. But Petrobas was not doing well and international financing was not forthcoming. The World
Bank, discouraged since the 1959 takeover of the
American and Foreign Power Company, had not approved
any projects for financing because "economic prospects are so uncertain." As a result of pressure on
foreign exchange, Brazil, like Castro's Cuba and Sri
Lanka, came to depend on Soviet crude oil. This
barter arrangement alarmed U.S. oil interests and
their friends in Washington. The role of the Soviet
Union was especially significant not only because
the Soviet Union, by then, had become the world's
second largest oil producer and an important exporter
of crude oil but also because the Soviet Union's low
oil prices and barter arrangements "particularly
frightened the major international oil companies
whose main source of profits was their oligopoly
control of crude-oil sales."[96] While the Goulart
administration was asking the oil companies to refine cheap Soviet crude oil, President Goulart threatened the seizure of the huge iron ore holdings of
Hanna Mining Company. In January 1964, he signed
into law a bill limiting profit remittances for
foreign-owned enterprises in Brazil. When the oil
companies rejected the government's order to refine
cheap Soviet crude oil, Goulart seized their refineries in March 1964, thus giving Petrobas a monopoly
over every phase of the oil industry except marketing. Less than a month later, Goulart was overthrown in a military coup. Washington was so enthu-
siastic about the overthrow of Goulart that it sent

off official congratulations even before the military junta took office.[97]

As was expected in Washington, the post-Goulart
administration took the following policy decisions.
First, it denationalized privately owned refineries
and dismissed officials of Petrobas who had actively
campaigned for their seizure. Second, it created a
favorable climate for DFI:

1. direct foreign investment was to be
   welcomed in the petrochemical sector, previously solely reserved for
   Petrobas. In late 1966, Phillips
   Petroleum, backed by the United
   States Government and the World
   Bank, invested $70 million in
   Brazil's fertiliser industry;
2. controls on profit remittances and
   tax concessions were considerably
   relaxed;
3. the development of oil shale reserves was opened to DFI for the
   first time. Ironically, Soviet assistance was to be used to further
   promote the private shale oil industry in Brazil; and,
4. an Investment Guarantee Agreement
   was signed in which Brazil agreed to
   surrender its rights to nationalise
   United States' property.[98]

Third, the overthrow of Goulart was followed not
only by a major mining concession to the Hanna Mining Company but also by major increases in the already large U.S. DFI in Brazilian manufacturing
($700 million in 1964, $1.4 billion in 1971).[99]

Coming to the abortive Bay of Pigs operation
in 1961, it is clear from documented evidence that
U.S. proxy intervention was due to pressures exerted
by the oil companies whose assets Castro seized in
June 1960; it can also be explained by the fact that
more than $1 billion in U.S. investments were in-
volved (Table 4.6). While it was apparent, given
the circumstances in which he took power on January
1, 1959, that Fidel Castro was determined to reduce

or terminate U.S. domination of the Cuban economy, it was not so obvious that "this would necessarily lead to a confrontation with the United States government."[100]

Meanwhile, some decisions which were decisive factors in the deterioration of U.S.-Cuban relations must be mentioned:

1. Agrarian Reform Law of May 17, 1959 which called for the distribution of large tracts of United States-owned land (including 300,000 acres owned by United Fruit) to squatters, tenants, peasants; compensation, which was based on the 1958 book value, was to be paid in twenty-five year bonds at 4.5 percent interest;

2. Cancellation of telephone rate increase, followed by "intervention" of the telephone company in March 1959 as well as reduction of electricity rates in the rural areas by 50 percent, resulting in a loss of $13 million by American and Foreign Power Company;

3. Imposition of a 60 percent royalty on foreign oil companies and promulgation of a law empowering the government to "intervene" in any companies in grave financial crises and/or had deliberately reduced production.[101]

While expressing sympathy for "the objectives which the government of Cuba is presumed to be seeking"--indeed, while recognizing that a state has a right to nationalize property within its territorial jurisdiction for public purposes and, more fundamental, that "soundly conceived and executed programmes for rural betterment, including agrarian reform in certain areas, can contribute to a higher standard of living, political stability, and social progress"[102]--a State Department note of June 11 to the Cuban government maintained that international law required "payment of prompt, adequate, and effective compensation," because the wording of the Agrarian Law raised "serious" questions about the "adequacy of the compensation" to U.S. nationals, adding that the 1940 Cuban Constitution made provision for prior payment of compensation for expropriated land and for the quantum to be determined by a law court. The point emphasized here is that insistence on the payment of "prompt, adequate, and effective compensation" confirmed Castro's "suspicions that the United States was exclusively concerned with property of its nationals which would be affected by his reforms."[103]

Meanwhile, key policy makers in the Eisenhower administration who were deeply concerned about the nationalization of U.S.-owned agricultural properties without compensation (and these included Richard Rubottom, Assistant Secretary of State for Latin America, Thomas C. Mann, Under-Secretary of State for Economic Affairs, and Robert Anderson, Secretary of the Treasury and a close confidant of President Eisenhower) responded to continuing corporate pressure on the State Department to take stronger action against Castro by giving serious consideration in September to reducing the Cuban sugar quota and arming the Batista exiles in Florida.[104] On October 11, anti-Castro forces, operating from Florida, dropped three fire bombs on a Cuban sugar mill. In its note to the Cuban government dated October 12, the U.S. government maintained that the Castro regime was required, under international law and the Cuban Constitution, to pay full and effective compensation, rejecting comparison of Cuba's agrarian reform with agrarian reform in postwar Japan under which payment had been made in bonds.[105] As anti-Castro forces continued their bombing raids over Havana, Castro reorganized his cabinet. He flushed out his "comrades" in the "July 26th Movement," named his brother, Raul, Minister for the Armed Forces, and named Che Guevara head of the National Bank. He denounced the United States, at a mass rally in Havana in December, for supporting and financing, through the CIA, bombing raids over Havana.

On January 11, 1960, a press release by the State Department summarized a note sent to its Cuban

opposite number protesting Cuba's expropriatory measures "without any sanction in Cuban law, without
written authority . . . and without court orders."
On January 12, Florida-based planes again carried
out bombing raids over seven Cuban sugar cane fields.
On January 21, Castro denounced, on television, the
U.S. note (contained in the press release of January
11) in such strong terms that Ambassador Philip
Bonsal was recalled to Washington for "consulta-
tion." A policy statement issued by President Eisenhower on January 26 expressed the hope, albeit vain
hope, that U.S. nationals would continue to contribute to the Cuban economy through "their investments."
Eisenhower maintained, first, that the United States
would "continue to bring to the attention of the
Cuban government instances in which the rights of
its citizens under Cuban law and international law
have been disregarded and in which redress under
Cuban law is apparently unavailable or denied" and,
second and more significant, that the United States
"has confidence in the ability of the Cuban people
to recognize and defeat the intrigues of international Communism."

Following contacts with the Soviet Union--made
through Soviet Deputy Premier Anastas Mikoyan in
Mexico in November 1959 as well as trade negotiations in Havana between Mikoyan and Cuban officials--
a Soviet-Cuban Trade Agreement was announced on February 13, 1960, introducing a new dimension into
U.S.-Cuban relations. Under the agreement, the
Soviet Union would:

1. purchase 425,000 tons of Cuban sugar
   in 1960 and 5 million tons of sugar
   in five years beginning from 1961 at
   approximately the world market
   prices, paying 20 percent of the
   purchase price in dollars and the
   rest in Soviet goods, presumably,
   crude oil.
2. grant Cuba a $100 million loan at
   2.5 percent interest, repayable in
   twelve years, to purchase machinery,
   equipment and raw materials, including crude and refined petroleum.[106]

The agreement to purchase Cuban sugar and pay 20 percent in dollars and the rest in Soviet goods was essentially a barter agreement. Additionally, it guaranteed a market for part of Cuban sugar export in the event of the U.S. sugar quota being reduced and/or eliminated; additionally, it provided Cuba with a source for petroleum and petroleum products.

That the U.S. Embassy in Havana viewed with alarm Mikoyan's visit to (and talks in) Havana was evident from a cablegram dispatched to Secretary of State Christian Herter on February 15, 1960. While taking the position that the visit was a "long step toward putting [Cuba] definitely in the Soviet camp" and that "there is little further hope that the United States will be able to reach a satisfactory relationship with the Cuban government as presently constituted," the Embassy opposed "drastic measures at this time" but recommended that Washington "concentrate on devising a means to correct the present intolerable state of affairs."[107] The strategy to damage and cripple the Cuban economy at least had a twin objective. First, it was hoped that "the Cuban people will sooner or later become disillusioned with their revolutionary leadership, thus setting the stage for a successful counter-revolution," and, second, and more fundamental, "the peoples of the underdeveloped countries are to be taught that revolution does not pay."[108]

At that time, it was agreed in the U.S. business community that the Cuban expropriations posed a threat to U.S. large investments in raw materials, agriculture, and telecommunications in Latin America. Many investors and their friends/supporters in the legislative and executive branches of government feared that failures to secure adequate compensation (when such investments are seized, ostensibly for public purposes) would encourage a domino effect. In a December 1959 Memorandum to Allen Dulles, Chief of CIA's Western Hemisphere Division, J. C. King observed that a "'far left' dictatorship now existed in Cuba which, 'if' permitted to stand, will encourage similar actions against U.S. holdings in other Latin American countries."[109] It was small wonder then that King recommended that "thorough consideration be given to the elimination of Fidel Castro."[110]

According to the Senate Assassination Report, the CIA Special Group first discussed the overthrow of Castro on January 13, 1960. During the meeting, Dulles

> noted the possibility that over the
> long run the U.S. will not be able to
> tolerate the Castro regime, and sug-
> gested that covert contingency planning
> to accomplish the fall of the Castro
> government might be in order.[111]

Reacting to comments by a State Department representative that "timing was very important so as to permit a solidly based opposition to take over," Dulles "emphasized that we do not have in mind a quick elimination of Castro, but rather actions designed to enable responsible opposition leaders to get a foothold."[112] At the March 9 meeting of the CIA Task Force on Cuba operation, King warned of an imminent attack on the U.S. Navy installation at Guantanamo Bay by the Castro regime, adding that unless Fidel, Raul, and Che were "eliminated in one package--which is highly unlikely--. . . the present government will only be overthrown by the use of force."[113] The National Security Council, which met on March 10 to discuss U.S. policy to "bring another government to power in Cuba," was informed by Dulles that "a plan to effect the situation in Cuba was being worked on"[114] by the CIA. In fact, the plan discussed by the Special Group on March 14 involved "sabotage, economic sanctions, propaganda, and training of a Cuban exile group for possible invasion."[115] At a meeting of the National Security Council on March 17, Eisenhower approved a CIA plan "to begin training twenty-five Cuban exiles, who might in turn train other exiles for an attempt to overthrow Castro."[116] The plan, evolved by Richard Bissell, Deputy Director of Plans, was more grandiose. It included a 50-milowatt radio station on Swan Island, a government-in-exile, a rebel air force based in Nicaragua, a rebel army to be trained in Guatemala, and an amphibious landing of 1,400 men in Cuba.[117] In essence, the "Guatemala scenario" was used as a model while the invasion was scheduled for November

or early December. On March 30, Castro accused the
U.S. government of attempting to overthrow his government, employing similar methods used in Guatemala
to oust Colonel Arbenz Guzman.[118]

While it may be said that the U.S. decision to
overthrow the Castro regime in March may well have
been influenced by the Soviet-Cuban Trade Agreement,
it was obvious that key individual policy makers
feared that uncompensated eminent domain seizures in
Cuba might encourage a domino effect. Consequently,
the Cuban expropriations strengthened the linkage
between economic and security issues. Additionally,
many business leaders believed, rightly or wrongly,
that the State Department was too "tepid in their
defence, too solicitous of other countries' problems
and insufficiently concerned with economic issues."[119]
To date, the role of the Soviet Union in Cuba's political economy was particularly significant because the
Soviet Union is not only the world's second largest
oil producer but also an important exporter of crude
oil. The Soviet-Cuban Trade Agreement introduced a
new dimension into U.S.-Cuban relations. First, low
Soviet oil prices and barter arrangements frightened
the oil majors whose main source of profits was
their oligopoly control of crude oil sales, while
Soviet oil exports and technology transfer left
their enormous equity interests exposed to dangers.
Second, and more fundamental, since Cuba's annual
crude oil imports (10 percent of Cuba's imports)
stood at $80 million, barter trade would clearly and
considerably reduce pressure on scarce and declining
foreign exchange reserves.

The Castro regime had advised Shell, Texaco,
and Exxon shortly after the February 1960 trade
treaty that each company would refine 11,000 barrels
of Soviet crude oil daily. It expected, as did Ambassador Bonsal, albeit naively, that the oil majors
would refine Soviet crude oil. The oil majors argued
that they had no obligation to refine Soviet oil;
the State Department maintained that their refusal
to handle Soviet crude was consistent "with the policy of the United States government." On June 11,
Castro advised the oil companies to refine Soviet
crude oil or accept the consequences: "Don't let
them say afterward that we attacked them, confiscated

or occupied them. The Government accepts the challenge and the companies must decide their own
fate."[120]

We have noted that it was naive for the Castro
regime to expect that the oil majors would handle
Soviet crude oil. To the oil majors, refining
Soviet crude oil was anathema. First, since most of
the profits in international oil came from crude oil,
the oil majors use their subsidiaries in oil-import-
ing DCs as outlets for the sale of their own surplus
crude oil. For example, Exxon's investments in pre-
Revolutionary Cuba totaling $62.3 million included
refining facilities and an extensive marketing system. Exxon's Cuban subsidiary bought its crude from
Exxon's Venezuelan subsidiary, Creole Petroleum, at
the high prices maintained by the oil cartel. Therefore, Exxon was reaping profits in Cuba and Venezuela
and on three separate operations--sale of crude, refining of crude, and sale of finished products. Second, there was the fear of the "demonstration effect
on other countries. As Tanzer put it:

> How could the international oil com-
> panies persuade the NATO nations to
> limit imports of Soviet crude oil, let
> alone dissuade other underdeveloped
> countries from forcing them to refine
> Soviet crude oil, once the companies
> accepted this crude oil anywhere? . . .
> It seems obvious that if the companies
> acceded to the demands of the Cuban
> government, they would find it almost
> impossible to resist pressures in . . .
> other countries to handle large amounts
> of Soviet crude oil (and even refined
> products).[121]

Let us explain the oil majors' anticipated
losses in dollar terms should they accede "to the
demands of the Cuban government." According to
Michael Tanzer,

1. annual profits from crude oil imports (which stood at 20 million
   barrels annually) alone totalled

$20 million, <u>given</u> a profitability
of $1.00 per barrel; and,

2. annual profits $132 million invest-
   ments by three oil majors ($62 mil-
   lion by Exxon and $70 million by
   Texaco and Shell) stood at $13 mil-
   lion, <u>given</u> an average annual profit
   of 10 percent.[122]

Thus, once the principle of accepting and/or refining Soviet crude oil was established, "the companies
could further lose some $30 million per year on
their imports into . . . other countries."[123]

Third, the oil majors had convinced themselves
that there were little prospects of making profits
or money in Castro's Cuba except importing crude oil.
This was because in November 1959 the Castro regime
had nationalized the subsoil and all oil that might
be found in Cuba.[124]   Furthermore, in May 1960 it
began building its marketing network for handling
Soviet refined products; it also cancelled exclusive
marketing contracts between the "three [oil] majors
and Sinclair on the one hand and their 2,500 outlets
on the other so as to provide markets for Soviet imports."[125]   Thus, once the Castro regime went into
oil marketing and cancelled exclusive marketing arrangements between the three oil majors and market-
ers, an intensive price war at the marketing level
would endanger profits within Cuba, which, from the
agrarian reform of early 1959, was increasingly mov-
ing in the direction of socializing the economy.

To sum up, if a stand must be taken against
Soviet crude oil by the oil companies which, not unnaturally, expect U.S. support given deteriorating
U.S.-Cuban relations, that was as good a time and
place as any.   In any event, what the oil companies
want "is <u>monopolistic control</u> over foreign sources
of supply and foreign markets, enabling them to buy
and sell on specially privileged terms. . . .   In a
word, they want to do business on their own terms."[126]
Consequently, since the oil companies are strongly
represented in important policy-making positions and
do influence U.S. public policy, and since it is U.S.
policy to promote and advance the interests of U.S.
corporate capitalism, it is understandable why U.S.-

based MNCs and their home government would react
violently to the Cuban Revolution through sabotage,
economic sanctions including a three-pronged oil
boycott,[127] and invasion.

What makes Cuba very important to policy makers
in Washington is precisely the fact that Cuba is
small and close to the United States, the world's
greatest exponent of the free enterprise system. The
fear of the domino effect of the success of Castro's
socialist democracy was forcefully put by Paul Baran
and Paul Sweezy: "If Cuba can defect from the 'free
world' and join the socialist camp with impunity,
then any country can do so. And if Cuba prospers
under the new set-up, all the other underdeveloped
and exploited countries will be tempted to follow
her example."[128] Therefore, what was at stake in
Cuba, as it was in Guatemala under Arbenz Guzman,
was "the very existence of the 'free world' itself,
that is . . . the whole system of exploitation."[129]

Confrontation with the U.S. government and U.S.
business interests was predictable for many reasons.
First, the refusal to refine Soviet crude oil was
seen as part of the conspiracy in Washington to destroy the Cuban Revolution. Second, Castro had come
to power through a revolution which had overthrown
the corrupt regime of Fulgencio Batista which had
depended on U.S. support for survival. Third, and
more fundamental, the decision in July 1960 by the
U.S. Congress and President Eisenhower to eliminate
the Cuban sugar quota in the U.S. sugar market was
"an act of economic warfare aimed at 'a change of
government' in Cuba."[130] The Cuban seizure of
foreign-owned refineries following the oil companies'
refusal to refine Soviet oil was equally predictable.
First, Soviet oil was essential for Cuban industry:
it was cheaper than oil imported by the oil majors
and bartered in exchange for Cuban sugar; the barter
arrangement would also relieve pressure on Cuba's
foreign exchange earnings. Second, on June 11 Castro
publicly warned the oil companies to refine Soviet
oil or accept the "consequences," ranging from expropriation or confiscation to "intervention" of the
refineries or all the companies' assets. Third, refining Soviet oil was regarded by the Castro regime
as a "test of sovereignty." As Maurice Zeitlin and

Robert Scheer asked, and rightly too: "Was the
Cuban Government to determine its own economic program or were U.S. (and British) oil companies to continue to possess a veto power over it?"[131] Fourth,
and more fundamental, Soviet oil was essential to
the Cuban program for economic independence.

It is obvious, then, that what was at stake in
the conflict between Washington and Havana was not
trade, since Havana "long after the socialization of
the Cuban economy . . . was vigorously promoting its
trade with Britain, France, Spain, Canada, Japan."[132]
Baran and Sweezy have noted:

> One can see that Cuba's crime was to
> assert . . . her sovereign right to
> dispose over her own resources in the
> interests of her own people. This in-
> volved curtailing and, in the struggle
> which ensued, eventually abrogating
> the rights and privileges which the
> giant multinationals had previously
> enjoyed in Cuba. It was because of
> this . . . that the corporations and
> their government in Washington reacted
> so violently to the Cuban Revolution.[133]

Given the raison d'être for wanting to cripple
the Cuban economy in every possible way, particularly ater the seizure of the refineries, President
Eisenhower and the U.S. Congress on July 6, 1960,
"declared economic war on Fidel Castro's Cuba by
slashing that country's [sic, Cuba] exports to the
highly profitable U.S. market by 700,000 tons."[134]
By reducing the Cuban sugar quota on July 7 as
amended, and setting it at zero for 1961, President
Eisenhower completed the economic weapon of the
sugar quota brandished by Senator Smathers of Florida
as early as June 1959.

Castro's reaction to the sugar quota cut, which
should have been expected in Washington, was swift
and decisive: "wholesale nationalization of American
industries and commercial properties in Cuba."[135] In
fact, in anticipation of the cut, the Castro regime
enacted Law No. 851 empowering the president and
premier:

to order jointly by means of resolution, whenever they may deem it convenient in defense of the national interest, the nationalization through
expropriation, of the properties or
concerns belonging to natural or juridi-
cal persons, nationals of the United
States of America or the concerns in
which said persons have a majority interest or participation even though
they may be organized under the laws
of Cuba.[136]

Law No. 851 made provision for the payment of compensation in 30-year Cuban bonds at 2 percent from a
special fund into which shall be paid 25 percent of
all dollar income accruing from sugar sales to the
United States in excess of 3 million tons at a price
of no less than 5.75 cents per pound. Since the
Cuban sugar quota had been completely wiped out and
since the quota before the cut had only been 119,000
tons above the 3 million mark, it was obvious that
the Castro regime had no intention of paying any compensation whatsoever. In any event, the bonds have
not been printed to date.

Acting pursuant to Law No. 851, the Castro regime on August 6 nationalized the assets of 40 U.S.-
owned enterprises including 36 sugar mills and two
utilities, followed by the takeover of the banking
industry. Under Laws No. 890 and No. 891 the regime,
on October 13, expropriated 382 U.S.- and Cuban-owned
commercial and industrial enterprises. A day later,
all existing mortgages held by U.S.-owned financial
institutions were cancelled under the Urban Reform
Law.

As was expected, the State Department sent a
note asserting that Law No. 851 was a violation of
international law because it was "discriminatory,
arbitrary and confiscatory," while the nonprovision
for "prompt, adequate, and effective compensation"
constituted an additional element of illegality.
Notwithstanding the three-pronged oil boycott of
Cuba which was aimed at bringing the Cuban economy
to a grinding halt,[137] the United States complemented
the oil companies' efforts on October 20 by imposing

an embargo on all exports to Cuba. In retaliation, the Castro regime expropriated 166 additional U.S.-owned enterprises. So by early 1961,

> Cuba was--in its economic structure, political allies, trade patterns, and social priorities--a socialist society . . . all the strategic sectors of Cuba's industry were nationalized. . . . The state sector produced ninety per-cent of Cuba's exports; state farms and cooperatives controlled the best lands; the whole pattern of trade had shifted from the United States to the socialist countries. Imports from the United States declined from $577 million in 1957 to $2.37 million in 1961. At the same time, the vast disparities between rich and poor, city and country, were being rapidly narrowed.[138]

In December 1960, President Eisenhower set the Cuban sugar quota for 1961 at zero, and in early January 1961, the United States severed diplomatic relations with Cuba after the Castro regime had called for a drastic reduction of the U.S. diplo-matic staff in Havana. By that time, the Bay of Pigs operation, an open secret in the Cuban commu-nity in Miami, had been reported in the press in Latin America and the United States and had already been denounced by Castro. Suffice it to say that the operation of April 17 was a dismal and disgrace-ful failure. The mercenaries were crushed at Playa Giron because they had no local base and there were no popular uprisings in Cuba, contrary to the hopes of the CIA. While CIA Director Dulles publicly ac-cepted responsibility for the invasion and its fail-ure, privately President John Kennedy blamed the CIA for the disaster, threatening to break the agency into a million pieces. He made good his threat, first, by removing Allen Dulles from office in Novem-ber 1961 and replacing him with John A. McCone, who held the post until April 28, 1965. On April 15, two days before the invasion, Castro for the first time referred to the Cuban Revolution as a "socialist

revolution carried out under the very noses of the
Yankees." In his "May Day" Speech on May 1, 1961,
Fidel Castro formally proclaimed that the Cuban Revolution was socialist.[139] In April, the United States
banned Cuban exports to the United States, followed
in June by additional restrictions placed on food
exports to Cuba. In February 1962, a total trade
embargo with Cuba was imposed, and in 1963 all Cuban
assets in the United States were frozen and all dollar transactions with Cuba prohibited.

To sum up, U.S. proxy intervention can be explained, partly, by the pressure by the oil industry
on the U.S. government; partly, by more than $3 bil-
lion in U.S. investments expropriated by the Castro
regime; and partly, by opposition to communism by
policy makers. As President Kennedy noted in his
State of the Union Message: "Questions of economic
and trade can be negotiated. But Communist domination in the Hemisphere can never be negotiated."[140]
Although the Bay of Pigs operation was a disgraceful
failure, the Senate Assassination Report noted at
least eight assassination attempts on Castro.[141]

While the details of the events leading to U.S.
military intervention in the Dominican Republic in
April 1965 need not detain us,[142] and although the
U.S. government justified intervention in terms of
protecting U.S. nationals on the island as well as
preventing "another Communist state in this hemisphere,"[143] behind the aggressive and the most vio-
lent U.S. military intervention in Latin America was
sugar interests, including the fact that several
policy makers and/or advisers to President Lyndon
Johnson and key officials who made the decisions
leading to the brutal suppression of the "constitu-
tionalists" or "rebels" were corporate lawyers and
directors who had close connections with the major
sugar corporations and, therefore, had a direct or
indirect stake in the status quo ante.

First, the chief architect of U.S. interven-
tion--Organization of American States Ambassador
Ellsworth Bunker, one-time stockholder in a Dominican
sugar mill--was the Chairman/President and for 38
years a Director of National Sugar Refining Corporation which was partially founded by his father and
depends on privileged access to Dominican sugar.

Second, Ambassador W. Averell Harriman's private in-
vestment house (Brown Brothers, Harriman) owns about
10 percent of National Sugar while his brother, E.
Roland Harriman, was a Director of National Sugar.
Third, Deputy Secretary of Defense Roswell Gilpatrick
was the managing executive partner in Cravath Swaine
and Moore, legal counsel to National Sugar. Fourth,
Supreme Court Justice Abe Fortas, a close friend of
President Johnson, was for 20 years a Director of
Sucrest Corporation, which imports molasses from the
Dominican Republic. Fifth, Adolf A. Berle, Jr., a
well-known specialist on Latin American affairs and
adviser to several U.S. Presidents, was a large
stockholder and for 18 years Chairman of the Board
of Sucrest. Sixth, Max Rabb, partner in Strook,
Strook and Lavan, legal counsel to Sucrest, was an
influential supporter of President Johnson while
molasses magnate J. M. Kaplan was a large contributor
and influential adviser to many Democratic Party candidates and Americans for Democratic Action. Finally, Joseph S. Farland, State Department consultant
and former Ambassador to the Dominican Republic, was
a Director of the South Puerto Rico Sugar Company
which owns 275,000 acres of the best plantation land
in the Dominican Republic and was the largest labor
employer on the island.[144]

Undoubtedly, these corporations, including
American Sugar (the largest U.S. sugar refiner), depended, as rightly noted by Fred Goff and Michael
Locker, "directly on the Dominican sugar and molasses
supply for their operations. Any disruption in the
supply would hamper price stability."[145] Thus, there
is a relationship between the U.S. decision to intervene in the Dominican Republic and the interests of
several policy makers and/or advisers to President
Johnson. In any event, "without these direct economic interests, it would be difficult for these
gentlemen in their 'neutral' decision-making roles
to escape the assumptions, inclinations, and priorities inculcated by their economic and social
milieu."[146]

It is clear from our examination that the
U.S. response to acts of nationalization and/or revolutionary change in Iran, Guatemala, Brazil, Cuba,
and the Dominican Republic can be explained partly by

the interests of policy makers who have a direct or
indirect stake in the status quo ante and partly by
the "political context of nationalization--the social
nature of the regime pursuing policies of state ownership, the area(s) of the economy subject to nationalization, and the extent of nationalization"[147]
rather than opposition to communism. It is therefore easy to understand and explain U.S. involvement
in the overthrow of President Allende given Chile's
economic dependence on the United States and Allende's
efforts to transform Chile into a socialist democracy
which include the socialization of the means of production.

We have noted that the Chilean expropriations
generated "a hostile and conflictive response on the
part of U.S. policy makers,"[148] eventually leading
to the overthrow of the Allende regime in the September 1973 military coup. Those who sought to ab-
solve the U.S. government and U.S.-based MNCs from
complicity in the coup have attributed Chile's internal economic problems to sheer governmental in-
competence. For example, Jack Jubisch, Assistant
Secretary of State for Inter-American Affairs, in
testimony before the House Foreign Affairs Committee
on September 20, 1973, had this much to say:

> The economic policies themselves that
> were pursued by the Allende government
> resulted in the steadily deteriorating
> economic situation. The unwillingness
> of the government to modify its poli-
> cies made it inevitable that interna-
> tional lending agencies would curtail
> their programs to Chile. . . . The
> Paris Club, consisting of various cred-
> itor nations, concluded that there was
> little that could be done to Chile un-
> less the government adopted policies
> they could support. . . . It was not
> the United States, but the institutions
> themselves, which made their decisions.
> In sum it is untrue to say that the
> U.S. Government was responsible . . .
> for the overthrow of Allende.[149]

Holding a similar view was Henry Kissinger who, during his confirmation hearings as Secretary of State before the Senate Foreign Relations Committee, noted, "It was the policies of the Allende government, its insistence on forcing the pace beyond what the traffic would bear much than our policies that contributed to their economic chaos."[150] Writing on the U.S. role in the overthrow of Allende, Paul Sigmund was very blunt:

> The argument that an American invisible blockade was responsible for or a major contributing factor to the overthrow of Allende is . . . not persuasive. . . . The basic causes of Allende's overthrow lie . . . in . . . (1) eventual runaway inflation . . . caused not by lack of foreign assistance but by a domestic economic policy, initiated well before the steps taken by the Nixon Administration in the latter part of 1971. . . (2) Allende's ideologically motivated policy of intensification of the class struggle . . . (3) an Allende . . . policy of circumventing the law through legal "loopholes" or non-enforcement of its provisions. . . and (4) complicity on the stockpiling of arms by leftist groups, the discovery of which finally moved the Chilean armed forces to act. . . . The economic and political policies of the Allende government were a failure, in and of themselves.[151]

The implication of the position taken by Kubisch, Kissinger, and Sigmund is that the September 1973 coup was inevitable and perhaps justified. It also meant that efforts at redistributing national wealth and income and transforming Chile into a socialist democracy were "doomed to failure because of their intrinsic impracticability."[152]

However, this position seemed to have been controverted by the revelations of CIA Director William Colby before the House Armed Services Subcommittee on Intelligence on April 22, 1974, concerning CIA covert operations in Allende's Chile[153] and by President Gerald Ford's comment at a press conference on September 16, 1974, that covert operations aimed at destabilizing the "constitutionally elected government of another country" are "taken in the best interests of the countries involved,"[154] meaning Chile and the United States. Indeed, President Ford's comment was consistent with one Kissinger made in June 1970: "I don't see why we need to stand by and watch a country go communist due to the irresponsibility of its own people." It was small wonder then that Petras and Morley have argued that the U.S. "sustained policy of direct and indirect intervention culminated in a general societal crisis, a coup and a military government."[155]

The truth of the matter is that Chile's national debt before Allende came to power stood at $3.83 billion. From 1946 to 1958, Chile received a total of $253.6 million from the United States, of which $154.8 million were Export-Import Bank loans. As Table 4.9 reveals, Chile received approximately $1.4 billion from the Alliance for Progress; $254.4 million from EXIMBANK; and over $290 million from the World Bank and the Inter-American Development Bank. Given the raison d'être for extending U.S. bilateral assistance to Chile, namely, to help avoid and/or prevent any swing to the left, loans chased old debts; indeed, loans poured into Chile at such a rate that by 1970, Chile had the second highest per-capita debt in the world, after Israel. Most of the debts were contracted with public, private, and international lending institutions subject to U.S. influence, and payments on these largely unproductive debts became due during Allende's incumbency. Additionally, U.S. DFI in Chile by 1970 amounted to $1.8 billion; in fact, Chile's dependence on U.S. private foreign capital was almost total as U.S. MNCs were increasingly becoming the dominant force in the largest and most dynamic sectors of the Chilean economy: manufacturing, insurance, banking, communications, wholesale and retail trade, and natural resources (copper, iron, nitrates, iodine, salt, and particularly copper, all of which accounted for 75.8 percent of the total value of Chile's commodity exports in 1970).[156]

TABLE 4.9

United States Bilateral Assistance to Chile 1961-70

Alliance for Progress Loans	Approx. $1.4 billion	
Agency for International		
Development Funds	1963	$41,300,000
	1964	$78,800,000
	1965	$99,500,000
Political Risk		
Insurance (OPIC)[a]	Approx. $1.8 billion (1965-70)	
Bilateral Assistance (1964)[b]		
Program Loan	$55,000,000	
EXIMBANK Credit[c]	$15,000,000	
Treasury Exchange Agreement	$15,000,000	
EXIMBANK Loans (1967-69)	$254,400,000	

Over-All Aid Program
Increased dramatically from $97.7 million in 1963 to
$260.4 million in 1964 (266.5 percent increase), followed
by a sharp drop to $92.5 million 1965

1964 allocation included a $40 million General Economic
Development Grant to alleviate unemployment in an
election year

United States' Support for Multilateral Assistance to
Chile 1965-70
World Bank $98,000,000
Inter-American Development Bank $192,100,000
Loan for Commodity Imports (1964) $15,000,000

Total Public and Private Debt End-1970 $3.8 billion

Source: Petras and Morley, How Allende Fell
(Nottingham, England: Spokesman Books, 1974), pp. 23, 24,
and 25.
[a]Overseas Private Investment Corporation is the successor to the Agency for International Development Special
Risk Investment Guarantee Agreement.
[b]1964 was an election year and Eduardo Frei's major
opponent was Salvador Allende Gossens, candidate of the
Left Coalition (FRAP).
[c]EXIMBANK--Export and Import Bank was established by
an act of the United States Congress in 1945.

That the United States regarded Chile as "a sober and steadying influence in hemispheric affairs" if she "remains on our side of the ideological fence" was evident from U.S. government and corporate intervention in the 1964 election. Approximately $20 million was channeled into the election campaigns of Eduardo Frei, candidate of the Christian Democratic Party, while the United States provided support services and top officials of Kennecott and Anaconda bolstered Frei's electoral fortunes by accepting Frei's program of Chileanization of the copper industry as the only viable alternative to nationalization, proposed by Allende and the Left Coalition.[157]

In any event, Frei became the President from 1964 to 1970. The Christian Democratic Party had succeeded in attracting support from both the right and left with its reformist platform. Commenting on Frei's victory, the New York Times noted:

> The victory is a great relief to every important capital in the Western Hemisphere. . . . Only Havana will fail to rejoice in it. The Chilean election had everywhere been rated as the most important in Latin America in years. . . . Hence Chile will remain an orthodox member of the Organization of American States, aligned to the West. Where the rival group, the FRAP (Allende's coalition of parties) would have nationalized the copper and nitrate industries (about 90% American-owned), the Christian Democrats merely plan to have all copper refined in Chile. . . . Frei's program is "revolutionary" only in the sense of the Alliance for Progress.[158]

Under Frei, the Chilean government acquired 51 percent equity interests in Anaconda and Kennecott. While it could be claimed that government majority equity participation in joint ventures between a host government and local MNC subsidiaries confers on the government the control inherent in such majority holding, many important decisions, as the ex-

periences of Zambia, Sierra Leone, and Ghana have
shown,[159] remained in the hands of Anaconda and
Kennecott. Compensation was high for the shares
bought, and a new tax agreement made it possible for
the companies to triple their profits. In 1969
alone, Anaconda and Kennecott made $79 million and
$35.3 million million profits, respectively; and be-
tween 1965 and 1971, Anaconda and Kennecott netted
$426 million and $178 million profits, respectively.[160] Under an expansion program presented to
President Frei and accepted by his government, the
copper enterprises contrived an astute strategy making nationalization of the copper industry politically costly and embarrassing by contracting a government-guaranteed loan of $632.4 million from a con-
sortium of public and private lenders in the United
States, Western Europe, and Japan.

It is true that the Chilean balance of trade
has remained positive, export revenues being greater
than imports of goods. Chile has had persistent
balance-of-payments deficits, primarily caused by
large profit remittances by local MNCs, necessitat-
ing massive foreign assistance and loans to cover
these deficits. In essence, the Chilean society was
living on borrowed money, more than half of which
was owed to the United States. To be sure, the standard of living of the heavily consumer-oriented upper
and middle class was based on foreign loans, credits,
and delayed debt repayments. As debt service charges
consumed about 30 percent of the total value of
Chilean exports, the Chilean government was forced
to obtain new foreign loans and aid plus negotiate
and reschedule debt payments. Unfortunately, by the
time Allende came to power, Chile was placed in "a
weak bargaining position over both internal and external policies with its main creditors, the United
States and the international financial community. . . .
This gave the United States, with its power to ensure
that the flow of aid and credits to Chile could cease,
a powerful tool for disrupting the Chilean economy."[161] Finally, and more important, because 70
percent of Chilean imports (which included crucial
spare parts and machinery for the most critical sectors of the economy--copper, steel, electricity,
petroleum, and transportation) came from the United

States, this gave the U.S. government added powerful leverage to disrupt the Chilean economy if it so desired. For example, almost one-third of the diesel trucks at the Chuquicamata copper mine were grounded by late 1972 because of lack of spare parts and/or tires. Again, over 90 percent of the spare parts used in the copper industry were imported from the United States, meaning that an embargo on the exports of these crucial spare parts to Chile could inflict unacceptable damage to the Chilean economy. In short, when the Allende government came to power in October 1970 in spite of efforts to stop Allende although not without costing the life of General Rene Schneider, General Officer Commanding the Chilean Armed Forces,[162] it was "confronted with a situation of external control over copper production, technology and spare parts, and manufacturing, making the economy extremely vulnerable to financial and commercial pressures."[163]

We have noted in Chapter 1 abortive efforts made by ITT to swing the September 1970 popular elections to Alessandri. Mention was also made of ITT's efforts not only to block Allende's victory in a congressional run-off election (since it has become a convention for the Chilean Congress to elect as the President the candidate with the largest number of votes and Allende had a plurality) but also to oust Allende from power through an "invisible economic blockade" of Chile (which included credit squeeze by private and public financial institutions; embargo on exports of spare parts to Chile and delaying the purchase of Chilean copper--the lifeline of Chile-- for six months). A major reason for ITT's involvement in Chilean politics, as we have noted, can be explained by its Chilean investments which stood at $153 million, and the fact that Allende had campaigned on a platform of the nationalization of the commanding heights of the economy, particularly public utilities (including Chiltelco, an ITT subsidiary), banks, hotels, and extractive industries.

The socialist experiment embarked upon by the Allende government represented a new nationalist challenge to the United States in Latin America. Chile's attempts to opt out of the capitalist orbit directly challenged the political and economic hege-

mony of the United States in Latin America. This is
because democratic socialism represented not only a
systemic challenge but also a conflict between capitalist and socialist modes of production. Because
the nationalization of U.S. investments in Chile was
carried out within the framework of a socialist economy, confrontation between the Allende government
and the U.S. government (under strong pressures to
act from business groups which had contributed to
the election campaigns of President Richard Nixon)
was therefore predictable. More important, the existence of capitalist development poles in Brazil
and Peru strengthened U.S. efforts to destroy Allende's socialist and anticapitalistic experiment.
A second consideration was the domino effect or rip-
ple effect of a successful socialist democracy in
Chile, particularly after the Allende government
announced in September 1971 that $774 million would
be deducted as "excess profits" from any compensation due to Anaconda and Kennecott for the nationalization of their Chilean assets, meaning that the two
copper corporations were not entitled to any compen-
sation--since most estimates placed the book value
of their nationalized assets at $500 million to $600
million. Concern was expressed "at very high levels
of government," first, that a successful socialist
transformation in Chile would encourage nationalists
everywhere and anywhere and, second, that a "soft"
response to the Allende doctrine of "excess profits"
deduction would encourage expropriations (without
compensation) especially in Latin America and Africa.

In official reaction, Secretary of State
William Rogers condemned the "excess profit" concept
as a "serious departure from accepted standards of
international law." In a discussion in October 1971
with top executives of six corporations with investments in Chile who had come to express grave concern
that the decision on the "excess profit" deduction
could have a domino effect throughout Latin America
in the absence of strong U.S. retaliatory action,
Rogers expressed the possibility of imposing an embargo on spare parts and materials to Chile as well
as suspending U.S. bilateral assistance to Chile
under the Hickenlooper Amendment unless Anaconda and
Kennecott received "swift and adequate compensa-

tion."[164] Supporting the U.S. position on the treatment of foreign governments expropriating U.S. investments without compensation, Robert S. McNamara, President of the World Bank and former U.S. Secretary of Defense, "warned developing countries that a 'disquieting' trend by governments to annul agreements with foreign governments could 'seriously imperil' their creditworthiness and inhibit investment in their entire region."[165]

In essence, since U.S. policy makers perceived Chile as "the linchpin in the Latin American struggle to redefine its political and economic relationships with the United States," it should not surprise anyone who has studied the role of the United States in Latin America and DCs in general that the overall U.S. response to the socialist experiment in Allende's Chile was two-fold:

> a combination of severe economic pressures whose cumulative impact would result in internal economic chaos and a policy of disaggregating the Chilean state through creating ties with specific critical sectors (the military) and supporting their efforts at weakening the capacity of the state to realize a nationalist development project. This sustained policy of direct and indirect intervention culminated in a general societal crisis, a <u>coup</u> and a military government.[166]

Pursuant to the policy of making the Chilean "economy scream," and following the Nixon policy statement of January 1972 threatening foreign-aid sanctions (which may include suspension of U.S. bilateral assistance and withholding U.S. support for loans under consideration in international banks) against any country expropriating significant U.S. interest "without making reasonable provision for . . . compensation," the United States responded with the following policy decisions:

> 1. Chile was denied EXIMBANK loans to
>   purchase three United States Boeing

passenger jets while EXIMBANK termi-
nated all loan guarantees to United
States commercial banks and exporters having business links with Chile
as well as "disbursements of direct
loans that had been previously negotiated by the Frei government."[167]

2. With the exception of two educational loans totalling $11.6 million
to the Austral and Catholic Universities, which were opposition strong-
holds, no IDB [Inter-American Development Bank] long-term development
loan was granted to the Allende government. An application for a $30
million loan for a petrochemical
complex was killed after the United
States Executive Director objected
to a plan by the IDB to send a technical team to evaluate the project.
Denial of IDB was consistent with
the provisions of the Gonzalez
Amendment.[168]

3. Although Chile continued to meet its
debt service obligations to the IBRD,
the World Bank did not extend new
loans to Chile because the "Bank
maintains a strict standard in the
matter of taking without compensation,"[169] and this should surprise
no one given the raison d'être for
the World Bank Convention on the
Settlement of Investment Disputes,[170]
and because "reasonable efforts" are
not "being made to reach a settlement" with Anaconda and Kennecott.

4. The United States government refused
to renegotiate Chile's public debt
to the United States except under
certain conditions which will seriously hamper Chile's freedom of action with respect to monetary, fis-

        cal, foreign and public sector pol-
        icies.[171]

5. The United States canvassed, albeit
   unsuccessfully, Chile's creditor-
   nations to make renegotiation of
   public debts conditional and impossible.

6. United States suppliers demanded
   "cash in advance for essential raw
   materials and spare parts to
   Chile,"[172] and this at a time of
   rising import prices, increasing
   domestic demand, declining world
   copper prices, credit squeeze by
   the United States government and refusal by the United States business
   community and United States to renegotiate Chile's public debt except
   on its own terms.

Interestingly enough, notwithstanding the
Nixon Doctrine enunciated in January 1972, the United
States, in addition to granting a Chilean request for
a $5 billion loan for military purchases in mid-1971,
announced in December 1972 a $10 million credit
agreement for the Chilean military. In a statement
justifying the extension of military assistance to
Chile, Secretary of State Rogers noted, "It is quite
interesting that in the case of Latin America we are
still providing some military assistance to Chile,
for the reasons we think it would be better not to
have a complete break with them."[173] To be sure, in
May 1973 President Nixon exercised his powers under
Section 4 of the Foreign Military Sales Act to allow
five Latin American countries including Chile to
purchase F-5E military fighter aircraft, on the
grounds that such action was "important to the national security of the United States."[174]

On September 11, 1973, a military coup overthrew the democratically elected government of Salvador Allende. According to a communiqué issued by
the junta, "the Chilean armed forces and carabineros
are united to initiate the historic and responsible

mission to fight for the liberation of the father-
land from the Marxist yoke."[175] Undoubtedly, the
"invisible blockade" was a major or contributory
factor in the Chilean economic crisis. Perhaps, and
as O'Brien noted, the Allende government should have
expected something like the invisible blockade and
presumably taken this into account when formulating
a socialist, anticapitalist development strategy.[176]
Although the facts of the U.S. role in the mechanics
of the execution of the military aspects of the coup
are scanty,[177] the U.S. government did play a crucial role in establishing the political and social
conditions for the coup through a well-coordinated
policy of credit squeeze and informal invisible
blockade.

As was expected, the United States denied any
involvement in the coup. Kubisch has forcefully
stated:

> I wish to state as flatly and as cate-
> gorically as I possibly can that we did
> not have advance knowledge of the coup
> that took place on September 11. . . .
> In a similar vein, either explicitly or
> implicitly, the U.S. government has
> been charged with involvement or com-
> plicity in the coup. This is absolute-
> ly false. As official spokesmen of the
> U.S. Government have stated repeatedly,
> we were not involved in the coup in any
> way.[178]

This statement seems to have been controverted by
the testimony of Colby before the House Foreign Affairs Sub-committee as well as the testimony of
Richard Helms before the Senate Foreign Relations
Committee. Asked to comment on whether the CIA's activities continued after Allende's inauguration as
Chilean President, Colby had this to say:

> If I might comment, the presumption
> under which we conduct this type of
> operation is that it is a covert oper-
> ation and that the United States hand
> is not to show. For that reason we in

the executive branch restrict any
knowledge of this type of operation
very severely and conduct procedures
so that very few people learn of any
type of operation of this nature.[179]

In his own testimony, Helms told the committee that
he lied in his earlier evidence that the CIA was not
involved in Chilean politics during the Allende administration. He stated: "I know that Nixon wanted
it [sic, the Allende administration] overthrown, but
there was no way to do it that anybody knew of."[180]

Assuming that the United States was not the
prime promoter of the coup, at least it assisted the
making of the coup. There is evidence that the CIA
spent $8 million (equivalent of $40 million to $80
million on the Chilean black market) on covert operations that were evidently approved at the highest
levels of government. The amount was devoted to
financing opposition parties, newspapers, and activities, especially strikes from 1970 through 1973. CIA
agents who operated under the front of the AFL-CIO
posed as the "friends of the workers." This was done
to mislead certain sections of the working people and
incite them against the government that was defending their interests. To be sure, the Report of the
Senate Committee on the Activities of Secret Services
in Chile admitted that the strikers enjoyed effective
support from many CIA-funded groups.[181]

INTERVENTION AND CHANGES IN
DIRECT FOREIGN INVESTMENT

What we would seek to examine here is whether
there are changes in foreign business activity as a
result of covert or overt intervention in a taking
state by an investor state on behalf of its nationals. Hence, our third hypothesis:

As a corollary to Hypothesis 2, foreign
intervention, whether overt or covert
(proxy) or foreign-directed and influenced coup d'état following expropriations of assets or acquired rights of

local subsidiaries of MNCs, more often
than not leads to increased foreign
"business activity," in terms of increased private foreign investments
and/or restitution of expropriated
assets.

Let us begin with the business climate in Chile
following the overthrow of the Allende government.
As was expected in Washington, the military junta:

1. announced a new development strategy designed to
   encourage direct foreign investment;
2. gave notice of Chile's intention to adopt a "low-
   profile" within the Andean Common Market;
3. agreed in principle to paying compensation to
   Anaconda and Kennecott;
4. offered compensation to other U.S. investors
   whose assets were expropriated by the previous
   regime;
5. denationalized a large number of foreign-owned
   enterprises expropriated by the Allende government;
6. invited Exxon to acquire La Disputada copper mine
   for $175 million, pursuant to a new investment
   enunciated by it following the overthrow of
   Allende; and
7. returned those enterprises whose management was
   taken over by the previous regime.[182]

As a result of these policy decisions, among others,
foreign credits poured into Chile within months of
the military junta's coming into power.   Table 4.10
shows foreign credits granted to Chile after Allende.
Approximately $470 million came from the United
States, Brazil, Argentina, and multilateral development banks; $124 million came from a U.S. banking
consortium; and $10 million came from the Banco de
Colombia and the Swiss Foreign Trade Financial Commission.   In addition, the U.S. government made available a $24 million credit for the purchase of "des-
perately needed wheat," followed by another $28 mil-
lion credit for the purchase of corn.[183]

TABLE 4.10

Foreign Credits Granted to Chile after Allende

1. From the U.S. government	$ 49,000,000
2. From Brazil	62,000,000
3. From Argentina	35,000,000
4. From the International Monetary Fund (contingency credit--stand-by)	95,000,000
5. From the World Bank	18,250,000
6. From the Inter-American Development Bank	201,000,000
7. From the Andean Development Corporation	8,550,000
8. From the U.S. government (military credit)	11,000,000
9. From a U.S. banking consortium	124,000,000
10. From Banco de Colombia	10,000,000
11. From Swiss Foreign Trade Financial Commission	10,000,000
Total	$621,800,000

Source: James Petras and Morris M. Morley, How Allende Fell (Nottingham, England: Spokesman Books, 1974), pp. 123-24,

The overthrow of Mossadegh in Iran paved the way for a new investment climate in that country. First, the Anglo-Iranian Oil Company received £25 million from Iran. Second, a new arrangement relating to the operation of Iranian oil was agreed upon between the Iranian government and the "Seven Sisters." Thus, although the National Iranian Oil Company would remain the owners of the oilfields and the refinery, an Iranian consortium would buy oil from the National Iranian Oil Company in the following proportion: British Petroleum, the new name for Anglo-Iranian Oil Company, takes 40 percent; the five Sisters in the United States would each take 8 percent; Shell takes 14 percent, while Compagnie Française de Petrole takes 6 percent. Third, Anglo-Iranian was released from a liability of undisclosed

size with respect to Iranian counterclaims. Fourth,
Anglo-Iranian secured substantial payments from
other members of the consortium.

In Guatemala, the overthrow of the Arbenz
Guzman government was followed by the restitution of
all the assets of United Fruit nationalized under an
agrarian law in June 1952. Following the overthrow
of the Goulart government, the military junta denationalized privately owned refineries. It created
a favorable climate for DFI. To this end, DFI was
welcomed in the petrochemical sector, hitherto reserved exclusively for Petrobas; control on profit
remittances and tax concessions was relaxed; the development of oil shale reserves was opened to DFI
for the first time; and an Investment Guarantee
Agreement was signed in which Brazil agreed to surrender its rights to nationalize U.S. property. Finally, and more significant, the overthrow of the
Goulart regime was followed by a major mining concession to the Hanna Mining Company. It is small
wonder then that the United States has responded
favorably to the Brazilian development strategy
"based on foreign multinational corporate investment,
political repression of the lower classes, the recon-
centration of wealth in the hands of the upper class
and a developing consumer-oriented middle class."[184]
To be sure, since the 1964 coup, the United States
has provided over $2 billion in economic and military
assistance to the military junta in support of a political environment conducive to U.S. economic penetration.

Undoubtedly there has been increased "business
activity" following the overthrow of nationalist regimes in Iran, Guatemala, Brazil, Dominican Republic,
Bolivia, and Chile, to name but a few. As noted
above, U.S. responses to economic nationalism or
revolutionary change or acts of nationalization in
Iran, Guatemala, Cuba, Brazil, Dominican Republic,
and Chile can be partially explained by the interests
of the policy makers who have a direct or indirect
stake in the status quo ante and partially by the
"political context of nationalization--the social
nature of the regime pursuing policies of state ownership, the area(s) of the economy subject to nationalization, and the extent of nationalization,"[185]
rather than opposition to communism.

The U.S. response to the Venezuelan expropriations was not confrontational because the expropriations were sectoral rather than structural; a sectoral and fragmented nationalization policy in Venezuela neither displaced other foreign capitalist interests nor encompassed measures threatening the
continued dominance of the capitalist mode of production. In any event, the business community welcomed the expropriations, and above all, the Perez
government paid appropriate compensation to U.S. investors whose assets were expropriated. Additionally, because petroleum revenues provided new investment opportunities, "the U.S. business community decided to adopt a more pragmatic approach to the new
rules. 'Constructive' behavior superseded a conflictive posture and became the basis for the continuing
relationship."[186] The point to emphasize here is
that U.S. MNCs moved into nonextractive areas of the
economy because the Perez government provided a political environment for such an entry. It was small
wonder then that the U.S. business community opposed
the exclusion of Venezuela from the Generalized
Tariff Preferences of the United States Trade Act of
1974 because of Venezuela's membership in the Organisation of Petroleum Exporting Countries.[187]
    It is true that U.S. policy makers adopted a po-
sition of hostility toward the Velasco government in
Peru following Peruvian expropriation of the assets
of U.S. MNCs such as the International Petroleum
Company (a subsidiary of Exxon), W. R. Grace Company,
and Gulf Oil Company. A change in U.S. policy became manifest in late 1971. Unlike the Chilean expropriations, the measures carried out by the Velasco
regime were not intended to result in a socialist
transformation in Peru but "to modify Peru's terms
of dependency and to provide a basis for industrialization" within the framework of a capitalist development strategy. Additionally, a compensation settlement providing relief for U.S. investors expropriated
since Major General Juan Velasco came to power in
October 1968 was signed on February 19, 1974.[188]
Further, the military junta imposed limited restrictions on profit remittances abroad. More significant, while exercising control over private foreign
capital, these restrictions were accompanied by new

concessions to private foreign investors. In fact,
international oil companies signed a number of ex-
ploration contracts with the military junta. To be
sure, increasing private foreign capital participation can be seen in new industrial and mining under-
takings. In essence economic nationalism in Peru
was not aimed at eliminating dependence on DFI; it
was aimed at redefining Peruvian dependence on DFI.
Perhaps, this explains why the Velasco regime sur-
vived for some seven years. More radical economic
measures begun by him (starting with the expropriation of the Marcona Mining Company) were halted when
he was ousted from office in August 1975 and replaced
by the more moderate President Francisco Morales
Bermudez, who immediately initiated compensation
negotiations with the U.S. government rather than
with the Marcona Mining Company.[189]

NOTES

1. G. Pope Atkins, Latin America in the International Political System (New York: Free Press,
1977), p. 132.
2. Ibid.
3. V. I. Lenin, Imperialism: The Highest
Stage of Capitalism (Moscow: Progress Publishers,
1966); J. A. Hobson, Imperialism: A Study (London:
George Allen and Unwin, 1938).
4. P. M. Sweezy and H. Magdoff, "Notes on the
Multinational Corporation," Monthly Review 5 (1969):
1-7; Id., "Notes on the Multinational Corporation,"
Monthly Review 6 (1969): 1-13. For a Marxist theory
of imperialism and a critique of Marxist theories of
imperialism, see Tom Kemp, "The Marxist Theory of
Imperialism," in Studies in the Theory of Imperial-
ism, edited by Roger Owen and Bob Sutcliffe (London:
Longman Group, 1980), pp. 15-34; Michael B. Brown,
"A Critique of Marxist Theories of Imperialism," in
Studies in the Theory of Imperialism, pp. 35-70.
5. H. Magdoff, The Age of Imperialism (New
York: Monthly Review Press, 1969).
6. W. M. Scammell, The International Economy
Since 1945 (London: Macmillan Press, 1980), p. 159.
7. Barnet and Muller, Global Reach, pp. 72-104.

8. Chile, Speech Delivered by President
Salvador Allende, President of the Republic of Chile
Before the General Assembly of the United Nations December 4, 1972 (Washington, D.C.: Embassy of Chile,
1972), p. 24.
9. William Diebold, The United States and
the Industrial World (New York: Praeger, 1972), pp.
199-200.
10. Hobson, Imperialism, p. 81.
11. Atkins, Latin America, p. 133.
12. Ibid.
13. See Akinsanya, The Expropriation of Multinational Property in the Third World, pp. 77-114;
Id., "Host Governments' Responses to Foreign Economic
Control: The Experiences of Selected African Countries," International and Comparative Law Quarterly
30 (1981): 769-90.
14. See Robert A. Pastor, Congress and the
Politics of U.S. Foreign Economic Policy 1929-1976
(Berkeley: University of California Press, 1980),
pp. 136-284; Akinsanya, The Expropriation of Multinational Property in the Third World, pp. 284-300;
Id., "Host Governments' Responses to Foreign Economic
Control," pp. 782-83.
15. See Andreas F. Lowenfeld, "Diplomatic Intervention in Investment Disputes," Proceedings of
the American Society of International Law (1967): 96-
107.
16. George Ingram, Expropriation of U.S. Property in South America (New York: Praeger, 1974), p.
116.
17. Bryce Wood, The Making of the Good Neigh-
bor Policy (New York: Columbia University Press,
1961), p. 194.
18. Lipson, "Corporate Preferences and Public
Policies, Foreign Aid Sanctions and Investment Protection," World Politics 28 (1976): 410-11. See
also Daniel S. Blanchard, "The Threat to U.S. Private
Investment in Latin America," Journal of International Law and Economics 5 (1971): 233-37; Ingram,
pp. 19-104.
19. David A. Gantz, "The Marcona Settlement,"
American Journal of International Law 71 (1977):
474-93.
20. Pastor, Congress, pp. 219-50.

21. Philip M. Brown, "Mexican Land Laws," American Journal of International Law 21 (1927): 295-96.

22. For the list of oil companies affected by the Expropriation Decree, see B. A. Wortley, "The Mexican Oil Dispute 1938-1946," Grotius Society Transactions 43 (1957): 25.

23. Hans W. Baader, "The Validity of Foreign Confiscations: An Addendum," American Journal of International Law 56 (1962): 505.

24. Akinsanya, The Expropriation of Multinational Property in the Third World, p. 119.

25. Wortley, "Mexican Oil Dispute," p. 31.

26. Canada, House of Commons, Debates, February 23, 1971, p. 3658.

27. Isaiah A. Litvak and Christopher J. Maule, "Nationalisation in the Caribbean Bauxite Industry," International Affairs 51 (1975): 54.

28. Because the U.S. government did not believe that Guyana was making "reasonable effort" to compensate Alcan, the United States Executive Director of the World Bank in June 1971 abstained, as a sign of disapproval, from voting on an application for a $5.4 million loan to Guyana for sea defense dikes. While the U.S. Department of the Treasury supports tough actions that would deter expropriation proceedings in the Third World, the Department of State, with respect to Demba's nationalization, argued against the abstention on the World Bank loan to Guyana, apparently believing that it was an inappropriate action in matters affecting Canadian government policy and Canadian companies. Additionally, the aluminum industry lobbied the State Department (which sent a statement to the Guyanese government) and the House of Representatives with a view to repealing Guyana's sugar quota for 1971-72 to the United States. See Litvak and Maule, pp. 53-55.

29. David A. Gantz, "The United States-Peruvian Claims Agreement of February 19, 1974," International Lawyer 10 (1976): 389-99.

30. Lars H. Thunnell, Political Risks in International Business: Investment Behavior of Multinational Corporations (New York: Praeger, 1977); Peter D. Bennett and Robert Green, "Political Instability as a Determinant of Direct Foreign Marketing

Investment," Journal of Marketing Research 9 (1972): 182-86; Yair Aharon, The Foreign Investment Decision Process (Boston: Harvard Business School, 1966).

31. See George Modelski, Multinational Corporations and World Order (Beverly Hills, Calif.: Sage, 1972), pp. 5-30, 52-69; Pastor, Congress, pp. 203-18, 251-353; Kurth, "The Multinational Corporation, U.S. Foreign Policy and the Less Developed Countries," in The New Sovereigns, pp. 139-53; Williams A. Williams, The Tragedy of American Diplomacy (New York: Delta, 1972); Id., The Roots of the Modern American Empire (New York: Random House, 1969); Magdoff, The Age of Imperialism; Michael Parenti, Trends and Tragedies in American Foreign Policy (Boston: Little, Brown, 1971).

32. Thomas E. Weisskopf, "United States Foreign Private Investment: An Empirical Survey," in The Capitalist System, ed. Richard C. Edwards, Michael Reich, and Thomas E. Weisskopf (Englewood Cliffs, N.J.: Prentice-Hall, 1972), p. 431 (emphasis in original).

33. United States, Department of Commerce, Survey of Current Business, November 1972, pp. 28-29.

34. See Akinsanya, "Host-Governments' Responses to Foreign Economic Control," pp. 778-79.

35. Kurth, "The Multinational Corporation," p. 143.

36. Fortune (New York), August 10, 1981, p. 205.

37. James F. Petras, Morris Morley, and Steven Smith, The Nationalization of Venezuelan Oil (New York: Praeger, 1977).

38. Kurth, "The Multinational Corporation," pp. 143-44.

39. Petras, Morley, and Smith, Nationalization, p. 95.

40. Henry Kissinger, "Strengthening the World Economic Structure," presented at Kansas City, Missouri, May 13, 1975 (United States, Department of State, Bureau of Public Affairs).

41. Petras, Morley, and Smith, Nationalization, p. 100.

42. Ibid., p. 97.

43. Ibid.

44. See Hartmut Brosche, "The Arab Oil Embargo
and United States Pressure Against Chile: Economic
and Political Coercion and the Charter of the United
Nations," in Economic Coercion and the New International Economic Order, ed. Richard B. Lillich (Charlottesville, Va.: Michie Company, 1976), pp. 285-
317; Paul E. Sigmund, "The 'Invisible Blockade' and
the Overthrow of Allende," Foreign Affairs 52 (1974):
322-40; Id., Multinationals in Latin America: The
Politics of Nationalization (Madison: University of
Wisconsin Press, 1980), pp. 131-78; Richard R. Fagen,
"The United States and Chile: Roots and Branches,"
Foreign Affairs 53 (1975): 297-313; Ian Roxborough,
Phil O'Brien, and Jackie Roddick, "Background to the
Military Overthrow of Allende," in Politics and
State in the Third World, ed. Harry Goulbourne
(London: Macmillan Press, 1979), pp. 232-42; Thomas
Powers, Richard Helms and the CIA (New York: Pocket
Books, 1979), pp. 281-308; Sampson, The Seven Sis-
ters, pp. 128-54; Id., The Sovereign State, pp. 230-
56; Petras and Morley, How Allende Fell; Robert
Engler, The Politics of Oil (Chicago: University of
Chicago Press, 1961), pp. 201-15; Carl Oglesby, "The
Free World's Corporate Empire," in Trends and Trage-
dies in American Foreign Policy, ed. Michael Parenti
(Boston: Little, Brown, 1971), pp. 75-90; Petras,
"United States Wealth and Power in Latin America,"
in Trends and Tragedies in American Foreign Policy,
pp. 90-104; Paul A. Baran and Paul M. Sweezy, "The
Containment of Communism," in Trends and Tragedies
in American Foreign Policy, pp. 105-17; John Gerassi,
"Destroying a Social Democracy: The Case of Guate-
mala," in Trends and Tragedies in American Foreign
Policy, pp. 121-27; Michael Tanzer, The Political
Economy of International Oil and the Underdeveloped
Countries (Boston: Beacon, 1969), pp. 319-76; Kurth,
"The Multinational Corporation, U.S. Foreign Policy
and the Less Developed Countries," pp. 139-53; Abra-
ham F. Lowenthal, "The United States and Latin
America: Ending the Hegemonic Presumption," Foreign
Affairs 55 (1976): 199-213; Jose M. Aybar de Soto,
Dependency and Intervention: The Case of Guatemala
in 1954 (Boulder, Colo.: Westview Press, 1978);
Richard A. Falk, "President Gerald Ford, CIA Covert
Operations, and the Status of International Law,"

American Journal of International Law 69 (1975): 354-58; Harold S. Kerbo, "Foreign Involvement in the Preconditions for Political Violence: The World System and the Case of Chile," Journal of Conflict Resolution 22 (1978): 363-91; O'Brien, "Was the United States Responsible for the Chilean Coup?" in Allende's Chile, pp. 244-72; Gordon L. Bowen, "American Covert Actions Against Castro's Cuba," read at the Annual Convention of the International Studies Association, Biltmore Hotel, Los Angeles, March 18-22, 1980.

45. Petras, "United States Wealth," p. 108.

46. Ibid., p. 109.

47. Ibid., p. 110 (emphasis in original).

48. Oglesby, "Free World's Corporate Empire," p. 79; Petras, "United States Wealth," p. 110.

49. Petras, "United States Wealth," p. 110.

50. Petras, Morley, and Smith, Nationalization, p. 97.

51. Petras, "United States Wealth," p. 101.

52. Ibid. See also Akinsanya, "U.S. Multinationals in South Africa and Policy Options for the United States," Third Press Review of Third World Diplomacy 1 (1982): 95-115.

53. Petras, "United States Wealth," p. 98.

54. Petras, Morley, and Smith, Nationalization, p. 98.

55. Akinsanya, The Expropriation of Multinational Property in the Third World, pp. 25-46.

56. Petras, Morley, and Smith, Nationalization, p. 98.

57. Thomas C. Enders, An Action Program for World Development (Washington, D.C.: Department of State Publication 8780, General Foreign Policy Series 289, 1975), p. 12.

58. See United States, Policy Statement on Economic Assistance and Investment Security in Developing Nations, January 19, 1972. Reprinted in International Legal Materials 11 (1972): 241.

59. Lipson, "Corporate Preferences," pp. 397-414; Pastor, Congress, pp. 251-300.

60. Petras, Morley, and Smith, Nationalization, p. 100.

61. Sampson, Seven Sisters, p. 132.

62. James A. Nathan and James K. Oliver, United States Foreign Policy and World Order (Boston: Little, Brown, 1976), p. 215. See also Tanzer, The Political Economy of International Oil and the Underdeveloped Countries, pp. 321-26.

63. Ian McDonald, Anglo-American Relations Since the Second World War (New York: St. Martin's Press, 1974), p. 93.

64. See Robert Scheer, "Eisenhower's Role Recounted: How CIA Orchestrated '53 Coup in Iran," Los Angeles Times, March 29, 1979, p. 6.

65. Nathan and Oliver, U.S. Foreign Policy, p. 216.

66. Ibid., p. 215.

67. Scheer, "Eisenhower's Role," p. 7.

68. Sampson, Seven Sisters, p. 141.

69. Scheer, "Eisenhower's Role," p. 1. For more on the CIA covert operations in Iran, see Richard Nixon, The Real War (New York: Warner Books, 1981), p. 83; Nathan and Oliver, U.S. Foreign Policy, pp. 215-16; Peter Calvocoressi, World Politics Since 1945 (London: Longman, 1977), pp. 172-78; Patrick F. Wilmot, In Search of Nationhood (Ibadan, Nigeria: Lantern Books, 1979), pp. 118-19; Oglesby, "Free World's Corporate Empire," p. 83; Powers, The Man Who Kept the Secrets: Richard Helms and the CIA, pp. 106, 110, 434.

70. Scheer, "Eisenhower's Role," p. 7; Sampson, Seven Sisters, pp. 142-51.

71. P. Lyon, Eisenhower: Portrait of the Hero (Boston: Little, Brown, 1974), p. 614 (emphasis in original).

72. Atkins, Latin America in the International Political System, p. 138; Nathan and Oliver, U.S. Foreign Policy, p. 217.

73. Petras, "United States Wealth," p. 94.

74. See Loftus E. Becker, "Just Compensation in Expropriation Cases: Decline and Partial Recovery," Proceedings of the American Society of International Law (1959): 341, 343-44.

75. Petras, Morley, and Smith, Nationalization, p. 98.

76. Lyon, Eisenhower, p. 590 (emphasis added).

77. Nathan and Oliver, U.S. Foreign Policy, pp. 217-18.

78. See United States, Congress, House, Select Committee on Communist Aggression: Hearings Before the Subcommittee on Latin America, 83d Cong., 2nd Sess., 1954 (Washington, D.C.: Government Printing Office, 1954), pp. 24-26.

79. See United States, Department of State, Tenth Inter-American Conference (Washington, D.C.: Government Printing Office, 1955), pp. 156-57.

80. Atkins, Latin America, p. 231.

81. Powers, The Man, p. 416, n. 19.

82. For more on U.S. intervention in Guatemala, see Powers, The Man, pp. 106-10; Philip B. Taylor, Jr., "The Guatemalan Affair: A Critique of United States Foreign Policy," American Political Science Review (1956): 790-92; Lyon, Eisenhower, p. 611; Gerassi, "Destroying a Social Democracy: The Case of Guatemala," pp. 121-27.

83. At the height of U.S.-backed invasion, Arbenz Guzman appealed to the United Nations Security Council which referred the matter to the Organization of American States, over the objections of the Soviet Union, thanks to the provisions of Article 52 of the United Nations Charter. In any event, Arbenz Guzman had gone into exile by the time that the Organization of American States fact-finding team arrived in the Guatemalan capital.

84. Powers, The Man, p. 418, n. 19.

85. Nathan and Oliver, U.S. Foreign Policy, p. 220.

86. Lowenthal, "The United States and Latin America," pp. 199-213; Tanzer, Political Economy, pp. 327-44, 355-61; Collier, "Expropriation," p. 1089; Atkins, Latin America, pp. 137-38; Kurth, "The Multinational Corporation," pp. 149-50.

87. Lipson, "Corporate Preferences and Public Policies: Foreign Aid Sanctions and Investment Protection," pp. 396-421.

88. Petras, "United States Wealth," p. 94.

89. Except otherwise stated, materials on foreign capital participation in the Brazilian economy are drawn from Henry J. Steiner and Deltev F. Vagts, Transitional Legal Problems (New York: Foundation Press, 1973), p. 440.

90. See Akinsanya, The Expropriation of Multinational Property in the Third World, pp. 333-42.

91. See Steiner and Vagts, Transnational, pp. 441-42.

92. Akinsanya, Expropriation, pp. 290-91.

93. Steiner and Vagts, Transnational, p. 442. In June 1967, ITT announced the sale of all ITT facilities in Brazil (including some in the state of Parana) for $12 million, half of which was invested in its telecommunications manufacturing facilities in the country.

94. Steiner and Vagts, Transnational, p. 443.

95. Tanzer, Political Economy, p. 358.

96. Lipson, "Corporate Preferences," p. 402.

97. Lowenthal, "The United States," p. 200.

98. Tanzer, Political Economy, p. 361; Petras, "United States Wealth," p. 99.

99. Kurth, "The Multinational Corporation," p. 150.

100. Sigmund, Multinationals in Latin America, p. 93.

101. Ibid., p. 98.

102. Ibid.

103. Ibid., p. 99.

104. It was Senator Smathers of Florida who in June 1959 first raised the question of the possibility of cutting the Cuban sugar quota. A similar suggestion was made by Secretary of State Christian Herter and other Senators (Sigmund, Multinationals, pp. 98, 103).

105. See Ian Brownlie, Loaves and Fishes: Access to Natural Resources and International Law (London: London School of Economics and Political Science, 1978), pp. 11-12.

106. Sigmund, Multinationals, p. 104.

107. Ibid. (emphasis added).

108. Baran and Sweezy, The Containment of Socialism, p. 115.

109. See Alleged Assassination Plots Involving Foreign Leaders: An Interim Report of the United States Senate Select Committee to Study Government Operations with Respect to Intelligence Activities, Introduction by Senator Frank Church, hereafter cited as Senate Assassination Report (New York: W. W. Norton, 1976), p. 92.

110. Ibid.

111. Ibid., p. 93.

112. Ibid.
113. Ibid.
114. Ibid.
115. Ibid., p. 114, n. 3.
116. Powers, The Man, p. 130.
117. Ibid., pp. 130, 133.
118. For an account of the planning, execution, and outcome of the planned invasion, see Powers, The Man, pp. 129-48.
119. Lipson, "Corporate Preferences," p. 400.
120. Tanzer, Political Economy, p. 329.
121. Ibid., pp. 329-30.
122. Ibid., p. 330.
123. Ibid. It must be noted here that the Indian government was making similar requests to the oil majors to refine cheap Soviet crude oil. See Tanzer, Political Economy, pp. 34-38.
124. Ibid., p. 330.
125. Ibid., p. 331.
126. Baran and Sweezy, Containment, p. 114 (emphasis in original).
127. Tanzer, Political Economy, pp. 334-40.
128. Baran and Sweezy, Containment, p. 115.
129. Ibid.
130. Sigmund, Multinationals, p. 108.
131. Maurice Zeitlin and Robert Scheer, Cuba: Tragedy in Our Hemisphere (New York: Grove Press, 1963), p. 176.
132. Baran and Sweezy, Containment, p. 114.
133. Ibid., pp. 114-15.
134. Martin Kenner and James Petras, Fidel Castro Speaks (New York: Grove Press, 1969), p. 68.
135. Sigmund, Multinationals, p. 109.
136. See American Journal of International Law 55 (1961): 823.
137. For the failure of the oil boycott, see Tanzer, Political Economy, pp. 335-40.
138. Kenner and Petras, Castro, p. 68.
139. Ibid., pp. 69-81.
140. Ibid., p. 69.
141. Powers, The Man, p. 186; Senate Assassination Report, pp. 71-180.
142. Atkins, Latin America in the International Political System, pp. 232-33.
143. Ibid., p. 233.

144. See Oglesby, "Free World's Corporate Empire," p. 84; Petras, "United States Wealth," pp. 95-96; Fred Goff and Michael Locker, The Violence of Domination: U.S. Power and the Dominican Republic (New York: North American Congress on Latin America, n.d.).

145. Petras, "United States Wealth," p. 95.

146. Ibid., pp. 95-96.

147. Petras, Morley, and Smith, Nationalization, p. 100.

148. Ibid.

149. United States, Department of State, Department of State Bulletin, October 8, 1973, pp. 465-66.

150. United States, Congress, Senate, Committee on Foreign Relations, Nomination of Henry A. Kissinger, Part 2, Executive Hearings (Washington, D.C.: Government Printing Office, 1973), p. 304.

151. Sigmund, "The 'Invisible Blockade' and the Overthrow of Allende," pp. 337-39.

152. Petras and Morley, How Allende Fell, p. 8.

153. See Seymour H. Hersh, "C.I.A. Chief Tells House of $8-Million Campaign Against Allende in '70-72," New York Times, September 8, 1974, pp. 1, 26.

154. See New York Times, September 17, 1974, p. 22; also Newsweek (New York), September 23, 1974.

155. Petras and Morley, How Allende Fell, p. 9.

156. Ibid., pp. 11-13, 21-26; O'Brien, "Was the United States?" pp. 220-24.

157. See Lauren Stern, "U.S. Helped Beat Allende in 1964," Washington Post, April 16, 1973, pp. A1, A12; United States, Congress, Senate, Subcommittee on Multinational Corporations, Multinational Corporations and United States Foreign Policy, Part 1 (Washington, D.C.: Government Printing Office, 1973), p. 290.

158. New York Times, September 6, 1964.

159. See Akinsanya, "Indigenisation or Nationalisation of Private Foreign Investments: Alternative Strategies for Dealing with Transnational Corporations in Member-States of ECOWAS," in Development Planning in the Economic Community of West African States (Priorities and Strategies), edited by R. E. Obogu, G. Adamu, and T. A. C. Gogue (Ibadan, Nigeria: Heinemann Educational, 1983), pp. 365-409.

160. O'Brien, "Was the United States?" p. 223.

161. Ibid., p. 224.

162. See Powers, The Man, pp. 281-306; Senate Assassination Report, pp. 225-54; Sampson, The Sovereign State, pp. 230-56.

163. Petras and Morley, How Allende Fell, p. 12.

164. See Benjamin Welles, "Rogers Threatens Chilean Aid Cutoff in Expropriation," New York Times, October 23, 1971, p. 1.

165. Petras and Morley, How Allende Fell, p. 64.

166. Ibid., p. 9.

167. Stern, "Aid Used as Choke on Allende," Washington Post, September 10, 1973, pp. A1, A14.

168. Akinsanya, The Expropriation of Multinational Property in the Third World, pp. 284-300.

169. Gillian White, Wealth Deprivation: Creditor Contractor Claims (Manchester, England: University of Manchester, Faculty of Law, n.d.), p. 23. See also Alfonso Inostroza, "The World Bank and Imperialism," in The Political Economy of Development and Underdevelopment, pp. 152-57.

170. For the convention, see A. Broches, "The Convention on the Settlement of Investment Disputes Between States and Nationals of Other States," Recueil des Cours 2 (1972): 333-405.

171. O'Brien, "Was the United States?" p. 235.

172. Petras and Morley, How Allende Fell, p. 71.

173. United States, Congress, House, Committee on Foreign Affairs, Foreign Assistance Act of 1972, Part 2, 93d Cong., 2nd Sess., March 14-23, 1972 (Washington, D.C.: Government Printing Office, 1972), p. 39.

174. United States, Department of State, Department of State Bulletin, July 16, 1973, p. 90.

175. Petras and Morley, How Allende Fell, p. 106.

176. O'Brien, "Was the United States?" pp. 235-36.

177. Ibid., pp. 236-41.

178. United States, Department of State, Department of State Bulletin, October 8, 1973, p. 465.

179. Petras and Morley, How Allende Fell, p. 109.

180. O'Brien, "Was the United States?" p. 241.

181. Falk, "Gerald Ford," pp. 354-58; Lowenthal, "The United States and Latin America," p. 199.

182. Chile has virtually left the Andean Common Market while compensation agreement was reached with Kennecott and Anaconda. Akinsanya, The Expropriation of Multinational Property in the Third World, p. 140.

183. United States, Department of State, Department of State Bulletin, October 8, 1973, p. 465; Jonathan Kandell, "Private U.S. Loans in Chile Up Sharply," New York Times, November 12, 1973, pp. 53, 55; Terri Shaw, "Blockade of Chile Diminishing," Washington Post, October 28, 1973, pp. A1, A17.

184. Petras and Morley, How Allende Fell, p. 47.

185. Petras, Morley, and Smith, Nationalization, p. 100.

186. Ibid., p. 107.

187. Ibid., pp. 112-13.

188. See David A. Gantz, "The United States-Peruvian Claims Agreement of February 19, 1974," International Lawyer 10 (1976): 389-99.

189. See Gantz, "The Marcona Settlement," American Journal of International Law 71 (1977): 474-93.

Conclusions

Economic nationalism in several Third World countries is often characterized by the desire to exercise control over their economies. It is often characterized by the desire to exercise greater control over foreign-owned enterprises, particularly local MNC subsidiaries. Several claims have been made on behalf of MNCs. First, it has been argued that MNCs operating in the Third World contribute resources that are generally not available or insufficiently available, namely, capital, technology, and marketing skills. Second, it has also been claimed that MNCs create jobs and, through import-substitution industrialization, alleviate balance-of-payments deficits of their host states. On the other hand, critics of MNC operations in the Third World have three general complaints. The first is that MNC operations generally have had an adverse impact on their host states. Second, multinationals have been accused of engaging in illegal political activity and offering bribes in order to circumvent local regulations. Third, MNCs are beyond national control; they constitute imperium in imperio and thus undermine the territorial nation state.

From this study emerges the following general conclusions. First, while it may be true to say that MNCs transfer capital resources from a capital-rich country to a capital-poor country, by and large, MNCs are vehicles through which capital resources are transferred from capital-poor countries

319

to capital-rich countries through such devices as
transfer pricing, sharp accounting practices, overinvoicing imports, and underinvoicing exports as
well as overpricing technology.[1]

Second, MNCs may well have created jobs; on
the balance, and when compared with domestic enterprises, MNCs do in fact destroy jobs because they
employ capital-intensive technologies which are inconsistent and inappropriate with the factor endowments of Third World countries.[2]

Third, while it is not denied that MNCs transfer technology to DCs, the technology so transferred
is inappropriate, obsolete, overpriced, and inconsistent with the factor endowments of host states.
More fundamental, extractive MNCs create enclave
economies, namely, they have few backward and forward linkages with the host economy.[3]

Fourth, MNCs encourage inappropriate consumption patterns through product differentiation (or
innovation) and/or marketing and advertising techniques, although some of the undesirable consumption
patterns may well be a reflection of an existing
uneven distribution of national income rather than
the effects of MNC operations.[4]

Fifth, because MNCs generally pay their employees higher salaries and provide generous fringe
benefits than do domestic enterprises, MNCs may
have, albeit unwittingly, contributed to the widen-
of the elite-mass gap and polarization of social
forces in the host states.[5]

Sixth, one of the costs of MNC operations in
the Third World is technological dependence. A
major danger posed by the state of technological
dependence of most Third World countries is that it
impedes and stifles local development. Not only
does the easy access of foreign technology prevent
domestic or state-owned enterprises from investing
in research and development. As Sanjaya Lall puts
it, it makes DCs "biased against using what innovations are produced locally. The effect is cumulative, since R and D generates considerable 'learning by doing' over time; the less research developing countries do, the less experience they gather
to do it in the future."[6]

As a result of new economic nationalism in the 1960s and 1970s, several DCs have taken measures against foreign-owned enterprises ranging from nationalization and majority equity participation in local MNC subsidiaries to indigenization of certain sectors of the economy.

Because it is the duty of a state to protect the person and property of its nationals abroad, investor states have responded in many forms to the waves of economic nationalism. In general, expropriations of foreign assets have not been questioned unless they are arbitrary, discriminatory, and are not accompanied by some compensation. Some investor states have intervened on behalf of their nationals by making diplomatic representations to the taking states; others have threatened foreign-aid sanctions against countries taking their nationals' investments without discharging their obligations under customary international law; and still others have intervened directly or indirectly and ousted the nationalist regimes, thus restoring the status quo ante. Because investor states have often intervened on behalf of their nationals through covert or overt operations and because the gap between the industrialized countries of the North and the agrarian countries of the South continues to yawn largely through MNC operations,[7] many Third World countries have used the instrumentalities of the United Nations to demand a new international economic order.[8] But as we noted in a study with Arthur Davies, it is impossible to have a new international economic order without a new national economic order.[9] This means that Third World countries will have to depend much more on their own resources and rarely on MNCs. They will have to develop their own technologies either through industrial spying and/or massive investment in education as well as R and D. More fundamental, they will need to undergo radical structural transformation so as to smash local allies of MNCs. All these measures can only be successfully implemented within the framework of a centrally planned (socialist) economy.

NOTES

1. Colman and Nixson, Economics of Change, pp. 224-34; Muller, "The Multinational Corporation and the Underdevelopment of the Third World," in The Political Economy of Development and Underdevelopment, pp. 136-46.

2. Colman and Nixson, Economics of Change, pp. 231-33; Muller, "The Multinational Corporation," pp. 132-36.

3. Frank, Foreign Enterprise in Developing Countries, pp. 73-93; Biersteker, Distortion, pp. 119-29.

4. Biersteker, Distortion, pp. 129-35; Colman and Nixson, Economics of Change, pp. 231-33.

5. Biersteker, Distortion, pp. 137-54.

6. Lall, Developing Countries and Multinational Corporations, p. 28. On dependence, see, generally, Lall, "Is 'Dependence' a Useful Concept in Analysing Underdevelopment?" World Development 3 (1975): 799-810; Theotonio Dos Santos, "The Structure of Dependence" in The Political Economy of Development and Underdevelopment, pp. 100-17.

7. See Akinsanya, "The United Nations Charter of Economic Rights and Duties of States," Annual of the Nigerian Society of International Law 3 (forthcoming).

8. Ibid.

9. Adeoye Akinsanya and Arthur Davies, "Third World Quest for a New International Economic Order: An Overview," International and Comparative Law Quarterly 33 (1984): 208-17.

Bibliography

BOOKS AND MONOGRAPHS

Akinsanya, Adeoye A. The Expropriation of Multinational Property in the Third World. New York: Praeger, 1980.

_____. Economic Independence and Indigenization of Private Foreign Investments: The Experience of Nigeria and Ghana. Columbia: University of South Carolina, Institute of International Studies (1982).

Asante, Samuel K. B. Transnational Investment Law and National Development. Lagos, Nigeria: University of Lagos Press, 1981.

Atkins, G. Pope. Latin America in the International Political System. New York: Free Press, 1977.

Barnet, Richard, and Muller, Ronald E. The Global Reach. New York: Simon and Schuster, 1974.

Biersteker, Thomas J. Distortion or Development? Cambridge, Mass.: MIT Press, 1978.

Boardman, Patrick M., and Schollhammer, Hans. Multinational Corporations and Governments. New York: Praeger, 1977.

Colman, David, and Nixson, Frederick. Economics of Change in Less Developed Countries. Oxford, England: Philip Alan, 1978.

Dunning, John H. International Production and the Multinational Enterprise. London: George Allen and Unwin, 1981.

Engler, Robert. The Politics of Oil. Chicago: University of Chicago Press, 1961.

Fitzgerald, Garret. Unequal Partners. Publication no. TAD/INF/PUB/78.6. New York: United Nations.

Frank, Isaiah. Foreign Enterprise in Developing Countries. Baltimore, Md.: Johns Hopkins University Press, 1980.

Helleiner, Gerald K. A World Divided. Cambridge, England: Cambridge University Press, 1976.

Ingram, George M. Expropriation of U.S. Property in Latin America. New York: Praeger, 1974.

Johnson, Harry G. Technology and Economic Inter-dependence. London: Macmillan Press, 1975.

Kegley, Charles W., and Wittkopf, Eugene. American Foreign Policy. New York: St. Martin's Press, 1979.

_____. World Politics. New York: St. Martin's Press, 1981.

Lall, Sanjaya. Developing Countries and Multi-national Corporations. London: Commonwealth Secretariat, 1976.

_____. Developing Countries in the International Economy. London: Macmillan Press, 1981.

Lall, Sanjaya, and Streeten, Paul. Foreign Investment, Transnationals and Developing Countries. London: Macmillan Press, 1977.

Leigh, Monroe. Expropriation of Foreign-Owned Investment--Recent Trends. New York: Matthew Bender and Co., 1973.

MacBean, Alasdair, and Balasubramanyam, V. N. Meeting the Third World Challenge. London: Macmillan Press, 1978.

McDonald, Ian. Anglo-American Relations Since the Second World War. New York: St. Martin's Press, 1974.

Modelski, George. <u>Multinational Corporations and World Order</u>. Beverly Hills, Ca.: Sage, 1972.

Nathan, James A., and Oliver, James K. <u>United States Foreign Policy and World Order</u>. Boston: Little, Brown, 1976.

O'Brien, Philip. <u>Allende's Chile</u>. New York: Praeger, 1976.

Parento, Michael. <u>Trends and Tragedies in the American Foreign Policy</u>. Boston: Little, Brown, 1971.

Pastor, Robert A. <u>Congress and the Politics of U.S. Foreign Economic Policy, 1929-1976</u>. Berkeley: University of California Press, 1980.

Petras, James, and Morley, Morris M. <u>How Allende Fell</u>. Nottingham, England: Spokesman Books, 1974.

Petras, James, and Smith, Steven. <u>The Nationalization of Venezuelan Oil</u>. New York: Praeger, 1976.

Pinelo, Adalberto J. <u>The Multinational Corporation as a Political Force in Latin American Politics</u>. New York: Praeger, 1973.

Powers, Thomas. <u>Richard Helms and the CIA</u>. New York: Pocket Books, 1979.

Rolfe, Sidney E. <u>Multinational Corporation</u>. New York: Foreign Policy Association, 1970.

Said, Abdul A., and Simmons, Luiz. <u>The New Sovereigns</u>. Englewood Cliffs, N.J.: Prentice-Hall, 1975.

Sampson, Anthony. <u>The Sovereign State</u>. London: Hodder and Fawcett, 1973.

_____. <u>The Seven Sisters</u>. London: Hodder and Stoughton, 1975.

Sauvant, Karl P, and Lavipour, Farid G. Controlling
    Multinational Enterprises. Boulder, Colo.:
    Westview Press, 1976.

Scammell, W. M. The International Economy Since
    1945. London: Macmillan Press, 1980.

Sigmund, Paul E. Multinationals in Latin America.
    Madison: University of Wisconsin Press, 1980.

Singer, Hans, and Ansari, Javed. Rich and Poor
    Countries. London: George Allen and Unwin,
    1978.

Spero, Joan E. The Politics of International
    Economic Relations. London: George Allen and
    Unwin, 1977.

Stauffer, Robert B. Nation-Building in a Global
    Economy: The Role of the Multinational Corpo-
    ration. Beverly Hills, Ca.: Sage, 1973.

Tanzer, Michael. The Political Economy of Inter-
    national Oil and the Underdeveloped Countries.
    Boston: Beacon Press, 1969.

Todaro, Michael P. Economic Development in the
    Third World. London: Longman, 1977.

Wilmot, Patrick F. In Search of Nationhood.
    Ibadan, Nigeria: Lantern Books, 1979.

Woddis, Jack. Armies and Politics. New York:
    International Publishers, 1977.

Wyden, Peter. Bay of Pigs. New York: Simon and
    Schuster, 1979.

JOURNALS AND PERIODICALS

Akinsanya, A. "Permanent Sovereignty over Natural
    Resources and the Future of Foreign Investment."
    Nigerian Journal of International Affairs 5
    (1979): 70-92.

_____. Host-Governments' Responses to Foreign
Economic Control: The Experiences of Selected
African Countries." International and Com-
parative Law Quarterly 30 (1981): 769-90.

Bell, R. David. "Sales of Foreign Affiliates of
U.S. Firms, 1961-65, 1967 and 1968." Survey of
Current Business 50 (1970): 18-20.

Blanchard, Daniel S. "The Threat to U.S. Private
Investment in Latin America." Journal of International Law and Economics 5 (1971): 221-37.

Bock, P. G., and Fuccillo, Vincent J. "Trans-
national Corporations as International Political
Actors." Studies in Comparative International
Development 10 (1975): 51-77.

Chandler, Geoffrey. "The Myth of Oil Power," International Affairs 46 (1970): 710-18.

Collier, Ellen C. "Expropriation of American-Owned
Property by Foreign Governments in the Twentieth
Century." International Legal Materials 2
(1963): 1066-110.

Craig, William Laurence. "Application of the
Trading with the Enemy Act to Foreign Corporations Owned by Americans: Reflections on
Fruehauf v Massardy." Harvard Law Review 83
(1970): 579-601.

Devlin, David T., and Kruer, George R. "The Inter-
national Investment Position of the United
States: Developments in 1969." Survey of
Current Business 50 (1970): 21-38.

Falk, Richard A. "President Gerald Ford, CIA Covert
Operations and the Status of International Law."
American Journal of International Law 69 (1975):
354-58.

Gantz, David A. "The United States-Peruvian Claims
Agreement of February 19, 1974." International
Lawyer 10 (1976): 389-99.

_____. "The Marcona Settlement." American Journal of International Law 71 (1977): 474-93.

Gilbert, Peter R. "Expropriations and the Overseas Private Investment Corporation." Law and Policy in International Business 9 (1977): 515-50.

Gilpin, Robert. "The Political Economy of the Multinational Corporation." American Political Science Review 70 (1976): 184-91.

Grover, B. S. K. "The Multinational Corporations and the Developing Countries." Indian Journal of Political Studies 1 (1978): 84-96.

Hanson, James. "Transfer-Pricing in the Multinational Corporation: A Critical Appraisal." World Development 3 (1975): 857-65.

Hymer, Stephen. "The Efficiency (Contradictions) of Multinational Corporations." American Economic Review (1970): 441-53.

Jackman, Robert W. "Dependence on Foreign Investment and Economic Growth in the Third World." World Politics 34 (1982): 175-96.

Kerbo, Harold S. "Foreign Involvement in the Preconditions for Political Violence: The World System and the Case of Chile." Journal of Conflict Resolution 22 (1978): 363-91.

Lall, Sanjaya. "Transfer-Pricing by Multinational Manufacturing Firms." Oxford Bulletin of Economics and Statistics 35 (1973): 173-93.

_____. "Is 'Dependence' A Useful Concept in Analysing Underdevelopment?" World Development 3 (1975): 799-810.

Lipson, Charles H. "Corporate Preferences and Public Policies: Foreign Aid Sanctions and Investment Protection." World Politics 28 (1976): 396-421.

Lowe, A. W. "Blocking Extraterritorial Jurisdiction: The British Protection of Trading Interests Act 1980." American Journal of International Law 75 (1981): 257-82.

Lowenfield, Andreas F. "Diplomatic Intervention in Investment Disputes." Proceedings of the American Society of International Law (1967): 96-107.

Lowenthal, Abraham F. "The United States and Latin America: Ending the Hegemonic Presumption." Foreign Affairs 55 (1976): 199-213.

Madujibeya, S. A. "Oil and Nigeria's Economic Development." African Affairs 75 (1976): 284-316.

Mikesell, F. Raymond. "Effects of Direct Foreign Investment on Development." Economic Impact 35 (1981-82): 36-41.

Ohly, D. C. "Covert Intervention in International Law." Proceedings of the American Society of International Law (1975): 192-216.

Okunpola, Akin, and Ojo, Oladeji. "The Role of Multinational Corporations in the Economic Development in African Countries." Nigerian Journal of International Studies 1 (1975): 67-88.

Sorensen, Theodore C. "Improper Payments Abroad." Foreign Affairs 54 (1976): 719-33.

Vernon, Raymond. "Storm over the Multinationals." Foreign Affairs 55 (1977): 243-62.

ARTICLES IN EDITED WORKS

Akinsanya, A. "Indigenisation or Nationalisation of Private Foreign Investments: Alternative Strategies for Dealing with Transnational Corporations in Member-States of ECOWAS." In Development Planning in the Economic Community of West African States (Priorities and Strategies), pp. 365-409. Ed. R. E. Ubogu, G. Adamu, and T. A. C. Gogue. Ibadan, Nigeria: Heinemann Educational, 1983.

Baldwin, A. "Foreign Aid, Intervention and Influence." In The International Political System, pp. 357-80. Ed. Romano Romani. New York: John Wiley, 1972.

Brosche, Harmut. "The Arab Oil Embargo and United States Pressure Against Chile: Economic and Political Coercion and the Charter of the United Nations." In Economic Coercion and the New International Economic Order, pp. 285-317. Ed. Richard B. Lillich. Charlottesville, Va.: Mechie, 1981.

Inostrosa, Alfonson. "The World Bank and Imperialism." In The Political Economy of Development and Underdevelopment, pp. 152-57. Ed. Charles K. Wilber. New York: Random House, 1973.

LaPalombara, Joseph, and Blank, Steven. "Multinational Corporations and Developing Countries." In The Foreign Policy Priorities of Third World States, pp. 113-50. Ed. John J. Stremlau. Boulder, Colo.: Westview Press, 1982.

Muller, Ronald. "The Multinational Corporation and the Underdevelopment of the Third World." In The Political Economy of Development and Underdevelopment, pp. 124-51. Ed. Charles K. Wilber. New York: Random House, 1973.

Roxborough, I., O'Brien, P., and Roddick, J. "Background to the Military Overthrow of Allende." In Politics and State in the Third World, pp. 232-42. Ed. Harry Goulbourne. London: Macmillan Press, 1979.

Santos, Theotonio Dos. "The Structure of Dependence." In The Political Economy of Development and Underdevelopment, pp. 109-17. Ed. Charles K. Wilber. New York: Random House, 1973.

PUBLIC DOCUMENTS AND UNPUBLISHED WORKS

Bowen, Gordon L. "American Covert Actions Against
     Castro's Cuba." Paper presented at the Annual
     Meeting of the International Studies Associa-
     tion, March 18-22, 1980, at Biltore Hotel, Los
     Angeles.

Chile, Speech Deliverd by Dr. Salvador Allende,
     President of Republic of Chile Before the Gen-
     eral Assembly of the United Nations, December 4,
     1972. Washington, D.C.: Embassy of Chile, n.d.

Cooper, George R. Beneficial Effects of OPIC In-
     volvement in Recent Claims Cases, April 26,
     1973, Washington, D.C.: OPIC, 1973.

Jordan, Robert L. Insurance Claims Experience to
     Date: OPIC and Its Predecessor Agency, November
     1977. Washington, D.C.: OPIC, 1977.

Pearson, Frederic S. "Foreign Military Intervention
     and Changes in United States Overseas Business
     Activity." Paper presented at the Annual Meet-
     ing of the International Studies Association,
     February 25-27, 1976, at Royal York, Toronto,
     Canada.

United Nations, Multinational Corporations in World
     Development. Publication no. E.73.II.A.11.

United States, Department of State, Bureau of In-
     telligence and Research, Nationalization, Ex-
     propriation, and Other Takings of U.S. and
     Certain Foreign Property since 1960, November 30,
     1971.

_____. The Overseas Private Investment Corpora-
     tion: A Critical Analysis, 93rd Cong., 1st
     Sess., 1973.

_____. Senate. Hearings before the Sub-Committee
     on Multinational Corporations of the Committee
     on Foreign Relations. 93rd Cong., 1973,
     Parts 1 and 2.

_____. Department of State, Bureau of Intelligence and Research. _Disputes Involving U.S. Foreign Direct Investment: July 1, 1971: Through July 31, 1973_. February 28, 1974.

_____. Department of State Statement on "Hot" Libyan Oil, May 7, 1974. Reprinted in _International Legal Materials_ 13 (1974): 767-82.

_____. _Disputes Involving U.S. Foreign Direct Investment: August 1, 1973-January 31, 1975_, March 20, 1975.

_____. _Disputes Involving U.S. Foreign Direct Investment: February 1, 1975-February 28, 1977_. September 19, 1977.

_____. _The Foreign Corrupt Practices Act of 1977_. Reprinted in _Federal Register_ 43 (1978): 36,064-66.

Wallace, Brian F. "Multinational Corporations and Governments in Developing Nations: Effects on the Distribution of Wealth and Power in Colombia." Paper presented at the Annual Meeting of the International Studies Association, March 18-21, 1981, at Franklin Plaza, Philadelphia.

Whiting, Van R. "International Aspects of National Regulation: Transnationals and the State in Mexico, 1970-1978." Paper presented at the Annual Meeting of the International Studies Association, March 21-23, 1979 at Royal York, Toronto, Canada.

Index

About the Author

ADEOYE A. AKINSANYA is a Professor in the Department of Government and Public Administration at the University of Ilorin, Ilorin, Nigeria, and was, during the 1980-81 academic session, a Visiting Professor of International Studies at the University of South Carolina, Columbia, and a Fulbright Scholar at the School of Advanced International Studies, The Johns Hopkins University, Washington, D.C.

Dr. Akinsanya has published widely in the areas of comparative politics, public administration, international law, international economic relations, and international relations. His articles have appeared in several edited works and such professional journals as African Affairs, Annual of the Nigerian Society of International Law, Geneva-Africa, International and Comparative Law Quarterly, International Problems, International Review of Administrative Sciences, Journal of Administration Overseas, Journal of African Studies, Nigerian Journal of Contemporary Law, Nigerian Journal of International Affairs, Public Administration and Development, and the West African Journal of Sociology and Political Science. His latest works include The Expropriation of Multinational Property in the Third World; Law of the Sea: Unilateralism Vs Multilateralism; and Economic Independence and Indigenization of Private Foreign Investments: The Experiences of Nigeria and Ghana, published by the Praeger Publishers, University of Lagos Press, and the Institute of International Studies, University of South Carolina, respectively.

Professor Akinsanya holds a B.S. from the University of Ibadan, Ibadan, Nigeria, an M.A. and a Ph.D. from the University of Chicago, and an M.P.A. from the University of Pittsburgh.